D0363797

LETTS Rip!

Quentin Letts

CONSTABLE • LONDON

GREENWICH LIBRARIES

3802 801973498	
Askews & Holts	06-Apr-2011
320.941	£12.99
3148807	BL

Constable & Robinson Ltd
3 The Lanchesters
162 Fulham Palace Road
London W6 9ER
www.constablerobinson.com

First published in the UK by Constable,
an imprint of Constable & Robinson Ltd, 2010

Copyright 2010 © Quentin Letts and the *Daily Mail*

The right of Quentin Letts to be identified as the author of this
work has been asserted by him in accordance with the
Copyright, Designs and Patents Act 1988

All rights reserved. This book is sold subject to the condition
that it shall not, by way of trade or otherwise, be lent, re-sold,
hired out or otherwise circulated in any form of binding or cover
other than that in which it is published and without a similar condition
including this condition being imposed on the subsequent purchaser.

A copy of the British Library Cataloguing in
Publication data is available from the British Library

ISBN: 978-1-84901-544-8

Printed and bound in the EU

1 3 5 7 9 10 8 6 4 2

PEFC
PEFC/16-33-111
CATG-PEFC-052
www.pefc.org

To my children Claud, Eveleen and Honor – this is what I was up to all those months away from home.

Acknowledgements

With thanks to numerous colleagues at the *Daily Mail* for their help, and particularly to my editor, Paul Dacre, who kindly gave permission for these articles to be reprinted.

Introduction

AT THE gates of Downing Street one day in early 2007, shortly before some prime ministerial photo opportunity, a Whitehall special adviser refused to admit us sketchwriters. She declared that the event was open only to 'real journalists'. Cheeky sod.

Qualms about sketchwriting are not uncommon at Westminster. Politicians and their grunts dislike the rude, unbiddable sketchers. Some of the lobby journalists regard us with suspicion, too. I can see their point. Sketchwriters do not have to be balanced or break exclusive stories. We must sometimes seem lazy lizards, licensed to editorialise.

I started writing sketches for the *Daily Telegraph* in the autumn of 1990. Simon Heffer, the incumbent, was on a sabbatical in Australia and I was asked to fill the gap. Simon was – is – a tremendous Thatcherite and while he was Down Under his heroine was toppled. Had he only been in London perhaps he could have saved her.

This book covers a later period, after I joined the *Daily Mail*. It starts at the height of Blairism and charts its slow, grotty demise. This has been a bad decade for Parliament and at times I felt my soul being corroded by anger. Occasional fury is allowable but sketches are better when they aim for understated bafflement.

Re-reading my efforts while making these selections, I realised that over the past 10 years I sometimes became swivel-eyed in my vexation at the way Blair and Co. were mistreating our legislature. You will find a few non-political articles to lighten the stew. Sketches have been edited to remove (some of) the boring bits. A few nuggets have been hurled into the mix to help create a flavour of the era.

The parliamentary sketch is open to accusations of frivolity and ephemerality. The only response is to raise a paw and say 'fair cop, guvnor'. Sketches describe the sights and sounds and smells of political debate. They take the view that politicians' policies are covered adequately elsewhere. Sketches succumb to the occasional feud. They are subjective. They do not tell the whole story. They are *sketches*, not oil paintings.

Yet sketchwriters, like canaries down the mine, can be the first to detect fatal gases. As early as June 2000 it was clear that Gordon Brown was opposed to defence spending (this became deadly, for him and our forces, nine years later). That same year, the sketch pointed out that the Tories needed to modernise to regain power. The point was grasped by the party only five years later. If the City had in October 2003 read a sketch which mentioned a man called Goodwin, investors might not have lost so many billions on bank stocks. Sketchwriters were also writing about MPs' abuse of expenses long before disaster hit in 2009.

Fainthearts sometimes accuse me of being snobbish, right-wing and unkind to female politicians. I would certainly like a smaller state, if only because it would give ministers less chance to meddle with our lives.

And I hope I am every ounce as unkind to female politicians as I am to male politicians. To be otherwise would be sexist. Would it not?

This mangy, splenetic old sketch is a journalistic rear gunner and seeks no greater station in life. It deals in the rackety theatre of manners and comportment and if that is snobbery, so be it. Politicians spend much time and money on such things because they know that voters are influenced by them. The newspaper writer who describes it is no more of a snob than the Leftist Prime Minister who glottal-stops his public school accent. Do I mean you, Tony Blair? I do believe I do!

And with a swerve and the squeal of burning rubber, Mr Byers was free

JAMMY devil, Stephen Byers. For weeks it has all been going horribly wrong for the Trade Secretary, to the point that people said he would be zapped in a reshuffle. But yesterday, with a last-minute swerve and the squeal of burning rubber, Mr Byers avoided disaster – for a few months, at least.

Life was surely never meant to be so interesting for this metallic-voiced former polytechnic lecturer, a fellow of such greyness that he would be hard to locate on a foggy morning. In the world of Byers, things are supposed to run to timetables. Careers are mapped. Promotion and success are plotted on graphs. Political crises are not meant to explode in one's face, catching you in the eye like the radiator cap of an overheated Wolseley Hornet.

But that is what happened with Rover this spring and Mr Byers handled the matter inexpertly, a sign possibly of inexperience, more probably of incompetence. He has not deserved much luck but yesterday a great dollop of it came his way and he was able to stand up in the Commons, announce that Rover had been bought and peacock himself as the saviour of West Midlands engineering.

Government backbenchers were ecstatic. They knew it had been a close thing not only for Rover but also for Labour's vote in the Black Country. Midlands MPs almost wept with gratitude. Our seats, our seats. Thank you! The likes of Ian Pearson (Lab, Dudley S), Lynne Jones (Lab, Birmingham Selly Oak) and Tony Wright (Lab, Cannock Chase) said hallelujah. Ken Purchase (Lab, Wolverhampton NE) came over all dewy-eyed and praised the trade unions for the part they had played in the Rover deal.

A Brylcreemed Leftie called Dennis Turner (Lab, Wolverhampton SE), chairman of Westminster's catering committee, said it was high time for 'a lovely party'. 'We should rejoice!' cried Mr Turner, becoming way overexcited. 'It is a lovely day!'

Some of the Labour lot spat fury at the Tories for, as they saw it, failing to show adequate delight at the Rover sale. 'Miserable sods!' snarled Peter Snape (Lab, West Bromwich E) under his breath. He pointed at the Tory front bench and called them 'cynics'.

There was more of this bitter fare from Mr Byers when he launched a nasty little attack on his shadow, Angela Browning. She, incidentally, boosted her matronly airs by wearing a blue and white outfit resembling a ward sister's uniform circa 1965.

Mr Byers claimed that 'while some of us were rolling up our sleeves' the Conservatives had done 'nuffing'. He noted that John Redwood, the former Tory frontbencher who made much of the anti-Byers running recently, was not present in the chamber. Mr Byers shook his fist in a rage of self-justification. He accused the Tories of trying to play 'party politics' with the Rover crisis. Er, so what was this, then?

It was left to the veteran Martin O'Neill (Lab, Ochil) to introduce chill, financial reality to proceedings. Almost apologetically, he noted that the backing for Rover's new owners is, at present, 'comparatively small' for an enterprise with such ambitions. Mr O'Neill is chairman of the Trade and Industry Select Committee and one fears he may have a point.

If that was the gloomiest moment, then the prettiest sight of the day was a glorious orange rose in the buttonhole of Tony Baldry (Con, Banbury). Mr Baldry could have picked better, mind you, for orange is the party colour of the Liberal Democrats, and at teatime Sandra Gidley, victor of the Romsey by-election, took her seat for the first time. Nearly the entire Lib Dem parliamentary force (if that is not too satirical a term) turned out to cheer Mrs Gidley. 'Tory loss!' crowed Bob Russell (Lib Dem, Colchester). Given that the by-election was caused by the death of the Tories' Michael Colvin in a fire, this was a crass thing to say. It reinforced one's view of the Lib Dems as the vultures of British politics.

10th May 2000

How right Martin O'Neill was about Rover. Its 'saviours' were to prove anything but, extracting millions for themselves before the company crashed. Stephen Byers left the Cabinet in 2002.

With a hunted glance at the Tories, Miss Drown sat down

DRIPPY by name, drippy by nature. That is the initial impression given by Julia Drown (South Swindon), the Labour MP who has been at the forefront of requests that breastfeeding be allowed in Parliament.

Miss Drown, 37, product of Hampstead Comprehensive and Oxford University, daughter of a picture restorer and a nurse, was yesterday on her feet in the chamber. This was a rare sight, for she is not the most assiduous of attenders. So how did she do? How did she sound? In a word: wet.

She wanted the Government to solve the problems of the world's poor and starving. Shoulders hunched, she brushed her long, straight fringe off her forehead and clutched an Order Paper close to her front, as though for strength. In tremulous, tinny voice she disclosed that lots of people in India are having a rotten time of things. The West should, well, do something about it. Yes. And with a sniffle and a fearful bite on lower lip, and a reproachful, hunted glance at the Tory benches opposite, she sat down.

It was more like a fourth-form essay than adult parliamentary debate. But perhaps it is too easy to be beastly to Miss Drown and her sisters on the Labour benches.

Perhaps there are some occasions when William Hague and his crack troops could do with a Julia Drown or two.

Looking across at the Opposition side of the House, one found only men. The old stereotype of a Tory MP was of an elderly military man, pinstriped, waistcoated, perhaps mustachioed, probably double gusseted. That no longer applies, but the modern counterpart, though sleeker and clean shaven, is barely any less clubby and male.

Their ringleader is Eric Forth (Bromley & Chislehurst), and there he duly was yesterday, second row back, screwing up his eyes in disbelief at the feebleness of Miss Drown's little speech. Around him sat the small knot of Tory parliamentarians who, with little recognition or thanks, keep the business of Opposition politics going at Westminster.

John Bercow (Buckingham), Graham Brady (Altrincham), James Gray (N Wilts), Nick St Aubyn (Guildford), Owen Paterson (N Shropshire), Julian Lewis (New Forest E), Desmond Swayne (New Forest W) and Stephen O'Brien (Eddisbury) are all in their first parliament.

Unlike Blair's Babes they have quickly picked up the complex rules of Commons debate. Forth's Furies, you could call them, though a Labour supporter might prefer Forth's Frothers. They have become highly competent debaters, acute scrutineers. They speak without notes, manage to cast their voices over the din, and are fearless in attacking Government obfuscation. Yet the contrast yesterday between them and droning Miss Drown was not entirely a happy one.

In their regulation dark-blue suits and with their intelligent airs Forth's Furies undoubtedly cut a striking dash, but one felt a twinge of sympathy for the lone woman. Down there on the floor of the House it must be nerve-racking to stand in front of such a squad. Some Labour women do better than our brittle heroine from South Swindon. A few minutes after Miss Drown's oration Shona McIsaac (Lab, Cleethorpes) jumped to her feet and made a tough, short speech in favour of distant water trawlermen.

Miss McIsaac, who is only a couple of years older than Miss Drown, said her piece with a grand twinkle in the eye and she was immediately rewarded with a ministerial promise that the matter would be given proper consideration.

Miss Drown, therefore, can not blame it all on some institutional sexism in Parliament.

In the chamber there is a real need for rigorous, robust analysis. So thank goodness Forth's Furies are there to defend our interests. But in the outside world the Tories need to realise that dark suits and intellectual toughness are not enough to win over an electorate. A little more sympathy would not go amiss. They could do with a woman's touch.

12th May 2000

When Gordon Brown lost power in 2010 he was felt, by many voters, to have neglected defence spending. This problem is noted by the sketch a decade earlier – not that anyone took much notice.

The Minister hurled everything overboard and paddled like mad

WHEN a member of Labour's Leftwing 'awkward squad' complains about cuts in defence budgets, it may be time to reach for the tin helmet and ask your builder's merchant to deliver sandbags. Gordon Prentice (Lab, Pendle) is about as pink as they come. He disapproves of the Monarchy, thinks the honours system stinks, and resigned a low position in the Blair Government on (extraordinary, I know) a matter of principle. He felt Labour was not doing its duty towards single mothers. Yet this was the man who in the Commons yesterday asked what the blazes was going on with the Royal Navy budget.

Could it really be true – 'I cannot for the life of me believe it is,' he said – that the Government had 'failed to order a single warship' since it took office? Not one. Nul points. Or 'zero', as Toy hecklers kept saying, forming noughts with their fingers and thumbs.

John Spellar, a bearded creature who occupies one of the ministerial berths at Defence, tapped out a nervous rhythm on the despatch box. 'Er, well,' he began, and cleared his throat. Mr Prentice peered magisterially at the Minister, head cocked, as he awaited a simple 'yes' or 'no'. Mr Spellar bit on that hairy lower lip and blinked, as tentative as the ward room orderly who has to tell a portly admiral that all the rissoles have been eaten.

'Er,' he said, 'er ...' And then out it came. Naval requirements, Mr Spellar claimed, had 'altered'. As a result, only half the number of ships is now required to do the same job. Conservative MPs cackled and Mr Prentice looked disappointed. It was true, after all. Oh dear.

Defence spending is in tatters. At one point yesterday MPs talked about the high number of unexploded bombs littering the Yugoslav landscape, but there is arguably no bigger ticking UXB than the one in Whitehall marked 'Labour's military neglect'.

The Armed Forces do not hold much of a grasp on the affections of the Chancellor of the Exchequer. After Oxford University, the military is probably Establishment bogey number two in the anguished subconscious of G. Brown. So when Defence Ministers have lobbied him for tax money in the past three years he has not given them much satisfaction.

As Menzies Campbell, for the Lib Dems, put it, there is little chance of the defence budget recovering while 'the shadow of the Chancellor' hangs over the MoD.

Jane's Fighting Ships, a military publication little given to hyperbole, has pointed out that we currently have the biggest gap in naval spending 'since the days of Henry VIII'. This coincides with the possibility that our new RAF fighters will not have guns (too dear) and with the fact that our soldiers in Sierra Leone are having to make do without significant armour. Iain Duncan Smith, improving as Shadow Defence Secretary, speculated that at this rate Royal Navy sailors will soon 'have to say bang instead of firing real bullets'.

Did he overstate his case? Well, it is reported that the frigate *Sheffield* has dismantled its Exocet loaders because there aren't enough rockets. Geoff Hoon, Defence Secretary, left the job of defending Government policy largely to our shaggy friend. Like many commanding officers, Mr Hoon knows when to duck.

Mr Spellar hurled everything overboard, paddled like mad, and was soon throwing up as much froth as the propellers of a dreadnought which is being parked by a trainee bosun. Eventually he lost his temper and wailed that the Opposition 'couldn't give a damn'. But the chap who couldn't give a damn may be rather closer to home for New Labour.

6th June 2000

Days later, an early sighting of the 'bottler Brown'.

She squawked like an oil-stricken guillemot

GORDON Brown performed one of the biggest bottle-outs since Peter O'Toole gave up strong drink. The Chancellor refused to take a Commons question about himself, Peter Mandelson and the euro. 'Frit! Frit!' yelled Conservative MPs, using Margaret Thatcher's old Lincolnshire word for 'frightened'.

Mr Brown ordered the Treasury's number five minister, Economic Secretary Melanie Johnson, to answer instead. Miss Johnson may speak like 'Woy' Jenkins but she is an inexperienced parliamentarian. She fluffed it.

Question 12 on the agenda for Treasury Questions was tabled by Julian Lewis (Con, New Forest E). 'What discussions has the Chancellor had with a) the Minister for Europe b) the Secretary of State for Northern Ireland on the timing of any move to replace the pound with the euro?' Crafty. Both the Europe Minister, Keith Vaz, and the Ulster Secretary, Mr Mandelson, are dead keen for us to join the euro soonest, whereas Mr Brown wants to suck it and see. The Cabinet is said to be riven on the issue.

Labour MPs tried to slow things down during the first 40

minutes of the hour's session in the hope that Mr Lewis's question would not be reached. We had had lengthy analysis of fiscal arrangements for voluntary sector bodies, of employment policies for the North-East and of Third World debt (Mr Brown shared with us some stuff about pupil/teacher ratios in Uganda). It was starting to look as though question 12 was doomed, especially when Keith Darvill (Lab, Upminster) stuck out his little pinky and expressed undying fascination with capital gains tax policy regarding long-term investments. The minutes were ticking by. But Speaker Boothroyd is a sharp old bird. She hurried things along and refused Labour any more supplementary queries. 'Question 12!' she barked. 'Hooray!' said the Opposition. Seven minutes left.

Ministers are supposed to give an answer to the question listed on the Order Paper but Miss Johnson had this to say to Mr Lewis: 'The Government's policy on membership of the single cuwwency wemains as set out by the Chancellor of the Exchequer in October 1997 and westated by the Pwime Minister in Febwuawy 1999.' There wasn't a word about Mr Brown's discussions with Messrs Vaz and Mandelson.

Tory and Lib Dem MPs slapped their knees. When Mr Lewis rose for a follow-up he was given a hard time. Labour regard him as something of a bulbous-eyed loony. 'Time for medication!' said one Brownite. Mr Lewis ignored it. With five minutes still left, the misery was not over for Miss Johnson. Nor could she even count on her own side. Burly Bill Rammell (Lab, Harlow) did his best to help her, claiming, loyally, that 'there is absolute unity of purpose in this Government'. Laughter. But the veteran Dale Campbell-Savours (Lab, Workington) gave the fire a poke by inviting Miss Johnson to discuss the possibility that we will have a euro referendum in the year 2002. Three minutes left, and the good ship Johnson was sinking.

Shadow Chancellor Michael Portillo now had a go. He was amazed that Mr Brown had dodged 'the central economic issue of the day'. Miss Johnson, squawking and flapping her arms like an oil-stricken guillemot: 'That's complete wubbish!' Matthew Taylor, for the Lib Dems, also weighed in. There was now little trace of Miss Johnson, save for a few last bubbles on the surface.

In rugby they talk of a 'hospital pass'. That is what a crafty player does when, seeing the approach of the opposing team's 18-stone fullback, he passes the ball to some unsuspecting innocent – who is duly flattened. Mr Brown looked at the expendable Miss Johnson and gave a dry chuckle. Some boss he makes.

23rd June 2000

The man wot makes the Queen laugh

HER Majesty was amused. At Buckingham Palace this week, sword in hand, she had just knighted Norman Wisdom. The atmosphere was sober and regal until, as Sir Norman returned to his seat, there was a clack of heels and a muffled 'Crumbs!' as the old trouper enacted one of his trademark stumbles.

No one else could have pulled it off. Any other comedian who sought to crack a joke at a royal investiture would have been castigated for trying to steal the show. But the Queen threw back her head and laughed happily. Good old Norman!

Aged 85, Sir Norman Wisdom remains incorrigible. You will not find him on satirical quiz shows such as *Have I Got News for You*, nor will you find him at any gathering of Cool Britannia icons. Among metropolitan sophisticates he is as unfashionable as polyester ties. But his monarch and many of her subjects still adore him. It could easily have been his best-loved film character Norman Pitkin, whose 'uniform' of cloth cap and several-sizes-too-small jacket became as much an image of the Fifties and Sixties as Ban the Bomb marches, who was knighted at the Palace on Tuesday.

Sir Norman and his loveable loser alter ego have long been

QUENTIN LETTS

interchangeable. Show business's newest knight still talks and 'ooohs' and gawps like the little man he played so many times. Playing the butt end of slapstick has not so much been a role for Norman Wisdom – it has been his life. He has been performing professionally since 1945, having started out in variety shows as Norman Wisdom – The Successful Failure.

If there was a banana skin, Norman slipped on it; if there was a laundry chute, he fell down it, head first; if there was a lorry, he would be found hanging off its tailgate; and if there was an open manhole within a mile of him, yep, Norman would step into it, followed by his cap and an echoing 'Aiee!' From 1953 to 1969 he made 19 films, usually starring as the clumsy, stoical, hapless Pitkin.

His hits included *Trouble in Store* and *A Stitch in Time*, which out-box-officed James Bond in *From Russia with Love*. He was nominated for an Oscar in *The Night They Raided Minsky's* and also produced his own theme tune, 'Don't Laugh at Me 'Cos I'm a Fool'.

One can over-analyse these things, but Norman Pitkin, in all his haplessness, was often the most rounded person in Wisdom films. In the stoicism of the little man, battling to be heard, fighting his way through official obstinacy to rescue the world from chaos, Norman Wisdom had lessons for us. Little Norman, hailed as the Everyman long before Tom Hanks's Forrest Gump, was bullied, barked at, fired and flattened. Yet every time he came back for more – and in the process he made women want to smother him in motherly love, while men jostled to extend him a friendly arm.

His own life has not been unlike that. Son of a chauffeur and a dressmaker, he had a rough childhood in Paddington, London, leaving school at 13 and running away from his drunken, violent father. On the advice of a stranger, young Norman joined the Army at the age of 15.

Before that there had been days and months when he slept rough in the streets. But it has never been the Wisdom way to

13

moan. Recalling the way his father would throw him around as a boy, Sir Norman once said that 'it taught me to fall'.

Nor did he become angry when remembering the time he worked as a cabin boy and, in port at Buenos Aires, was sent off to box against a professional prizefighter. At 5st 9lb, the 14-year-old Norman was duly knocked out cold and his crewmates stole his money. He told one interviewer that he was simply glad when, on returning to his ship, he was greeted with laughter and camaraderie. He always ached to be accepted. He found that opportunity in the Army, where he used to amuse his fellow squaddies by pretending to trip while square-bashing. This led to him being cast as an act in Army revues. Rex Harrison happened to see him in one Army show and that is how his career took off.

So top hats off to the new Knight Bachelor. Perhaps the only surprise on Tuesday was that he did not try to run away from the Queen when she prepared to dub him. If it really had been his alter ego Pitkin, he would have squinted at her with an uncertain laugh before accusing her – with an ''Ere, wot you up to?' – of trying to do him a mischief with her sword.

23rd June 2000

Back to the world of pantomime villains.

Mr Kaufman seethed

A THERMOMETER would have shown that it was warm – sticky high 60s, shirtsleeve order – around midday in Westminster's Committee Room 15. But the atmosphere was as cold as Ice Station Zebra.

Alan Howarth, Arts Minister, was before the Culture Committee, which is chaired by Gerald Kaufman (Lab, Gorton). They belong to the same political party but these two are not close. Ginger Rogers and Baldrick or Fred Astaire and Clarissa Dickson-Wright would make more convincing duos than Kaufman and Howarth.

The verb 'chair' fails to convey the *droit de seigneur* which emanates from Mr Kaufman over this committee. He preens himself like a Burmese cat and likes visitors to place foreheads to the carpet and chant salaams.

Mr Howarth used to be a Tory MP but in 1995 jumped to Labour. Commons floor-crossers tend not to be popular at Westminster. Feline Gerald's second problem with Mr Howarth, arguably, is that he occupies a job Mr Kaufman might once have fancied. Third, Mr Howarth and his aides have consistently failed to enact the Kaufman Committee's advice. Last month Mr Howarth tried to bypass it by creating a separate advisory group. The new panel will, said Mr Howarth yesterday, be 'eminent' and will be manned by 'very distinguished historians, lawyers and philosophers'. In other words: much better calibre people than your lot.

Mr Kaufman seethed. With his mouth forming the shape of a plump prune, it was not hard to discern his pique. The subject under discussion was historic art thefts. This includes the Elgin Marbles (which some think we pinched from Greece). The committee has yet to announce its conclusion, but it is possible it may recommend that art reparations are overdue. The Government does not want to lose the Marbles, but should it place principle above political expediency?

Labour's Lin Golding certainly thought so, and wanted Mr Howarth to make a decision. 'I can't see what else ministers are for,' she told him briskly.

Mr Howarth is a man of fastidious habits, physical and intel-lectual. His short hair is so neat you can see the lines left by the teeth of his comb. A marathon runner, he is slim. His lean hands are lightly tanned, his calcium-rich fingernails manicured.

In speech he maintains a moderation, in volume and tone, that would be the envy of NASA's mission control. All consonants are enunciated and his vocabulary is lawyerly. He prizes reason above rhetoric and may consider emotion a weakness.

'My predecessor was disinclined to ratify the convention,' he said at one point (i.e. it was too hot a spud). He spoke of 'the burdensome nature of compliance' to a treaty (translation: too much work). And 'it is a fairly loosely drafted convention' (translation: sloppy, appears to have been written by some monkey).

So when he paid smooth compliments to the committee, one looked for the hidden meaning. 'An enormous amount of spadework has been done,' he said. 'Very many thanks.' This translated as: 'All right, push off now. You've had your fun.' Mr Kaufman's voice drooped with sarcasm as low as an autumn tree laden with plums. 'We are thrilled by that,' he said.

Next time he sees Tony Blair I imagine the words 'please', 'sack' and 'Howarth' may well cross his cold lips.

9th June 2000

Betty Boothroyd had been Speaker since 1992. She was magnificent: objective, humorous, distinctive, imperious. No spin doctors for her. When she rises to make a statement in July 2000, there has been no advance briefing as to its content.

Be happy for me, said Madam Speaker

GOOD Lord, they're clapping. Applause! In the House of Commons! This was the sensation of the day – the decade – when Speaker Boothroyd told the Commons that she had decided to retire. No one had expected her to step down so soon and the imminence of her departure made some MPs gasp. Others just looked wretched, distraught, as miserable as small children on being told that the family labrador has been run over by the post van.

Applause is not normally permitted in the Commons. Traditionalists chose not to join in, but no one tried to stop it. The clapping lasted for a good minute. One Labour MP told me afterwards that it was started by Helen Southworth (Lab, Warrington S), but I thought it began in the packed Strangers' Gallery, where members of the public sit.

Miss Boothroyd stared in amazement at this spontaneous tribute. Several members on the Government front bench clapped, as did a couple of Tories (Oliver Heald and Bernard Jenkin). Even the civil servants in their little box behind the Speaker's Chair put their soft palms together.

More traditionalist-minded MPs, mostly Tories, did not. Were they being stuffy? I don't think so. Their reluctance to clap in the Commons can be compared to the discomfort some people feel about clapping in church.

There was a catch in Speaker B's voice as she made her brief statement. The House groaned as soon as it realised what she was going to announce. 'I have undertaken on a number of occasions, as Members will recall, that the House will be the first to know when I decided to retire.' MPs: 'Oh!' If it had been an American Thirties film, some flat-capped Irish New Yorker would have raced in from the wings and shouted: 'Don't do it, Mac!' But Miss Boothroyd had made up her mind and there was no stopping her.

'I now wish to inform the House of my intention to relinquish the office of Speaker immediately before the House returns from the summer recess.' MPs: 'Oh!' She gripped her script between fingernails painted scarlet. It shook slightly. She added that she will be stepping down as an MP. The House sustained this further blow with a deep moan.

'Be happy for me!' said Miss Boothroyd, throwing wide her robed arms. She smiled benevolently and it was at this point that the clapping began. To Margaret Beckett, Leader of the House, fell the task of responding to the heavy news. Mrs Beckett's voice wobbled with emotion. Granite bleeds.

After Mrs Beckett's remarks, the House emptied into the

lobbies to speculate about Betty's successor. Miss Boothroyd blew a kiss to someone on the Labour side. Several MPs approached the Speaker's Chair to press her hand, among them the Education Secretary, David Blunkett. Nicholas Soames (Con, M Sussex) stood to attention at her side and bowed his head as he took his leave. Miss Boothroyd's good friend Gwyneth Dunwoody (Lab, Crewe and Nantwich) gave her an affectionate pat.

A young Tory, David Prior (N Norfolk), removed his spectacles and rubbed his eyes. Miss Boothroyd herself dabbed at the skin below her left eye. Was it a tear she was brushing away? But there was still work to be done. 'Order!' she said. 'Order!'

13th July 2000

As one old hoofer departs, another arrives, in the altogether.

The Graduate, Gielgud Theatre

AFTER weeks of anticipation, the moment when Jerry Hall was to take off her clothes for the first time in front of a West End audience arrived last night.

Not since Lady Godiva rode through Coventry in the altogether has so much fuss been made. Would she perform the Texan version of the Full Monty? And how would her previously derided acting skills cope with the role of Mrs Robinson in *The Graduate*?

For erotic thrills it fell some way short of a What the Butler Saw machine. For dramatic poise, think Trumpton on a slow day. But at 8.19 last night, London's theatreland stopped in its tracks when Jerry Hall dropped her towel and bared her breasts to a gawping, gaping throng. With the stagelights dimmed, the strip was as genteel as a Women's Institute calendar. Two fried eggs in the gloaming – that's all I saw. Voyeurs will have left the Gielgud

Theatre frustrated. But Miss Hall's opening night in *The Graduate*, playing vampish Mrs Robinson, filled the theatre with a static buzz. Jerry in her birthday suit!

Her acting may at times have been as wooden as a toothpick and she was hard to hear. But no one seemed to mind. With Miss Hall's ex, Mick Jagger, in the audience and an almost full house willing her on every inch of the way, the evening could only be a success.

Suspension of disbelief is said to be essential in the drama business, but last night no one really believed they were watching Mrs Robinson. It was tall, Texan Jerry they had come to see – and they weren't going to let a little am-dram acting stop their pleasure.

Crowds of slightly sweaty blokes were forming outside the theatre almost two hours before the curtain rose. Kate Moss turned up with a strange old man in a pirate bandana. It turned out to be the socialite Nicky Haslam.

In the foyer of the venerable Edwardian theatre, a stall did disgustingly brisk business selling *The Graduate* tee-shirts (£16), *Graduate* keyrings (£8.50) and, at £25, *Graduate* 'bath sheets' (as they call a towel in California). 'Would you like me to seduce you?' runs the show's motto – Mrs Robinson's line to young Benjamin Braddock. Would you like me to fleece you?, more like.

Miss Hall made her entrance in a slinky blue cocktail frock, with a drink in her hand and her hair up. Those celebrated blonde tresses did not stay in a bun for long. Soon they were unlocked, flowing gorgeously over the satin sheets in the hotel room where Mrs Robinson makes young Benjamin a man. Though the stripping was done in a trice, we did get to see a lot more of Miss Hall's long, lean upper arms and her supermodel ribcage – worthy of a prime butchered baron of beef. For those with an interest in theatrical detail, the strip itself lasts eight seconds.

Unexpectedly, Miss Hall was less convincing as the seductress than she was in the scenes where Mrs Robinson turns into a self-reproachful drunk. Maybe those recent scenes with her straying husband have taken their toll. Mr Jagger himself, just in front of me, sat bewitched, sucking hard on a Murraymint as though in a trance. No one clapped the leading lady more enthusiastically.

1st August 2000

Talking of hams …

Shades of Portia

CORNIER than Kansas, more sugary than an urn of navvies' tea, but Tony Blair's speech to the Labour conference was a brilliant turn.

He was sweating like a garden sprinkler. Not only was the conference hall hot, but he was also warmed by a barrage of stage and TV lights. A saveloy under the lamps at a chippie.

From the first word – 'y'know' – this was vintage Blair, the arch Mister Sincere, Mister Earnest Salesman. His goods for sale? A drifting political party which entered this week fretful for its prospects. This extraordinarily personal, pseudo-confessional speech perked them up no end.

By way of a warm-up we were given endless renditions of a pop song 'Let's Work Together'. Tough-guy security guards with earpieces prowled the stage area and a party hearty who resembled Sir Les Patterson guided VIPs to their seats. The atmosphere was part rock concert, part Papal visit.

The hall was packed. Surviving Labour leaders were all there – avuncular Lord Callaghan, Michael Foot in a leather biker's-style jacket, and Neil Kinnock, who walked in combing his ginger hair. Revolting habit to do your hair in public. No wonder he lost.

Cherie Blair dispensed continental kisses. Cherie has yet to master the soufflé-light air kiss. She grabbed hold of one old dear by the chops and set about her like a fairgoer with a toffee apple.

And then Blair was with us. Or should I say among us? For he had a remarkably messianic gleam.

He spoke of his 'mission', of his 'moral crusade', his firm beliefs and of how Labour's 'vision' was 'morally right'. Some passages of his text were liturgical in their metre: 'I am listening. I hear. And I will act.' There would be a Small Business Service to act as people's 'advocate and protector'. Pure Book of Common Prayer.

He told us we all had 'God-given ability' and it was his duty to nourish the country's 'soul'. A baby squawked and was jolly lucky not to be baptised there and then. One expected to be given a toll-free number somewhere in Alabama to make credit card donations to this most plausible of telly evangelist's pastoral funds.

Talking of cash, he ran through a long list of cuts which would allegedly need to be made to raise the £16 billion worth of cuts suggested by the Tories. They sounded awfully scary. But just how hard *is* it to trim state spending? A minute later Mr Blair blew a cool £1 billion on some dubious PT scheme to be run by Trevor Brooking.

He departed from his released text to give us a long spiel about his 'irreducible core'. He didn't mean that nuclear waste we had to ship back from Japan recently. These were his non-negotiable beliefs. It was a bold ploy, as fine a spell of off-piste skiing as you will ever see at Klosters or St Moritz. He hammed it up like Portia doing the 'quality of mercy' speech. He placed his right hand over his heart. It was fantastically over the top, which probably means the electorate will love it.

27th September 2000

The following week, ambitious Michael Portillo thought he might try to match Blair.

How the hombre came to us as an 'umble man

BRAVE hombre, Michael Portillo. In a coochie-coo speech, he not only poked fun at himself, jabbered in Spanish and told Tory activists that they should be more tolerant of gays (pass the smelling salts, Thelma!). He also, amazingly for a modern politician, delivered his entire oration from memory.

Intellectually, the speech was airy. Some of my brainier colleagues were left unsatisfied, like trenchermen served hole without the toad.

But it was never designed for eggheads. This was a mood piece, a dim-those-lights-baby-and-try-this-for-hot-pash number.

Everything depended on the delivery. So the Shadow Chancellor committed it to memory, spurned the lectern, and thereby won the day.

He entered the hall with a male-model sashay and introduced us to his front bench team. It could have been the start of *Blankety Blank*, except this lot were even less well known than the C-grade celebs on that show these days.

The stage set at Bournemouth is retro-groovy in a *Blake's 7* sort of way. The fixtures and fittings are all at queer angles. Talking of which, Mr Portillo knew he had to refer to his sexuality. So he declared: 'We are for people whatever their sexual orientation!'

Your average steak tartare might expect a warmer reaction at a rally of militant vegetarians. There was a sticky silence.

Two other things had to be addressed: his personal defeat in May 1997, and rumours of his leadership ambitions. The latter was done when he hailed William Hague's 'composure and courage'. Cue thunderous applause (Tories are terrific clappers). Mr Hague is much liked by his party, in a way his poor predecessor never was.

That dark hour at the Enfield election count gave Mr Portillo his best passages, and provided the semi-repentant theme. He came to us an 'umble man. He recalled that during his 'sabbatical' he worked briefly as a hospital porter. He was wheeling a very ill patient one day when the fellow suddenly came to. On seeing Mr Portillo, he 'sat bolt upright like Frankenstein's monster'.

It was a remarkably smooth performance. For years one has grown used to the Tories being naff and galumphing while the Blairites did the earnest, personal agony stuff. Earlier yesterday, when I saw a handlebar-moustached man bearding Ann Widdecombe at a bookstand, there was no reason to believe things had changed.

But here was a gooey, user-friendly politician, strolling around the stage like Kilroy, looking the cameras right in the eye and daring the voters to disbelieve him. His lacquered fringe curved like a Hispano-Suiza's mudguards.

A burst of fluent Spanish – '*antes de que te cases, mira lo que haces*' – explained his doubts about the euro, and made you think, 'Hmmn, this guy's fairly handy.' He didn't quite go weepy when he told us that his Spanish father came to Britain as a political refugee, but he has certainly had further to rise than Lady Jay. When speaking of poverty, Mr Portillo's gaze narrowed with actorly concern. He nodded to reinforce his sincerity. At one point he even echoed Tony Blair's 'I just can't do it' line from last week – although Mr Portillo was talking about breaking budgets, rather than cutting welfare.

Was he mocking the great Downing Street ham? Or mimicking him? Hard to say.

But you fight like with like, and this was certainly a speech for the Blairite age.

4th October 2000

The start of a long acquaintance …

The Members have spoken. Let's pray they haven't made a horrible mistake

PITY about the whiff of class envy, chippy as a burger bar. Pity, too, that MPs voted with such mule-headed, lumpen-massed party loyalty.

But after six and three quarter hours they – or rather the parliamentary Labour Party – plonked for Michael 'Gorbals Mick' Martin to be their next Speaker. We must now hope he lifts his game.

Our compère for the day was Sir Edward Heath, magnificently creaky, his eyes as watery and mournful as an elderly labrador's.

At his side sat the clerk of the House, whispering prompts out of the side of his mouth and nudging the old boy when to stand.

Once the selection process got under way it proved less complex than we had feared. Gorbals Mick was set up on the shy and it was the job of rivals to dislodge him. None did.

'Clear the lobbies!' sang Sir Edward, in a frail but pleasing tenor each time a division was called. After ten minutes he would then sing 'Lock the doors!', his pale eyebrows lifting as he searched for the high note. Costumed attendants sprang to bolt the doors and bar the way to the voting lobbies.

Mr Martin gave a dog of a speech, having scribbled a few notes and mumbled his way through them in a Billy Connolly accent. He slipped in his humble background, but then insisted that should have nothing to do with anything.

Oh sure. The subtext was clear: I'm a puir, wee Glasgow lad, whereas Sir George Young is an Eton toff.

It was embarrassing that he had not found a non-Labour MP to propose or second his candidacy. Instead we heard from the Old Labour veteran Peter Snape – who snarled at the Tories – and from the Labour MP Ann Keen. She is big on homosexual rights. Not so Mr Martin.

His was the least persuasive of all the candidates' sales pitches. On sheer rhetorical merit he didn't deserve more than a capful of votes. But that's not the way things work in this sorely unbalanced parliament. Labour MPs gave the impression they saw this as a chance to rub the Tories' noses in it.

'Clear the lobbies!' crooned Sir Edward, doing better than Sinatra in the twilight of his career. As soon as we got the result of the first vote – against Sir Alan Haselhurst – it looked likely Mr Martin would coast it. 'Lock the doors!' tweeted Sir Edward, almost snapping his fingers in Cliff Richard-style syncopation.

We were honoured with some rare sightings – Michael Heseltine in the chamber, and Ken Livingstone in the upstairs gallery. Good Heavens, there was Mohamed Al Fayed's friend Charles Wardle, MP for Bexhill and a man as infrequently seen as a marsh harrier on the Fens. Vast Tommy Graham appeared, first time for ages.

A pale Peter Mandelson looked in. Tony Blair sat on the front bench throughout, his hair perhaps less grey than a few months back. 'Lock the doors!' foghorned Sir Edward, now a fluffy phonograph of vintage Caruso.

As soon as Sir George was beaten there was no point continuing, but the minor players wanted their compliments aired.

Richard Shepherd's was the most acute speech. And Gwyneth Dunwoody gave a super little cameo, beautifully poignant. One was reminded of the young Judi Dench as a Shakespearean heroine. Gwyneth was sporting a new hairdo and she looked longingly at the empty Speaker's chair. But no dice. Speaker Martin was 'dragged' to his new chair, as is the custom, at 9.21 p.m., Mrs Keen biting back tears and other Labour MPs gloating as they ought not to have done. Mr Martin must now prove himself his own man.

At 6 p.m. there had been a brief break, perhaps to allow a technician to wind Sir Edward's spring. It worked. 'Clear the lobbies!' he kept hooting, only occasionally fading like Hilversum on long wave on a stormy night. As for the Commons, its

Members have spoken. Let us pray they have not made the most horrible mistake.

24th October 2000

Speaker Martin's first day in the Chair. And look. Who's that backbencher being ignored?

Mrs Laing winked heavily at him. Thrice.

SPEAKER Martin's first day in the Chair! He arrived wigless, sporting black trousers rather than the traditional stockings and plus twos, with a normal pair of black Oxfords (sans buckle and Tudor heel).

But he did wear a starched white legal collar and a black gown, which made him look a bit like one of those slightly queasy Italian judges in a big mafia trial.

After all that talk on Monday about modernisation, things got under way with a member of the Whips' Office dancing prettily towards the Chair, holding a wand of office. They resemble billiard cues, the sort you get in the rougher snooker halls where someone has eaten the tip. Labour modernisers loathe these small touches of tradition, and I would not give the wands much longer for this world.

The Whip proceeded, in medieval language, to advise the House that Her Majesty the Queen had been pleased to convey 'some signal mark of her Royal favour' on Betty Boothroyd. In a modernised House he would no doubt have simply said: 'All right you lot. Buck House latest: Brenda's made her Baroness Betty.'

Mr Martin will soon learn that the Speaker's is a lonely life, for it is an Office whose holder is cut off from the camaraderie of the Commons. So one hopes he will stop winking.

Yesterday he winked repeatedly at his Labour chums, a whole side of his florid face scrunching up as his right eye squished shut.

It really is a very red face. If he was not teetotal you'd think he was a two-bottle-lunch man.

Labour MPs kept going up to him and congratulating him. They were sucking up like mad. Rather than maintain a distance, perhaps acknowledging the sycophants with a magisterial nod, Mr Martin chattered back to them. This happened so much that he frequently lost track of proceedings. He was noticeably slow in shouting out the names of the next person to speak, but we must forgive him this. It is one thing to supervise major business debates, as he so often did when a deputy Speaker, but it is quite another to supervise the rapid proceedings of the daily Question Time.

The Conservatives wore glum little faces. Not many of them showed up for Mr Martin's debut, and some of those who did probably wished they had not made the effort.

I saw only three Tories – John Redwood, Bernard Jenkin and Eleanor Laing – go up and congratulate him. Mrs Laing, in a role reversal, winked heavily at him. Thrice.

Christopher Gill (Con, Ludlow) became the first MP to get a ticking-off from Speaker Martin. His crime? To ask too long a question. Yet later Mr Martin allowed big Jimmy Hood (Lab, Clydesdale) just as long – if not longer – to ask a question in which he paid lavish tribute to the new Speaker.

John Bercow (Con, Buckingham) made repeated efforts to contribute to proceedings, bouncing up and down. Boing! went Mr Bercow. Mr Martin called a Tory frontbencher. Boing! went Mr Bercow. Mr Martin found that his eye had been caught instead by an Ulster Unionist. And now by a Liberal Democrat. And now by a different Tory backbencher. Young Mr Bercow must have spent half the session boinging and trying to catch the Speaker's eye. Without success.

Mr Bercow, one of the most assiduous of parliamentary contributors, voted against Mr Martin in the final vote on Monday. One does hope this is not going to be held against him.

25th October 2000

A cautious pussycat

THE first ever press conference by a Speaker of the Commons. It was held in the Crimson Drawing Room of the Speaker's House at Westminster, its red silk wallpaper matching the purpling complexion of our brand-new Speaker, Michael Martin.

Huge oil paintings of bewigged 17th- and 18th-century Speakers gazed balefully down at us. One, Speaker Williams of 1680, looked not unlike Ann Widdecombe.

Mr Martin was expected to declare his hunger for parliamentary change, but in the event he came across as tepid on reform. It was for others to initiate changes. Classic – the Blair Babes voted for him because they thought him a radical, whereas in fact he may be a cautious old pussycat.

It soon became clear why the Crimson Drawing Room was so named. The heating was on full blast and, with 50 or so bodies in the room, it fast became as hot as a sauna. He seemed tetchy when the name of Betty Boothroyd was raised. 'Betty has gone and I am now here!' he snapped. 'It makes no difference what Betty said. I am a different personality.' Oooh. Touchy. At one point he appeared to refer to his predecessor as an obstacle. He also compared the Commons and its procedures to 'a clapped-out machine'.

It was the same in his days as a pressed metal worker. 'If the foreman told me to do a job, even with a clapped-out old machine, I still had to do it.' That was the attitude he intended to take with the Commons.

I asked: 'Are you a staunch monarchist?' There was a hideously long silence. You could almost hear the whirring and clicking as his brain sought a diplomatic answer.

Then, slowly, it emerged from his mouth like a slow-transmitted fax: 'We have a constitutional monarchy in this country. That sits well enough with me.' Someone remarked that that hardly sounded very enthusiastic. 'It's the best I can do,' he said, with little warmth.

26th October 2000

And after that, I'm afraid, Speaker Gorbals and I never really did get on. I threw verbal custard pies at him. He glowered and grunted and soon it was made known to me that I could be ejected from the press gallery. The managing editor of the Daily Mail had to take the Sergeant at Arms to lunch at the Garrick Club and tell the Westminster authorities, politely, to get lost.

How could heavy toping be so grievously besmirched?

FIRST, like one of those newscasters adopting a sorrowful tone, I voice a warning: this sketch contains material some may find offensive. Got you hooked? Then we'll begin.

The House of Lords held its nose and again debated the Sexual Offences Bill – all about the homosexual age of consent. Or as I heard one of the House's orderlies saying to his mate: 'It's the fruits' debate.' No Blairite he.

That great newspaperman Bill Deedes has an expression for explicit phrases: 'marmalade droppers'. He imagines readers at breakfast being so astonished that they literally let the marmalade pot fall from their fingers. In the Lords yesterday it was raining Cooper's Thick Cut.

We opened with the formidable Lady Young (Con), her salt and pepper hair cropped like a loo brush. As always, she spoke with glacial calmness, urging the protection of children. To hear the word 'buggery' from her Christian lips is a curious sensation. Imagine Sir Edward Heath speaking rappers' jive talk.

Quaintly placing the emphasis on the second syllable of 'condom', she quoted warnings from contraceptive packets. Presumably some young research assistant was despatched to Boots to buy a packet of three.

She offered the Government a 'compromise' – rather an awkward term, in the circumstances. It was, in short, to permit milder gay fumbles at 16, but to outlaw more eye-watering activities until 18. From the expressions on some noble lords' faces, 98 would be too early. The 94-year-old Earl of Longford (Lab) was sorry Lady Young had conceded a deal. He felt she should have stuck to her blunderbuss. Lifelong homosexuality was 'a sad disorder, a handicap – sinful'. Lord Longford compared it to 'schizophrenia and a tendency to alcohol'.

Several peers gasped. How could heavy toping be so grievously besmirched?

Lord Alli, perfectly open about being gay, told Lady Young she was an old granny who should let the young do their thing. Lord Selsdon (Con), in a sporty sort of speech, noted that in his Navy days he would frequently remark to himself, 'Well, I'll be buggered!' I'm not sure quite where that took us, but it raised a much-needed laugh. He added that he had done plenty of fast things in his day – 'I've even eaten the private parts of a green monkey' – but none of them matched gay sex for danger.

Loitering near the Throne was Lord Bragg (Lab), thin and scruffy. High time that young man was introduced to a hairbrush.

Lady Thatcher arrived – always a sign things are hot. She perched neatly beside Lady Young to show support. On Lady T's other side sat the dashing Earl Ferrers, white moustache twitching with dismay as he dwelt on gay goings-on. Lady Thatcher found something utterly fascinating to stare at on the carpet.

For detail no one outperformed Lord McColl (Con), a surgeon. He talked of the tightness of certain muscles, anatomical canals and unpleasant germs. The chairman of the debate, sitting at the committee table, drained a beaker of water, and the Attorney General rubbed his face. Lord McColl cited learned medical journals to reinforce his concerns. He even recommended us to a magazine called *Rubber Chemistry and Technology*.

Lady Jay, Leader of the House, did not attend. She had been in earlier, looking superior. Oh, and on a day the Blairites lectured us about 'tolerance', they outlawed fur farming.

14th November 2000

Most male eyes followed the ascent of her swanlike neck

JACK Straw is the Robbie Williams of the Cabinet. That is, he attracts crowds of female fans. All right, so they may not quite be screaming, bra-hurling teenyboppers, but there is no doubting their adoration. And they might come in useful one day, should he ever want to seek the Labour leadership.

Behind him in the Commons during Home Office Questions sat several women. They included jovial Rosie Winterton (Doncaster Central), big-boned Fiona Mactaggart (Slough) and Gillian Merron (Lincoln).

With her pre-Raphaelite curls and a pair of dimples deep as inkwells, Miss Merron is the most beautiful of the Blair Babes. She is a stalwart of the Cats Protection League. Miaow!

Beside her sat Sally Keeble (Northampton N), who has a Clive Anderson jaw and the nannyish zeal you get only from old girls of Cheltenham Ladies' College.

Mr Straw's coven also included kindly Betty Williams (Conwy), disco-dancing Oona King (Bethnal Green & Bow) and the slightly scary Helen Jones (Warrington N), whose metallic adherence to New Labour orthodoxy has not yet – surely to her own puzzlement – secured her a Government job.

Mr Straw was in a skittish mood, eager to show off to his 'girls'. His Tory opponent, Ann Widdecombe, has had some difficulties of late with her ill-received pronouncements on the undesirability of drugs. 'If I was not such a fair man,' said Mr Straw humorously, half turning so that he almost faced the shiny little faces, 'I would say that the Rt Hon. Lady (i.e. Miss Widdecombe) had, er, gone to pot.' Not since *New Faces* had one heard such a laboured gag, but it was good enough for the groupies. They tittered like nestlings, with the exception of Miss Mactaggart, a stolid sister who would look at home in a boiler suit. She let rip a huge honk of laughter which ricocheted off the ceiling and shot back down as sharp as a thunderbolt. Anyone sitting in the wrong place could have been crisped.

Miss Merron got to her feet and most male eyes followed the ascent of her swanlike neck. She put some slender question about crime trends. Mr Straw thanked her for her invaluable contribution and congratulated her on the fact that Lincoln is one of the safest cities in the country. Miss Merron gave a Zuleika Dobson smile, touched her dark fringe and resumed her seat with feline exactitude. A good student, Miss Merron listens closely to debates. She writes on her Order Paper with a pen, makes an apparently attentive note of what is said – even when it is being uttered by chumps such as Bob Blizzard (Waveney).

Who knows? She may be writing her shopping list; perhaps a billet-doux. But as far as her fellow MPs are concerned she is recording their brilliant *bons mots*. Every time she does it she wins another admirer. Clever.

21st November 2000

Throughout the Blairite years our political class declined to act its age. As Blair's first term nears its end the same hedonistic delusion, the same Peter Pan syndrome, is evident in popular culture.

Madonna in Brixton

THEY were paying £500 a ticket on the Brixton black market last night to watch a 42-year-old mother of two gyrate her hips and shriek about the meaninglessness of love.

Madonna, three months after giving birth to son Rocco, presented a firm tummy and a busy pelvis to 3,000 fans in south London.

She turned up on stage three hours late, sang for little more than 30 minutes, and frequently panted for breath – shades of a no-hoper in the 2.30 at Kempton Park. But the audience loved it.

The American singer, based in Britain these days with her fiancé Guy Ritchie, gadded about like a girl half her age. She wore a black leather jacket and flared black trousers, separated by an inch or two of creditably taut flesh.

'Tell me love isn't true, it's just something we do,' crooned the putative, big-biceped Mrs Ritchie. At times she was accompanied by four male dancers – bare-chested Charlies enacting 'erotic' routines.

According to no less an authority than the opera critic of *The Times*, her voice has dropped an octave in recent years. It remains powerful enough – Dame Margaret Rutherford on steroids. The electricity required for last night's multi-decibel performance must have sapped the national grid.

Her PR people had been busy. Such was the hype that one tout was asking £500 for tickets. The Metropolitan Police treated the occasion like the state visit of a US president.

Although the doors opened at 7 p.m. she arrived on stage only at 10 p.m., and managed the merest handful of songs. The audience? Sedate and fairly posh. Average age must have been close to 40 although many were trying to look younger. Grown men, probably company directors by day, drank American beer by the neck. A portly girl in a stetson chomped on a Twix. Those of us in pinstriped suits were in a minority. I spotted only two teenagers.

Jemima Khan floated upstairs to a VIP suite. Mick Jagger was expected. Ross Kemp, once Grant Mitchell of *EastEnders*, skulked by. Barbara Windsor flashed her teeth at the cameras.

The stage was decorated with bales of straw and a Chevrolet pickup truck which had been draped by a vast Union Jack. The flag lifted and there was our star, huge mouth agape, gap teeth bared. 'I let the music take me,' she wailed, before throwing herself into abandonment. She jiggled her bits, propelled her groin towards the dress circle and popped a cowboy hat on her dyed blonde hair.

It was noisy, mildly naughty, and the middle-class audience swooned at the din. She is not half the singer Aled Jones used to be, but five times the star.

Thank goodness she managed to find a babysitter.

29th November 2000

The Whip's wife wore a jewel like a giant Strepsil

THERE were empty seats at yesterday's Queen's Speech. Blairite peers perhaps find they have better things to do than listen to the person still acclaimed in the match programme as 'Her Most Excellent Majesty'.

Absentees missed some good sights, particularly among the diamond-studded peeresses. Peers' wives only get an airing once a year and they give it the full mustard.

Sixtyish Lady Wolfson, holding up well, presented a bold front in risqué blue lace. Lady Burnham flashed a tiara that could probably solve Third World debt in one go. Lady McIntosh, wife of a Labour Whip, had a jewel stuck on her forehead. It looked like a large Strepsil. Raven-haired Lady Saatchi had poured her cleavage into a tight little black number. Lord Bragg kept finding reasons to engage her in cross-eyed conversation.

Was it my imagination or were MPs noisier than usual when they ambled in after Black Rod's summons? Sir Peter Emery, one of three Tories in morning coat, arrived like a man to a cocktail party. He 'coo-eed' to a chum among the Lords Temporal.

Some of the Labourites growled approval when the Queen read the sentence which could signal the end of hunting.

HM's expression at this moment would not have discredited a poker table, but the Duke of Edinburgh maybe gripped the handle of his sword a little tighter.

The man is a stoic to endure as much as he does. For compensation he could yesterday gaze at the shimmering spectacle before him – not least youthful Lady Northbrook, who has the look of a Texan beauty queen and had opted for a silvery dress as shiny as Bacofoil.

Perhaps the most glam peeress on parade was Lady Pearson. A long dress of cool ivory silk was draped over her lithe frame and at moments it seemed she must pop out of it. Lady Pearson is what used to be called 'a little cracker'. She balanced out her colleague in the fourth row back – a bejewelled old boiler who was a ringer for the late Sir Michael Hordern.

The modernisers have not yet robbed the State Opening of all its pomp and splash. Beefeaters and Household Cavalrymen stood erect along the approach to the Throne. The Master of the Horse was there (on foot), as were the Captain of the Yeomen, the Mistress of the Robes, Clarenceux King of Arms and many more. Sweet Lord Maltravers, aged 13, was one of four pages of honour. He looked at the assembled scene and his mouth fell open.

In the ambassadors' box, the Omani representative wore a sky-blue turban that may mark him down as a Coventry City fan. Georgia's man was in national costume – a white coat with tassels – while the Yemeni envoy sported a turquoise smoking jacket. Very Noël Coward, my dear.

The Moroccan had a Tommy Cooper fez and the Iberians did not skimp on gold braid. Senegal sat there, a huge black chap in brilliant white robes. The Norwegian's chest clanked with medals. The Holy See looked glum.

Her Majesty's speech, all 12 short minutes of it, was bound in a slender booklet. Think of the wine list at an Angus Steak House. Lord Irvine, Lord High Chancellor, produced it from a saddle bag after executing a creaky genuflection to his Sovereign Lady.

Lady Jay, to one side, stood holding the Cap of Maintenance and looked a proper prune. One sometimes wonders if these ancient titles were devised simply to exact a little satirical revenge on our over-proud legislators.

Cherie Blair, watching from a side gallery, wore a royal-blue hat with grey feathers – Whitehall pigeon? She was in a trouser suit, as was the President of the Council Margaret Beckett. For much of the year Mrs Beckett wears elegant dresses, but for some reason it's always trews for the State Opening. I fear she may be trying to make a point.

7th December 2000

A frail figure stood before scores of full-bellied elders

NOT since the six-year-old Mozart played his first concerts can so many old men have listened so closely to a boyish figure with a piping voice and delicate bone structure.

Yvette Cooper, Health Minister and (reckon some – but not yet me) a future Labour leader, was opening last night's big debate on embryology.

Miss Cooper is the size of a jockey. Clip her on to the back of a well-fuelled racehorse and she'd be worth a fiver at William Hill. Her smallness was yesterday accentuated by the fullness of the Chamber. She stood there, one frail figure before scores of full-bellied parliamentary elders.

Some of the troglodytes on Labour's 'awkward squad' bench smirked as she approached the despatch box. Privately they think Yvette is a bit of a little Miss Perfect who needs the shine taken off her ego.

Over on the Tory benches her path to the Commons Table was also tracked with interest. Looks like a choirboy, y'see. But they listened. She held the House in the palms of her neat, red-scrubbed hands and spoke her piece in a clear, confident voice.

Were I her oratory coach I might counsel less wobbling of the head. And the northernish accent seems fake, as though she might be trying to sound more working-class than, as a daughter of

Hampshire and Balliol, she can realistically claim to be. Daddy was a big shot in the Engineers and Managers Association, and before she became an MP Miss Cooper was a rather earnest journalist on something called the *Independent*. It has not exactly been a life story of unremitting hardship.

Her aim was to persuade the House to give scientists greater freedom to dabble around with human embryos. MPs had been given a 'free' vote, allowing them to vote according to their conscience. Shouldn't they always do so? I only ask.

Miss Cooper's case, in short, was that ethical queasiness about the use of human 'stem cells' (which are taken from embryos) should not have precedence over medicine. It is possible that stem cells might be used to help find cures for some people suffering from Parkinson's disease, multiple sclerosis and Alzheimer's. Miss Cooper may have slightly hyped this aspect.

For the first half-hour the debate was civilised and intelligent. Miss Cooper was quizzed by the likes of Michael Fabricant (Con, Lichfield), Ruth Kelly (Lab, Bolton W), Ian Gibson (Lab, Norwich N), Edward Leigh (Con, Gainsborough) and an arm-waving, Magnus Pikesque doctor called Howard Stoate (Lab, Dartford). When Dr Stoate speaks, you hold on to your inkwell.

Often they seemed to know more than Miss Cooper but she managed not to be pushed off course. Some passages of her speech were overripe, particularly when she described some of the patients who could be helped by stem cell research – e.g., the Parkinson's sufferer 'who cannot sing nursery rhymes to her children'. Yeurrrch!

Mr Gibson, a scientist, started heckling Tories. Ann Winterton (Con, Congleton) came in for particular flak, but given her reluctance to take interventions, she probably deserved it.

Some of the Blair Babes – accompanied by honorary girlie Ben Bradshaw (Lab, Exeter) – tutted and twittered about Mrs Winterton's speech being 'disgraceful! disgraceful!' No doubt we'll have a lot more of that type of thing today in the fox-hunting debate.

Thank goodness treacly Miss Cooper won't be speaking in that. If she ever got on to the plight of little furry things she'd give us all diabetic highs.

20th December 2000

Skewered by the Hindujas passport affair, Peter Mandelson makes his second unhappy departure from Cabinet. And minutes later has to appear in the Commons.

The front bench slunk in to sit well upwind of the rotting carcass

NOT SINCE decapitating days at the Tower of London has a public figure been so publicly chopped. Less than an hour after leaving Number 10, a pale-necked Peter Mandelson entered the Commons to bid his world a cold adieu.

His resignation, at 1.33 p.m., had been met by an almighty roar in Westminster. It must have been like this in Neanderthal days when caveman spearchuckers bagged a mammoth.

Here was a big, big beast laid low. And 57 minutes later the parliamentary afternoon began with Northern Ireland Questions – Mandy's call! It was followed immediately by Prime Minister's Questions and the wretched leper had no option but to sit beside his beloved leader, the leader he had so grievously diminished.

Northern Ireland Questions normally draws a sparse crowd but this was standing room only. I feared one of those dodgy-Spanish-hotel-collapse disasters, such was the weight of hot humanity as Fleet Street's jackals craned over the balcony for a gander.

At first Mr Mandelson seemed sanguine. His fringe had redis-covered its Brylcreemed aplomb and he brushed some lint from his elegant trouser knee. He was in Ulster little more than a year but he did bring a certain style to the province.

He praised the 'typical resilience and professionalism' of the Royal Ulster Constabulary, yet the words could equally have applied to himself as he applied his sleek mind one last time to paramilitaries and the 'peace process'.

Gone for good, the bright prospect of playing host at Chevening. Gone for good, the happy chance of holding Tony's hand aloft at the start of a second term. He had lost, lost for evermore, his position, power, patronage. How, as he gripped that precious red folder with its engraved crown, how he must have ached to say boohoo.

Boo-hiss, reckoned the Tories. A few of them laughed at his misery.

Mr Mandelson's composure was tested when Mr Blair praised his dear friend's 'courage and sense of duty'. Was that a little wobble, the start of a crumple on poor Peter's chin? Mr Blair himself seemed close to tears at times. Had someone started humming the theme tune to *Love Story* we'd all have blubbed buckets.

Well, nearly all of us. Down on the Government bench there was more jockeying for position than you get at a St Trinian's school photo when the girls are vying to avoid Vaseline-thighed Miss Muscle, the lacrosse teacher.

Geoff Hoon, Defence Secretary, was the only senior minister to support Mr Mandelson by attending the whole of Northern Ireland Questions. Other colleagues appeared at a dishonourable dribble.

Alan Milburn, Alistair Darling and Stephen Byers slunk in, to sit well upwind of the rotting carcass. Gordon Brown entered, as reluctant as a racehorse being pushed into the stalls. Jack Straw, whose officials may have been the ones to trigger the scandal, took a seat beside Mr Mandelson with so deep a gulp he almost swallowed his tongue. He happily moved out of the way for a (just) straight-faced John Prescott. Margaret Beckett lingered by the double doors, delaying till the last moment the shimmy towards her seat.

But the Education Secretary, David Blunkett, was good enough to shake Mr Mandelson's hand. It was one of those diplomatic drinks party handshakes when the other man won't let go. So long did Mr Blunkett grip and squeeze – perhaps seeking signs of a pulse – that it seemed he must have put his palm in super glue. A full minute later it was still going on, with Mr Mandelson wondering when he could have his paw back.

When Mr Blair himself arrived, there was the oddest of moments. The PM seemed to offer the sad heap a half-smile of sympathy. Mr Mandelson, by way of return, shot him a sideways glance. It looked like a darting glance of wounded betrayal.

Before long the chamber went wild as William Hague waded in and the Tories yabba-dabba-do'd. Labour backbenchers returned the decibels with gusto. But their shouts were for the endangered Prime Minister, not for the fallen schemer at his side.

25th January 2001

DOWN in Committee Room 16 a white-robed delegation from Nigeria, led by His Excellency Prince Bola A. Ajibola, was given a hard time over corruption. The Prince was accompanied by General Alhaji Aliyu Mohammed, national security adviser to President Obasanjo. They were appearing in front of the International Development Committee, along with Dr Usman Bugaje, a Mr Ebenezer Obeya, a Mr Ayo Oke and one Enrico Monfrini, lawyer. MPs quizzed these stalwart lads about Third World corruption. The Nigerians listened with the greatest tact and replied in rather chewy west African accents that had the stenographer in a terrible tangle.

General Mohammed, a short fellow with a passing resemblance to the late Sid James, adjusted his national costume hat and rubbed his brow. From the sound of his grunts and the semaphore of his arm movements I would say he was being as helpful as could be, like a country farmer giving directions to a townie motorist.

Would the Nigerians not have been justified, however, in saying: 'Corruption? But I thought you lot at Westminster were the experts.' After the Mandelson/Hinduja scandal, can we ever again lecture the Third World about the purity of our political system?

26th January 2001

Silken disloyalty

LAST year the election of the new Speaker was conducted by Sir Edward Heath in his role as Father of the House. Few held it to be Parliament's finest hour (seven hours, to be exact).

The Procedure Committee is considering ways to improve the election system. We may be stuck with Speaker Martin, but the hope is that in future we have a better procedure.

Sir Edward, who appeared before the committee yesterday with former Speakers Lady Boothroyd and Lord Weatherill, does not hear as well as he used to. It would have been a kindness had the room been equipped with loudspeakers, or even an ear trumpet. High-ceilinged Committee Room Eight has the acoustics of a hangar at Duxford.

His eyelashes have moulted and he is a little stooped, but at 84 Sir Edward remains in possession of a good mind.

It took some time for the questions to get through from Aix to Ghent. The committee chairman, Nicholas Winterton (Con, Macclesfield), shouted at Sir Edward like a backseat passenger in a Tiger Moth talking to the pilot. But once the Father of the House heard them they were dealt with in the customary manner – a shrug of the shoulders, a faint hint of derision/dismay/humour, and a creaky reply which managed to patronise and rubbish in equal measure.

It will be gathered that, on the whole, Sir Edward was moderately satisfied with the existing system. As ever, the ruder he was, the more lovable he was. At one point he spoke of 'our side of the House', but immediately clarified this to 'my party's side of the House'. Was rank disloyalty ever so silken, so subtle?

A Labour MP, Clive Efford, complained about powers that the House of Lords retains over the Commons. Was this not an outrage? Sir Edward was unfussed. 'All I want to do is have a decent House of Lords,' he croaked. Lady Boothroyd cried: 'Come and join us!'

Cogent, twinkly Lord Weatherill, brown as a coffee bean, was the most radical of the trio. And he was aghast at the rotten press Gorbals Mick has received. Hear hear! How dare journalists mock so fundamental a public servant?

Lord Weatherill also felt that MPs should vote in secret for their Speaker and he wondered if it might soon be time to have a Speaker chosen from the Liberal Democrats. Again, a splendid idea. Let's kick out Gorbals Mick and have a Liberal as soon as possible.

31st January 2001

In private, the late Lord Weatherill was far less complimentary about Michael Martin. Around this time I went to see him in his office at the Lords. Martin's name came up in conversation. Jack Weatherill raised his eyebrows and groaned. I invited him to be bold and voice some criticism in public of a Speaker who clearly needed a steer. But he would not do it, arguing that it would be bad manners.

At this rate, we won't have many laws predating Lord Longford

ANOTHER lump of constitutional masonry came whistling off the ceiling yesterday. The Government pushed through something called the House of Commons (Removal of Clergy Disqualification) Bill.

This bins the long-standing rule that men/women of God cannot become MPs. A few pulpit thumpers such as the Reverend Ian Paisley (DUP, N Antrim) and the more mild-mannered Reverend Martin Smyth (UUP, Belfast S) dodged the ban because they are Nonconformists. The current laws apply only to clergy ordained by a bishop.

Nor would the existing laws have prevented the flying mystics of the Natural Law Party from taking their seats, had they ever managed to land on one.

But until now a person could not sit on the green benches from Monday to Friday and then, on Sunday, don cassock and surplice and administer Holy Communion to his or her voters. It may not have stopped Lambeth Palace being staffed by wet-palmed pinkos from the Sixties onwards, but it at least meant that the clergy were generally seen as non-partisan. Now the Government has decided to incinerate leathery old statutes including the House of Commons (Clergy Disqualification) Act of 1801 and section 9 of the Roman Catholic Relief Act 1829.

I confess that a little bit of me perishes whenever a 200-year-old tradition bites the dust. At this rate we won't have many laws that predate Lord Longford.

At first inspection yesterday's debate looked like one for history buffs, but it also showed how jumpy the Labour party managers are, despite their vast majority. They imposed a three-line Whip on this arcane little Bill, even though it had cross-party support. The Tories happily gave it a free vote.

The Bill, introduced by Peter Mandelson's assassin Mike O'Brien, was not inspired by any great principle. This is no personal criticism of Mr O'Brien, who was only acting under orders (as is his wont).

The Government wanted the law changed because it had discovered that one of its prospective candidates could be blocked because he has worn a dog collar.

A man called David Cairns, Labour's candidate in Greenock and Inverclyde at the next general election, is a former Roman

Catholic priest. So was the former CND leader Bruce Kent, who stood for Labour in the 1997 election. But the ex-Monsignor Kent is a man of infuriatingly independent views and somehow the Blairites were less exercised about making sure he had a fair run. Which is the greater inconvenience? Find another stooge to stand in the Greenock and Inverclyde constituency? Or rip up constitutional laws, some of which go back to the 16th century? You get no points for guessing the answer.

Ann Widdecombe, Shadow Home Secretary, was magnificent. In opposing the Bill she was witty, sharp and refreshingly cerebral. Mr O'Brien, who takes the orthodox new Labour view that every story needs a victim, claimed that the old laws reflected 'bigoted anti-Catholicism'. Utter bilge. He was duly put in his place by Miss Widdecombe, herself a Roman.

She felt priests had no place in Parliament. 'I find intriguing the possibility of a priest from Holy Orders, which demand poverty, chastity and obedience, functioning in this place,' she said. There's certainly something unsporting about politically active prelates. They make you want to swear terrible oaths. Even if they're losing an argument they will lay claim to some moral force, doing so with a patronising smile.

Just like Tony Blair, really.

7th February 2001

To the maestro of linguistic spaghetti, this made sense

ONE of our few parliamentarians to be fluent in Swahili (she once did a teaching stint in Kenya), Hilary Armstrong, can be adjudged something of a linguist. Lord knows what language she was speaking yesterday.

Miss Armstrong, worthy if dull, is Minister for Local Government and Regions. She has held this turgid brief since May

1997. No one else much fancies the job. Yesterday she arrived in the Commons along with John Prescott's numerous other minions for Questions on the Environment, Transport and the Regions. It is such a large department that when they enter the chamber it is like a rugger team sprinting on to the pitch before a big game.

Blackpool North's Joan Humble shook her fluffy mane and asked Miss Armstrong about 'local strategic partnerships'. You would be within your rights to ask me what these are, what they concern, if they are a Good or Bad Thing. Being a broad-brush sort of man, I haven't a clue. Nor, after listening to the following answer from Miss Armstrong was I much the wiser.

'Mister Speaker,' she began.

Alas, those were about the last comprehensible words. At that moment some higher hand seemed to activate the radio scrambler. 'Local strategic partnerships,' uttered Miss Armstrong, 'will provide a single, overarching, local, coordinated framework which will enable local stakeholders to address issues that really matter to local people. They will prepare and implement local community strategies and local neighbourhood renewal strategies. They will allocate local neighbourhood renewal funds which will double to £200 million and rationalise local partnerships working to deliver better services.'

Mrs Humble nodded, but surely not because she understood the Minister's reply. It was more the nod of a polite tourist who has asked a thick-accented Cypriot restaurateur to describe his dish of the day and has been unable to digest the stream of imperfect English that smuggles its way past his luxuriant moustache.

Being a Russian-speaking Slav (it's true), Mrs Humble was not to be outgibberished. She fearlessly invited Miss Armstrong to dwell at greater length on the 'successful existing partnership Blackpool has developed, which will form the basis of the new local strategic partnerships'.

Miss Armstrong fought back. With the aplomb of a drunkard reading from the Esperanto phrase book, she assured us that the

Government was committed to a 'cross-sector, cross-agency umbrella partnership which will offer real opportunities for strengthening existing partnership arrangements and make them more effective by making better connections between individual initiatives'.

Bletchley Park's finest would have had trouble with this enemy signal. Sir Patrick Cormack (Con, Staffordshire S), in plaintive tone, asked: 'Could the Minister's answer please be put in to plain English?' Miss Armstrong reacted peevishly. 'I am very sorry,' she cried, 'that the Hon. Gentleman was not able to hear because of the noise being made by the Opposition front bench.' (There had been a certain amount of guffawing from the Tories.) The Great Communicator was not finished. 'We are establishing,' she said, 'local strategic partnerships, each local authority working out how to work most effectively an overview of the whole area to really make sure that they identify strategic priorities, who will act on them and how they will ensure that services work better in their area.'

Beside her sat Mr Prescott, beaming with pride. To the maestro of linguistic spaghetti all this clearly made perfect sense.

14th February 2001

Speaker Martin again clashes with young John Bercow. I used to talk to Bercow occasionally in those days. He happily encouraged me to attack the Speaker. 'It is possible to respect the Chair and not esteem its occupant,' as he said.

He went ballistic. 'Withdraw that remark!' he snapped

VARIOUS forms of behaviour are forbidden in the Commons. MPs may not hiss, boo or crow like cockerels (ever since the night of 19th March 1872 when over-refreshed Hon. Members screeched 'cock-adoodle-dooooo' during a particularly dull speech).

Erskine May's Parliamentary Practice lists unparliamentary insults ranging from 'stool pigeon' to 'cheeky young pup'. Anyone using such words can expect to be reprimanded by the Speaker. Today's Conservative MPs have found a way of getting round this. Instead of actually saying 'cheeky young pup' they have simply started behaving like impertinent young dachshunds. There is a reason for this: the inadequacy of Speaker Martin. Gorbals Mick is increasingly a figure of slim authority. His calls for 'order!' go ignored. His scowls bounce off their targets. Many Tories laugh at him almost openly. The old booby's writ runs short.

Yesterday, during Treasury Questions, Gordon Brown and Michael Portillo were arguing about the euro. The Government is spending £9 million on preparations for the single currency. Mr Portillo, cross about this, suggested that the Chancellor intended to pull a fast one on the euro referendum.

'Con man!' muttered John Bercow (Con, Buckingham).

The only person in our gallery who heard him was a bat-eared chap from Hansard. But Gorbals Mick, who has loudspeakers in his chair, picked it up all right. He went ballistic. 'Withdraw that remark!' he snapped.

A little plot exposition may help you here. Mr Bercow, who is aged about 15 and a half, is a Tiggerish Rightwinger blessed with a photographic memory. This faculty for figures helps him make formidably detailed interventions. He is the sort of man who could memorise a telephone book, so you will not need telling how clever-clever he is with political statistics.

Should the voters of Buckingham ever tire of him Mr Bercow could find useful employment as one of those Memory Men popular on the vaudeville stage in the Thirties.

Old Gorbals Mick, who could not memorise a bus ticket, has little time for young Bercow. 'Dislike' is not quite the term. It is more a combination of seething hatred, disgust, and bitter, bitter envy. That explains why he came down so hard on Mr Bercow yesterday, even though the 'con man' slander was sotto voce, and probably true.

It could easily have been thrown not only at Mr Brown but also at fellow ministers.

The veteran Sir Michael Spicer (Con, Worcs W) wondered why productivity was down. Andrew Smith, Treasury Chief Secretary, replied that it was, in fact, 'rising'. Nicholas Winterton (Con, Macclesfield) fretted that the savings ratio was as low as it has ever been. Mr Smith, strangulating vowels without mercy, replied that 'the savings ration is rising'.

Edward Davey (Lib Dem, Kingston & Surbiton) had no more joy when he dared suggest, using official statistics, that Labour has spent less on public services than the Tories. He was simply told he was wrong.

Someone must have been telling lies. Rather than engage in debate, ministers just bring down the shutters, effectively saying 'you're wrong – we're right'. In such circumstances you need a strong-willed Speaker to allow backbenchers a little leeway.

So did Mr Bercow withdraw his slander? He did, but with such palpable sarcasm that I fear it will only have infuriated Gorbals Mick all the more. His fellow Tories grinned and threw contemptuous glances at Mr Speaker. Mr Bercow spent the rest of Treasury Questions trying to make a contribution. He was ignored by the Chair.

30th March 2001

If this lot really are the People's Peers, then I am a Swahili pot noodle salesman

AN OLD friend of Peter Mandelson ('known him since our early 20s') yesterday told us the names of the lofty elite who will help govern Britain in future.

The announcement was held in a cosy room off one of

Westminster's most chichi arrondissements. Welcome to democracy in the Blairite age. Over coffee and upmarket biscuits Lord Stevenson of Coddenham, an Establishment schmoozer of the first water, unveiled what Downing Street calls 'the People's Peers'.

Lord Stevenson was uncomfortable with that slightly sweaty term – and you could soon see why. The worthies on his list, published last night in the august *London Gazette*, have little in common with what New Labour patronisingly calls 'ordinary people'. This lot, almost to a button, are part of 'the game': adroit insiders, established movers in modern London's tight-knit political firmament.

They even include Lady Howe, wife of the former Deputy Prime Minister. Poor Geoffrey. The House of Lords was one of the few places he was safe from bullet-nosed Elspeth. Now she'll be near him on the red benches, scowling at the world.

Lord Stevenson, who owns four properties and has links, past and present, with 36 companies, is a fit, busy little fixer: wiry of build, an inexhaustible networker. Tony loves him. Like Mr Blair he attended a Scottish public school. 'Off' is pronounced 'orf'.

The 15 new peers appointed by Lord Stevenson's unelected commission comprise three professors, seven knights, one Lady, one think-tank chief, two charity chief executives and one prominent businessman. Downing Street had been happy for us to believe that there was a possibility of frontline teachers, ambulance drivers, midwives and the like being appointed to the Lords to freshen up Westminster.

It gave every impression that this was what it wanted; staging meetings around the country, launching a web-site, strewing information packs like confetti, contacting 10,000 organisations. That has proved a cruel mirage.

If this was about the democratisation of politics, the broadening out of parliamentary engagement, I am a Swahili pot noodle salesman.

Lord Stevenson, 55, who made his name in market research, is the embodiment of Britain's new brahmins. He said how 'very pleased – extremely pleased' and 'delighted' (five times) he was with his list. Well of course. They are just his caste.

Repeatedly he boasted that this was a 'transparent' selection operation, yet he declined to explain why the individuals had been chosen. He was asked why were there no bus conductors or hairdressers. Ah, he said, that was because we need to have people who feel 'comfortable' in the Lords. So that's it: unless you feel 'comfortable' under the Upper House's high, gold-leafed ceilings, unless you are 'comfortable' in the company of bishops and barons, you can kiss goodbye to the thought of joining the new ruling class.

Lord Stevenson said he did not know what 'the great and the good' means. Look about you, man! Alongside him sat most of his fellow commissioners – figures plucked mysteriously by a firm of accountants who were appointed by Mr Blair and his henchmen.

The Roman satirist Juvenal once asked: '*Quis custodiet ipsos custodes?*' Let's tweak that a bit and ask: Who selects the House of Lords selectors? The answer? A bunch of suits from a highly secretive City headhunting firm.

The commissioners include the head of No Smoking Day, a social exclusion expert and a member of the Home Secretary's Race Forum. The No Smoking Day woman became distinctly stroppy when asked to justify her position on this commission.

Lord Hurd, former Foreign Secretary, did his best to look intelligently ruminative. From time to time he would deliver a patrician *bon mot*, having pondered the philosophical posers thrown up by this democratic outrage. Sitting on this commission has not been Douglas's finest hour.

Lady Dean, sometime print union leader and more recently a member of the blind trust fund for Tony Blair's Labour leadership office, sat beside Lord Stevenson. She glowered at those of us who dared ask impertinent questions.

What right do Lord Stevenson and his ilk have to choose our legislators? This should be a job for either an elected, accountable head of government or for direct voting. This contracting-out of patronage stinks. How will we in future be able to scrutinise the commission's work?

Mr Mandelson 'just happens to be a friend', claimed Lord Stevenson, his plastic enthusiasm fading. He had 'never had any political involvement' with Peter. How good to know Mr Mandelson observes such a clear distinction between his political and personal lives.

A man at the back of the room suggested that the old system of hereditary peerages was more effective at throwing up people who had experience of humdrum, 'ordinary' life. Lord Stevenson hummed for a while before saying: 'This takes us on to very interesting conceptual territory.' Another reporter was upbraided for being 'too simplistic' in expecting 'ordinary' people to have made it on to yesterday's list.

Lord Stevenson stressed that he expects the new peers to be regular attenders and to work hard in the House. What might be the benchmark?

Might it be Lord Stevenson's own attendance record? In the 1999–2000 session of Parliament he managed to attend 22 days out of a possible 177.

Downing Street later sought to clarify the term 'People's Peers'. A spokesman averred: 'They are People's Peers in the sense that they are people who put themselves forward for peerages.' How foolish of us ever to have expected anything else.

27th April 2001

Clammy with sincerity

CHEESY as a Cheddar bap, Tony Blair yesterday opened Election 2001 in front of 600 bare-kneed, pigtailed London schoolgirls. At first they greeted him with teenybopper screams – particularly when he whipped off his jacket.

Mr Blair hijacked afternoon assembly at St Saviour's and St

Olave's, a school Harriet Harman once considered insufficient for her family's needs. Mr Blair had no such qualms about using the place. Use them he did, big time. This was the tackiest, tinniest political event I have (yet) been to.

He entered after an African freedom song, which swelled in an heroic crescendo for our hero's arrival. His speech followed the multicultural school choir's warbly rendition of a song called 'We are the Children of the Future'.

'The children are our future,' said Mr Blair, clammy with sincerity. 'That's very pertinent.' Hymn books were distributed and he stood at the lectern in front of some ecclesiastical stained-glass windows and a large cross.

His speech was delivered like an American telly-evangelical sermon and concluded with an echo of the Parable of the Talents. This guy really does defy satire sometimes.

'We're on our way to Heaven,' sang the girls of the choir. From the wings, Alastair Campbell watched with jaw twitching, eyes narrowed, a Doberman guard dog alert for Tory fifth columnists.

The school's headmistress, a bulletproof type called Irene Bishop, sat on the stage alongside Mr Blair. The two of them wore gottle-of-gear grins, chins held high for the cameras. A tattooed school janitor had told reporters to move out of a row of seats on the grounds that they were needed by the children and 'the kids are more important'. 'I'm not sure the PM's flunkeys would agree with you,' growled a senior television journalist.

One later learned that Mrs Bishop is a fanatical Blairite who considers him 'the most wonderful Prime Minister in the world'.

The seven-page speech did not exactly grip the audience, few of whom looked old enough to vote, this time or next. One girl covered her head with her pullover. As Mr Blair rambled on about devolution and mortgage rates, another girl leaned on her neighbour's shoulder to doze. Mr Blair made little effort to address the audience in front of him. They were only there for the TV cameras.

As soon as his speech was over, we had hymn 330, 'Here I am, Lord'. Tony sang the first few words until the TV arc lights started to switch off. Then he left, stiff-grinned, grabbing young girls by the hand as they tried to sing their hymn.

Opposite the school gates was a dusty-looking premises which identified itself as Pan African Legal Advisory Services. Next to that was an empty building with a 'Principle To Let' sign. Principle was the name of the letting agent.

As we filed out of the assembly hall, I asked a group of young-sters what they had made of the Prime Minister's speech. One, about 13 years old, wrinkled her nose and replied: 'Bunch of lies. He's a big crook.' Oh dear.

9th May 2001

Modern election campaigning is a bizarre activity. The political leaders are cocooned from the public. Having covered the last three general elections in some detail, I don't suppose I have met more than a handful of voters who have been swayed one way or another by all the frantic campaigning.

He struggled like a bluebottle on treacle

FROM several thousand feet up in a Titan Airways Boeing 737, call sign G-ZAPM, the clouds parted momentarily to betray snow-speckled Highland hills below. This was about as close as Tony Blair got to real earth yesterday.

We were en route with the Labour leader to Inverness, 570 miles from London. Sadly it proved the briefest of calls. Mr Blair flogged to one of Britain's most northerly cities to appear for little more than 20 minutes. The only place he visited was a building site to gawp at 'the biggest hole in the Highlands'.

He put on a Bob the Builder hat and yellow jacket, met a few pre-selected workers and burbled small talk which we could hear on a feed from a microphone in his tie. The hole was the start of a shopping centre.

'Yeah,' the Premier said to the construction staff, 'wow! aha!' The ten or so employees were on best behaviour – their guvnor was looking on.

One was a crane driver. Mr Blair gave a sticky grin. What to say to a crane driver? 'Er, amazing things, cranes!' he said. 'Great! Aha!' The fellow agreed.

Next up was an engineer. 'Yeah!' said the PM. 'I've always wanted to know what an engineer does.' On to a bricklayer and ganger. 'Aha!' said our helmsman, struggling like a bluebottle on treacle. 'Er, yeah!' The bricklayer gave him a slightly uncertain look, as though he might have been expecting slightly more.

And that, on the day Mr Blair boasted about his desire for 'a sensible and serious dialogue with the nation', was the morning's work. He returned to the airport.

Day seven of the Labour campaign, which also included a visit to a plastics factory in Aberdeen and a question and answer session chaired by the Victor Meldrew actor Richard Wilson, was about TV pictures and image bending.

Propaganda, we used to call it. Now it is called sophisticated campaigning.

At the plastics factory some uniformed employees stood respectfully in a row, like squaddies on parade. Their boss had gone to the trouble of donning his kilt. He duly became another in the growing band of decent folk who have been ruthlessly used in this campaign. TV soundmen swung pendulous microphone booms right over their heads, wrecking any attempt at normal conversation.

Sweating photographers clambered on stepladders. The factory workers looked perplexed and a little scared. In the background a large rotational oven turned slowly in a corkscrew motion. Here was a big machine, spinning and manufacturing something plastic and moulded. Labour's Millbank operation does much the same with politics.

The campaign 'message for the day', since you ask, was 'prosperity for all'. It was certainly a good day for security goons and limo drivers. Kevlar-jacketed police and bossy jobsworths were everywhere.

At the building site a mustachioed little man, name of Magson, bossily told reporters to behave or skedaddle. 'I wish you weren't here,' said the old charmer. Ah, you can't beat Scottish hospitality.

At Inverness airport, most of us walked the 80 or so yards from the terminal building to the plane. It took a three-car convoy, headlights and hazard lights blazing, to convey Mr Blair.

On the short flight to Aberdeen he wandered back in to our part of the 737 to spin a line about his desire for a campaign based on policies rather than personalities. Oh, come off it, I snorted. How can voters tell you their policy concerns if you never meet them face to face in unguarded, uncontrolled environments?

Mr Blair, who is chunkier up close, and a little less boyishly charming, angrily denied that the campaign was being conducted in a vacuum. 'I'm answering lots of questions that are difficult,' he claimed. On arrival in Aberdeen the telly cameras were positioned to catch him walking over to a small group of spectators.

Real people! Or maybe not. Peeling away from the herd I took the opportunity of talking to them, too. They were all ardent Labour supporters who had come to the airport specially to greet the PM.

15th May 2001

He wafted £20 in the greasy air of the Happy Haddock

FOR four and a quarter glorious minutes yesterday Tony Blair did something radical. He went walkabout 20 yards down a west Yorkshire street and shook hands with a few 'real' people. Showing us what a straight-up, geezerish Mister Ordinary he is, he darted into a fish and chip shop called the Happy Haddock.

From an à la carte tariff, which included spam fritters (50p) and chip butties (£1.10), the Prime Minister selected haddock and chips twice – for himself and the local Labour candidate. Mr Blair wafted £20 in the grease-scented air. Proprietress Teresa D'Arcy would hear nothing of it. 'On the house!' she declared. When it came to applying salt, Mr Blair betrayed a certain lack of expertise. The indomitable Mrs D'Arcy said he had ruined his lunch with such a heavy hand. Mr Blair assured her he would enjoy her fare, no matter what!*

The excitement of his foray outside the protective bubble of party aides, his first such adventure this campaign, was wondrous to behold. The words 'bun' and 'fight' do not start to capture the ferocity of the mêlée.

The event occurred at about 1.30 p.m. in Bradford Street, Brighouse, after Mr Blair paid the briefest of visits to a Labour club. This was a drab place, under the Sundaze Tanning Studio which advertised 'eight-minute sessions'. That's longer than a Blair walkabout.

The Happy Haddock was five doors down. Around Mr Blair was a phalanx of thick-necked bodyguards. Protection also came in the form of local party activists.

Trouble came primarily from two sources: a small but determined knot of elderly Tory partisans, led by a blonde. She turned out to be the local Tory candidate, Sue Catling. The other troublemakers were the photographers. When Mr Blair started his walkabout they went crazy, cantering after him amid a clatter of equipment, as the crowd of 100 bodies surged towards the Happy Haddock. I found myself pressed against the armpit of a burly detective. The next second, my nose was pointing towards the deep bosom of a Tory matron. A camera fell to the ground, I heard a dress rip, a muffled scream.

At one point Mr Blair stuck out his arm to shake someone's

When the PM made it back to his bus he was photographed eating one chip. He then handed the packet to an aide. I later saw it in the bus's bin, the food untouched.

hand. A Tory stalwart gamely filled the Prime Ministerial paw with a wad of leaflets.

'Tony!' yelled numerous voices. At that point I took a blow to the head and the world stopped spinning. Yes! Electioneering! A real campaign! At last!

At times, the PM would disappear from view and you feared that, like a surfer under a monster wave, he had been engulfed. But then his super white grin would bob back to the surface, borne high by the slow-moving scrum of humanity as it moved, crab-like, down the street. The scene was something akin to the Eton Wallgame, in which schoolboys huddle around a pig's bladder in one vast, muddy mess.

Mr Blair's day, starting early in Aberdeen before he flew south to Manchester, had opened in characteristic style – with a stunt. Spin doctors discovered our trusty Boeing 737, nicknamed Prime Minister One, would later fly Liverpool players to Europe for today's UEFA Cup Final. We were told Mr Blair had drafted a chummy letter wishing the lads luck. In Manchester we stood on a rainy airfield while Mr Blair opened a new runway by taking a pair of kitchen scissors to a ribbon.

And then came a visit to a police training school where we saw recruits doing physical jerks. This took place in a gym which smelled faintly, as do they all, of sweat and dust. Plimsolls thudded and squeaked on the parquet floor. Punch bags swung and the recruits did a series of 'muscle memory' exercises to help in the future apprehension of villains.

Mr Blair entered with a senior copper who looked like the late actor Deryck Guyler, Corky in the old TV series *Sykes*. As he watched, Mr Blair commented: 'I've never been great at running.' Running for election?

The police listened politely to him, but a more representative view, perhaps, came in Brighouse. Minutes before his arrival, a middle-aged housewife, Manuela Wilson, laid down her shopping bags to survey the scene. 'You haven't got any rotten tomatoes in there, have you?' said a policeman.

'No,' said Mrs Wilson. 'Pity,' said the officer. 'Would you like me to go and fetch you some?'

16th May 2001

How the toff whose butler has a butler suffered a dire sense of humour failure

LABOUR'S newest and richest parliamentary candidate swanned straight past a *Big Issue* salesman yesterday and straight into trouble, when he was confronted by a tailcoated butler.

Shaun Woodward, the former Tory frontbencher who has been shoehorned by Tony Blair into the 'safe' Labour seat of St Helens South, once remarked that 'even my butler has a butler'. But when we offered Mr Woodward the services of a butler in his working-class constituency he had a severe sense of humour failure, and ran away.

We were only trying to make him feel at home in his chosen new environment, for St Helens is a place where a man can go for weeks without sight of a manservant.

Butler Ashley Powell, 38, who has worked in some of London's finest houses, including Kensington Palace, approached Mr Woodward while he was canvassing shoppers in the Merseyside town's Church Street. Jaws dropped when Powell, with all the shimmering serenity of Jeeves, walked towards the unsuspecting New Labour multimillionaire.

Woodward was seeking the vote of an elderly lady when the butler did it.

'Excuse me, madam, excuse me, sir,' said the white-gloved Powell, holding a silver tray with a half-bottle of Albert Etienne brut champagne, a flute glass, and an ironed copy of the *Daily Mail*.

'May I invite you to enjoy a drink?' The lady – I regret that in the ensuing fracas we were never introduced – squinted at the champagne with interest. She was tempted. But Woodward, who took a moment or two to react, did a runner. With an 'oh come off it!' he bolted, as fast as a motorised rabbit at the greyhound track, straight for the nearest shop. It was a Littlewood's, and he entered at speed. The words 'your nuts, your crackers, sir' were still fading from Powell's lips when Woodward's political aides moved in.

A Millbank minder wanted to push Powell out of the way. 'If I could respectfully invite you to refrain from personal contact, madam,' said the impeccably mannered Powell, who works for the Ivor Spencer International School for Butler Administrators.

It was a good few minutes before Woodward re-emerged. He was steaming. 'Why? Why?' he glowered. 'How dare you?' It is, I fear, the end of our friendship.

It was incongruous to see Shaun Woodward in a hard-up former mining town such as St Helens. In the past we have lunched at Princess Diana's favourite London restaurant, Le Caprice, where Shaun sucked a huge cigar. We once had drinks in a well-appointed apartment off New York's Upper West Side. The Shaun Woodward I used to know was a man of bountiful tastes.

His current billet, a £44-a-night room at the Raven Lodge Hotel, is a change of pace. The décor in the bar is tired, a dusty air vent clacking in the wall and beer stains on the floor. He could have stayed in the nearby Hilton, and for one week's worth of interest on his fortune he could buy a house in the constituency. But the Raven Lodge suits his scheme at present.

In its dingy bar he met a delegation of sacked workers from the nearby Ravenhead glass factory. He was smoking cigarettes – perhaps he has gone off cigars. The workers had real grievances about pensions and future employment. As Woodward listened to them he posed for a BBC film crew.

Three lads were playing pool. What did they make of the plutocrat exile from down South? 'We get all sorts in 'ere,' shrugged John Norman, 26, a Labour voter in the past who this time felt he might vote for an independent candidate.

Earlier, I had visited Woodward's campaign HQ where I found his wife, the delightful Camilla Sainsbury (of the supermarket family). The office was chaos: maps of the constituency everywhere and a photograph of Tony and Cherie Blair on the mantelpiece, a bit like the way foreign embassies always have a portrait of the Queen.

Frank Faulkner, retired, watched the dust swirl as Woodward legged it off towards the Town Hall to hand in his election nomination papers. 'He's a fool, that bloke,' said Mr Faulkner. And the *Big Issue* salesman, Paul McCarthy, 31, was miffed that the immensely rich Woodward had not bought a copy of his magazine. He declared our stunt with the butler to be 'sound'. Would he vote for Woodward? He pulled a face. 'Tory, wasn't he? Nah!'

18th May 2001

Charles Kennedy as George Clooney

LET'S have a big hand for Alexander Loudon, a 60-year-old heart patient from Hampshire who yesterday allowed his hospital operation to be interrupted for a general election photo call by Charles Kennedy. Mr Loudon was on the slab at Southampton General when the Liberal Democrat leader, dressed in George Clooney 'greens', burst through the door with two of his local parliamentary candidates.

Health was the Lib Dem 'theme of the day'. And here was a party supporter prepared to make almost the ultimate sacrifice.

'I have my qualms,' said Steve Livesey, surgeon, as he watched the politicians seize Mr Loudon's frail hand and give it a good pumping. 'But the patient agreed to being visited.' Like any good Liberal Democrat, Mr Loudon knew exactly what to say. 'I'm voting for you lot,' he croaked to Mr Kennedy and Co., 'and when I get out of here I'm looking forward to paying very much more in taxes.'

Mr Loudon was kept waiting fifteen minutes for his angiogram while Mr Kennedy got into costume and scrubbed up. Mr Livesey insisted that the patient was in no pain.

The Southampton visit came towards the end of another feverish day in the Lib Dem campaign. We started in Edinburgh, flew to Manchester, bussed it to Oldham, ricocheted back to Manchester, then were catapulted down to the south coast before the drive to London. Time in the air: two hours ten minutes. Time in the bus: three hours thirty minutes. Live campaigning time: one hour twenty.

And that was a good day. On Tuesday he flew to Cardiff for a twenty-minute session. Today it will be north Norfolk and Guildford, lucky them.

The idea is to visit two regions a day, preferably at such a lick that people mistake young Gingernut for a man of genuine importance without actually having time to pummel him hard on his policies. This is a toe-dipper of a campaign. The politician has become a marble in a pinball machine, flicked from here, flapped to there, with no tilting. Certainly not: it is soft drinks only on the campaign plane.

24th May 2001

William Hague having resigned immediately on losing the general election, the Tories need a new leader.

Quiff like the bow wave from a surging speedboat

FINE speech, I'm sure – but no one who turned up yesterday morning could hear a word of what Michael Portillo said when he launched his campaign for the Tory leadership.

Mr Portillo did his stuff on the steps of shiny new Portcullis House, roughly ten yards from one of the noisiest road junctions in Westminster. 'I wish to put my name forward ...' began the likely new Leader of Her Majesty's Opposition.

Peep peep! tooted a taxi and a double decker dusted us in soot.

'I want to make some remarks about what sort of party we should be ...' said Mr Portillo, with that slight air of indigestion that screams out for a dose of Rennie's. PARP! burped a ruddy great construction lorry driven by a bloke with a bare chest.

An unladen artic' clattered over a pothole and a despatch rider's scooter mosquito-snarled off in the direction of the Embankment. From the television satellite trucks parked on the kerb came a loud throb. Throughout all this we strained to catch what the great new hope for the Right was saying.

'What's 'e bangin' on about?' enquired an elderly woman at the back, holding on to her wheelie shopping bag.

It was a bit like watching a pre-talkies motion picture. The hero's ripe lips were moving open and shut and he narrowed his eyes beautifully although that might simply have been a reaction to the din. The bit-part actors were rapt.

Mr Portillo's aides listened with just the right mixture of sobriety and confident enthusiasm. The rest of us hadn't a clue what he was saying.

He had appeared punctually, just as the last bong of 11 o'clock from Big Ben was fading. A few Tory MPs, among them Nigel Evans and James Paice, had formed a little support knot inside Portcullis House, squeezing their hands in excitement.

When Mr Portillo emerged from the building he was accompanied by a slick-backed Francis Maude who followed a step or two behind the master like a well-trained geisha. Mr Maude stood uncommonly close to Mr Portillo while the latter spoke. It was reminiscent of Prince Charles standing next to Diana on the day of their engagement.

Mr Portillo had memorised the speech, just as he memorised that speech to the Tory conference in Bournemouth last autumn. His latin hair was immaculate, fringe swept up and over like the bow wave from a surging speedboat.

As he spoke he held his arms wide apart and pulled the air towards his body with spadelike hands. It was the gesture of a restaurateur encouraging evening strollers on the Avenida Electorate to, *por favor*, step inside and examine his *menu del dia*. He grinned, just shy of greasy, and his tongue roamed his mouth for moisture.

Following Mr Portillo's speech outside Portcullis House, Mr Maude said a few words. The old dear with her shopping trolley butted in again. 'Is that Ancram?' she enquired.

As he disappeared one of his little helpers started to give journalists a list of senior Tories who had 'come out' for Portillo. Not the most felicitous of expressions, perhaps.

14th June 2001

His wife wore a cardigan and a look of worry

ALL this stuff about how brave Michael Portillo was to talk about his gay days is tosh. Iain Duncan Smith, another of the Tory leadership contenders, yesterday did something far more risqué. He started quoting 18th-century philosophers.

Has the man no shame?

Does he not realise, furthermore, that this is Blairite Britain, where voters – so the spin doctors reckon – have the intellectual capacity of Highland midges?

Mr Duncan Smith is the bald one with the large family, crackly voice and that slightly rabbitty upper lip. He is a v. decent guy. The only problem is that as far as the public goes he is as recognisable as one of those yashmaked Middle Eastern Sheilas you see in the souks on London's Edgware Road.

Tory leadership (re)launches are a bit like BBC programmes. If you miss one, it will soon be repeated. Yesterday we had two. Mr Duncan Smith's effort took place in a St James's hotel. On arrival, one was greeted by coffee and biscuits. I chose a Jammie Dodger, if only because the person who wins this election will need a few jammy dodges up his sleeve.

It is not automatically easy to see Mr Duncan Smith as that person. For all his abilities, he just seems musty and high-domed. First, he quoted John Wesley (1703–91), clergyman and founder of Methodism. The dictum was 'earn all you can, save all you can, give all you can'. Mr Duncan Smith talked of the importance of volunteers in society.

Although grand stuff for a Wesleyan sermon, it is less plausible as an electoral sales pitch to the nation of Posh and Becks, Sunday supermarket materialism and me-me values. He then spouted Edmund Burke (1729–97), philosopher and writer about the sublime. It is a courageous politician who willingly introduces the word Burke into a public discussion.

There were quite a few MPs in attendance, mostly ardent Thatcherites – the shoulder-twitching, facial tic tendency. Gentle Mrs Duncan Smith, name of Betsy, was also on parade. She wore a hair clip, a pretty yellow cardigan and a look of desperate worry for her Iain. We all listened politely to what he had to say. The man from Sky TV had gone to the trouble of wearing a monocle, such was his desire to fit in with the crowd.

The second Tory event was held by David Davis, who managed to fill a large hall at Church House. All you cynics out there will say that the venue was chosen because Mr Davis hasn't a prayer of success and needs all the divine assistance he can get.

DD looks like Bill Clinton with a bust nose. He may be an uninspiring speaker, but in accent and approach he is that rare thing in the modern Tory Party: a normal bloke. He also happens to believe in low taxation and British sovereignty.

He had persuaded novelist Freddie Forsyth to be his warm-up man. Mr Forsyth, having recently undergone surgery to an eye, took to the stage in a pair of splendid, wrap-round sunglasses. He looked like a pall bearer at a Cosa Nostra funeral.

The crowd of 300 were mainly students. One of the sideshows of this contest is seeing all the young political groupies trying to work out which candidate to support. Where lies the best career advantage? Westminster is awash with scheming nerds.

Hardly any MPs turned up, however, and that is why the competent DD, a former Europe Minister and ace scrutineer of New Labour, is said to be DITW (dead in the water). Pity.

29th June 2001

Face turning as red as a sauna bather's bottom

TWO gnarled tuskers yowling across the Rift Valley: that was the bizarre, inglorious scene in the Commons yesterday teatime shortly before the Father of the House, Tam Dalyell, was booted out of the chamber by the Speaker, Michael 'Mick' Martin.

The two old elephants were swaying on their feet, issuing subterranean grunts that were outwardly courteous but had a sharp subtext. What we saw was a brutal demonstration of the feebleness of this House of Commons.

Auld Tam was trying to make a point of order that reached into the very gizzards of our political system. Gorbals Mick, to whom we supposedly look as a defender of Parliament, wanted none of it.

Mr Dalyell was outraged that the Government had given the Commons an Iraq dossier whose contents, we now learn, were in large part nicked from some Californian PhD. The Commons had been misled. Tam wanted a minister to tell the House why. MPs felt the Government had lied to them and they damn well wanted explanations.

Who can say MPs are wrong to be enraged? But rather than let that anger be heard, Gorbals got in a low-brood strop. 'Please be seated while I'm standing,' he growled at Tam. That is certainly proper form. When a Speaker is on his pins, everyone else must siddown. A strong Speaker would not have to remind people to do so.

Mr Martin, bad at the start of his Speakership, has in recent months seemed to improve. Hoping to set Saddam Hussein an example, I signed a non-aggression pact and promised myself that I would not attack the old booby. Mistake.

The title 'Father of the House' goes to the MP with the longest continuous record in the Commons. It has generally been held by Establishment worthies who, by dint of a cushy seat and sparse physical exercise, had managed to outlive their contemporaries. Normally they were ex-ministers. Mr Dalyell's predecessor was Sir Edward Heath. Other Fathers have included Jim Callaghan and the late Bernard Braine. Fathers could be relied on not to rock the canoe.

Mr Dalyell is less orthodox. He worries away at officialdom like a dog with eczema on its spine. Time and again he will return to it to have another frantic chew. That is why he was on his feet yesterday, refusing to shut up.

'I tell the Hon. Gentleman to sit,' said Gorbals now. The 'please' had gone. 'I'm instructing him to resume his seat.' Tam refused. 'He has tested the patience of the chair,' said Gorbals, face turning as red as a sauna bather's bottom. 'I tell the Father of the House to resume his seat.' Tam, with one of his stubby-vowelled syllables: 'No.' 'I insist on my right as Speaker,' barked Gorbals. 'And I insist on my right as an MP to put a Point of Order,' said the grizzled Eeyore who, throughout his career, has said his piece, like it or not.

The impasse lasted minutes. We all looked on in astonishment. John Gummer (Con, Suffolk C) urged Mr Dalyell to yield and the Speaker momentarily allowed his attention to be deflected by his clerk, perhaps allowing Tam to sit with honour. There was no point. Seconds later Mr Dalyell was told that unless he shut up he'd be shown the red card.

'Very well,' he grunted. 'If this is what you want.' And with that, leaving behind his trademark green cushion, he headed slowly for the exit. As he departed, watched with dismay by almost everyone, he rasped that 'The House of Commons has been appallingly treated.' And so it has, by Alastair Campbell, who is so contemptuous of the voters who send MPs here. And by a Speaker who is not prepared to use his muscle to defend the Commons, but instead attacks its most senior, stalwart Hon. Member.

11th February 2003

Time for lunch.

R.I.P. the blood-red velvet banquette

HANS Blix and his chemical weapons inspectors would have donned protective suits at the sight of my Angus Steak House prawn cocktail. Rusty pink, it shimmered like the Baghdad bypass on a hot day. But silly them, and silly the rest of us who regard these restaurants as a national joke. The prawn cocktail was terrific. A humdinger.

Aberdeen and Angus Steak Houses, last redoubt of Seventies gastronomy, are threatened with closure. A rescue looks as unlikely as a request from table nine for a second flagon of Mateus Rosé. Profits have nosedived, allegedly because American tourists (who like steak houses) are staying away from London until the Iraq war is done. That sounds like an excuse to me. Fashion is to blame. Weak, impressionable, follow-the-flock fashion has seen the me-too crowd move on to raw, pricey sushi bars and poshed-up curry houses.

Aperitifs of Bristol Cream sherry and appetisers ('starter' might be a safer term, legally) of deep fried mushrooms in breadcrumbs at £4.60 are no longer 'now'. Tournedos Rossini and Duck à l'Orange and the Japanese Torpedo Prawn appear to have had their day.

There weren't many of us lunching at the Angus Steak House

next to London's Victoria Station yesterday. In fact, I was the only one. When I entered, the lone waiter gave me the sort of glassy gaze, part wonderment, part hazy recollection, with which you imagine Livingstone greeted Stanley that day in Africa.

'Sit by the window, please,' pleaded the fellow. 'Please!' He was desperate to show passers-by that the place was open for business. Anxious lest a friend spot me – even though the windowpanes were smoked glass, as found in swankier models of the Triumph Stag – I opted instead for a single banquette booth to the rear. Nearby an air vent pumped out the smell of singed dishcloth.

A loudspeaker lurked behind a pot plant, tinkling forth a medley of accordion muzak that would not have disgraced a Corsica Tourist Board promotional film of the late Fifties. The blood-red velvet-style seating squished gratifyingly under my bottom and the laminated cocktails menu winked. Go on, it seemed to say. Be a devil.

Aberdeen Steak Houses were once the height of elegance with their mirrored walls and dance floor lighting, triangled paper napkins and Escalopes of Veal Holstein. To this day they evoke an England of three-day weeks, sideburned likely lads and Desmond Bagley thrillers.

The company's origins were slightly aristocratic. With meat rationing still a memory, it was co-founded in the early Sixties by Reginald Eastwood, father of the Duke of Edinburgh's close friend the Countess of Romsey. He and his associates sold it in 1965 to Golden Egg cafeterias. In 1984 it was bought by a Turkish businessman, Ali Salih, and as recently as 1998 it was still selling about 700,000 steaks a year and turning over £20 million.

Customers liked the big portions and predictable flavours. You never got a surprise at a steak house, at least not unless a mouse scampered across the floor. There was a sorry incident two years ago when mouse droppings were found in a Chateaubriand sauce. But that can happen to anyone.

Last year the steak houses lost more than £3 million. Mr Salih finds he must now sell. As I contemplated this yesterday, the

Musak changed to a twangy guitar lament, Portuguese fado crossed with Vangelis. 'You have wine, please,' instructed my desert island companion, the waiter. If I refused I feared he would burst into tears. A glass of Muscadet arrived, cold and zingy. I have not had better at the Savoy. Enter an 8oz fillet steak, perfectly cooked, as tender as a poet's heart. Unlike so many modern restaurants there was not a single mention of 'roquette' or 'jus', nor a whisper of a mincing lisp from some Herbert pronouncing 'oregano' the Californian way. The service, throughout, was exemplary.

In a world that now pooh-poohs pineapple juice starters and the sturdy banana split, the Angus Steak House had the courage to persist. Black Forest gateau, at £4 a slice, was another heroic survivor. The lettuce-bedded, £4.60 egg mayonnaise withstood the Edwina Currie row but could now find the bean counters of Messrs BDO Stoy Hayward, administrators, a tougher prospect.

Pictures of smudgy cows in Highland settings stared down from the walls. Each footfall of my friendly waiter could be heard as he padded up with my pud: pink ice cream, smeared in shaving foam cream. Spot on again!

The place was empty but blameless. If this is the end, Aberdeen Steak Houses, what can one say, but thank you. And 'Well done'.

5th March 2003

Sometimes – quite often, actually – Establishment apologists accuse sketch-writers of nihilism and cynicism. Sometimes I almost wonder if they are right. But then I remember the day Tony Blair took us to war.

His speech to the Commons that day was well delivered but it was, we now know, based on highly dubious evidence. I'm afraid my instincts went awry. I fear that I had listened too much to the Establishment stooges and worried that opposition to war would be unpatriotic. The Tory Party made the same mistake. I – and they – should have been more sceptical.

A ladylike parp from Beckett

SOME physical argy bargy, plenty of well-sluiced heckles, and then a look of boyish relief from the Prime Minister as he mouthed 'So we're okay, then' on hearing the result from his Chief Numbercruncher.

It did not all go Tony Blair's way late last night. Nor, during a full-galleoned day of debate, did the Government escape without splinter shots to its main mast. But Parliament has had its say and with the 10.14 p.m. vote it fired the poop deck cannon for war.

Mr Blair himself contributed magnificently. This is not an easy thing to write, for his normal attitude to the Commons is rank, but yesterday he was first-rate.

He was so effective he had Margaret Beckett in tears. 'This is not the time to falter,' the PM was saying, and old maid Beckett was dabbing her eyes with a hanky. 'We must do ...' (gulp, pause, sincere search round the House) '... what we know to be right.' Another dab-dab, and now there came a ladylike parp from Mrs Beckett's delicate nose.

It really was an extraordinary speech. Mr Blair was furious with intent, fizzing with conviction, at times imploring, at others raging against the recklessness of inaction. Ah yes, recklessness. Clare Short, who threw that charge against Mr Blair a few days ago, sat a few feet down on the Government front bench. She looked like Faustus after striking his bargain.

Mr Blair rose at 12.35 p.m. to a chamber so full that they were standing nine-deep by the double doors. Peter Mandelson (Lab, Hartlepool) slunk upstairs like a household cat denied its favourite spot.

For the next 48 minutes the House's breast heaved as it grappled with the Prime Minister's reading of war. MPs sucked on their fists. Some chewed their fingers. He began slowly. It was as though each phrase was being weighed before being passed for muster. Some words were staccato. Other passages were given a thump of defiance.

Barely more than three minutes in, someone on the Lib Dem benches murmured dissent. Mr Blair fed off it in an instant. 'Of course, the Liberal Democrats!' he snorted. 'United in opportunism and error!' He immediately received a huge, prolonged cheer, from Labour and Tory alike. Just before the 10 p.m. vote Jack Straw launched a ferocious and funny assault on 'Charlie Chamberlain's' troops. It earned many drunken cheers.

Much of Mr Blair's speech, by contrast, was heard in a hush. So rapt was the House's attention that it was 14 minutes before anyone ventured to intervene. Mr Blair had statistics, lots, about Saddam's poisons. The figures were pinged out, melon pips hitting a spittoon. His disgust was even more apparent towards France, or 'the French' as they are now known. A susurration of disapproval fluttered across the benches at their name.

We had a few snipers: John Owen Jones (Lab, Cardiff C), Llew Smith (Lab, Blaenau Gwent), Simon Hughes (Lib Dem, N Southwark). Mr Blair admitted them with courtesy but had little trouble knocking them away. Glenda Jackson (Lab, Hampstead) was rebuffed. A Croydon bore, name of Davies, made to intervene and was sharply dissuaded by colleagues.

Blair, watched from the gallery by his wife, was by now talking in Biblical terms – 'There are two begetters of Chaos' – and about the world's looming new poles of power. The House was gripped.

Some, unlike tearful Mrs Beckett, will have found his peroration a touch over-sugared. But no one watching this stonking, tumultuous performance can have much doubt that yesterday Tony Blair produced a parliamentary classic.

Shortly before the vote there was some pushing and shoving just behind the Speaker's Chair, involving Peter Hain, Welsh Secretary, and the Labour rebel leader Graham Allen.

But for now the Commons tussles are done. The fighting moves to Iraq.

19th March 2003

A fashion outrage

SHOCK has been the tone of the Commons for the past week or so, but there was something different about the level of disquiet yesterday. I heard one man gasp. Another shielded his eyes. The word 'atrocity' suddenly acquired new triffid-talons of menace.

Gerald Kaufman's summer wardrobe had struck again!

Mr Kaufman (Lab, Gorton) had come along to hear Defence Questions. One admires him for his assiduous attendance. Manchester's Gorton district can settle back today warm in the knowledge that its elected Member was there, immersed, engrossed, enwrapped by the matters of the day. Yet Mr Kaufman was also enwrapped – buttoned in as tight as a pink chipolata in its plastic casing – by a Seventies disco-style black shirt and a necktie of astonishingly Technicolor stripes.

This barely does the thing justice. Staring at its sun-spots glare for just a few seconds, I made out a shocking-bright medley that ran from yellow to canary via scarlet, olive, custard, mackerel silver, blue, diesel grey, green, red and purple. At this point the survival mechanisms kicked over and I wrenched my throbbing retinas away to give them a swim in Optrex. Another few seconds and it would have been Peters and Lee time.

Adam Ingram, one of the two understrapper ministers at Defence, was being quizzed by Labour MPs about the ethics of using cluster bombs. Few Conservatives joined in the discussion, but that is perhaps because they were sitting on the opposite benches – opposite, that is, the Kaufman tie.

Her Majesty's Opposition had been reduced to a line of O-shaped lips, gaping mouths testament to the destructive power of a Gerald K fashion outrage.

It should be noted that this highly motivated man has form in such matters. A year ago Mr Kaufman entered the Commons chamber in a lightweight, chevron-shimmering, summer suit the exact colour of Somerfield supermarkets' English mustard. As with yesterday's pungent tie, it killed off all conversation within several yards.

Like all the best agents, Mr Kaufman betrayed no awareness of the mayhem he was causing. He listened to the exchanges with apparent innocence. All I could think of was the merchant who had sold Gerald the tie. I bet he couldn't believe his luck someone had finally bought the horror.

Mr Kaufman's neighbour, Jim Cunningham (Lab, Coventry S), stood no chance, poor swine. The tie's fallout had zapped him, and his voice had almost completely gone. Nicholas Soames (Con, Mid Sussex) rose to speak, but made the schoolboy error of looking at Kaufman mid-question. The tie glinted like a fifth columnist's mirror. Mr Soames appeared to forget what he was saying.

Regarding the political content of Defence Questions, Mr Hoon was again the embodiment of unflappability, although with the war started his personal exposure to political danger is much reduced. His shadow, Bernard Jenkin, is now so loyal Mr Hoon looks almost embarrassed.

Both Tory and Labour MPs demanded that Tony Blair come to the Commons to make a Statement about his latest talks with President Bush. These complaints had some intellectual coherence, but that was perhaps because by now Mr Kaufman had slunk out of the chamber, taking himself and his black shirt and his killer necktie elsewhere. Knot to be forgotten.

1st April 2003

Miss Widdecombe was by now in deep, cold storage

NEWS flash: nudist appearing at a parliamentary committee! It was still early, a goosepimplish chill in the breeze, when I got my orders to 'scramble, scramble' and dashed to the Home Affairs

Select Committee meeting on the Sexual Offences Bill. Witnesses included a big shot from British Naturism.

In the corridor outside we all looked at one another with shifty appraisal. Who was the representative from the nudist lobby? Was it that beaky chap with the briefcase? Or the butch woman with the close-mown grey hair and the hint of a grudge?

The Sexual Offences Bill could make it illegal to expose yourself in public. This, naturally, is of concern to naturists.

When we filed into the meeting it transpired that the beaky bloke was a leading QC, while the grey grudge was an outrider to a rather bossy woman from the Rape Crisis Federation. The other expert witnesses were a lawyer with an antipodean accent, a big-boned lady who looked like Ronnie Barker in drag, and a subdued little man who, with his modest gulps and downward glances, called to mind Mr Pooter proceeding to work in a suburban railway carriage. You guessed it. The naturists' leader was Mr Pooter.

The name was in fact Mick Ayers, president of British Naturism and one of our representatives on the world's leading nudist body (if that is the word), which is based in Antwerp. Mr Ayers, 56, is a former trade union official who lives in Lowestoft. He said he was there to represent Britain's 2.5 million nudies.

The meeting opened with detailed discussion about exact definitions of rape. The QC and the Rape Crisis woman deployed eye-watering terminology that I will not repeat here. They kept talking about 'the act' but I think they meant the Act. Ann Widdecombe (Con, Maidstone) listened with the frigid visage of a breakfast guest who suspects her plate of haddock kedgeree has gone off.

At one point the QC talked about 'the camp I come from' and Mr Ayers showed a flicker of interest, but it turned out the Bar whizz was merely using a figure of speech to describe his position on some legal matter. Mr Ayers relaxed.

Behind him sat two research assistants – a chinless fellow with an Edwardian centre parting and a plump matron who could have been a farmer's wife. At intervals they passed notes to Mr Ayers to assist the thread of his arguments. They were all, since you ask, fully dressed.

Chris Mullin (Lab, Sunderland S), chairing the meeting, briskly unveiled Clause 70 of the Bill, dealing with indecent exposure. Mr Ayers whipped off his glasses (nothing more) and gave an eloquent exposition of his case. In short, naturists want the wording of the Bill tweaked so that it only outlaws exposure done with dishonourable intent. Otherwise, they fear, innocent nudists could be having their collars felt. Or something like that.

He pointed out that bona fide nudists carry 'naturist passports' at all times. He did not explain quite where they kept these, but he disclosed that they bore photographs for swift identification purposes. From the sketchwriting bench there came, at this moment, a disgraceful ripple of mirth. 'There is,' said Mr Ayers, frowning, 'a need to differentiate between a very moral and proper way of life, which is a family activity' (he meant naturism), and those who hid behind trees, to leap out, naked, at strangers.

'People who expose themselves for sexual gratification,' he continued, in a slightly nasal voice delivered from one side of his mouth, 'tend to be very obvious – and if you are a male person it's very obvious in certain cases.' Miss Widdecombe was by now in deep, cold storage, limbs and facial muscles utterly frozen. Handsome David Cameron (Con, Witney) tried his best to concentrate on his paperwork.

Mr Mullin looked as though he had just swallowed the top of his Biro.

9th April 2003

A trip to Brussels ...

Three minutes to speak (and a chance to gaze adoringly at Giscard)

GISCARD d'Estaing lifted a liver-spotted hand and the House hushed. Owing, said Giscard, to the gravity of the meeting, members would be permitted to speak for longer. *Oui.* They could go on for three minutes rather than two. 'You can let your hair down,' said Giscard, himself nut-brown bald.

Welcome to the European Convention. They were discussing the creation of a United States of Europe. Want to say something? You've got 180 seconds, starting – now!

For Andrew Duff, one of five Brits, the time extension was insufficient. Lib Dem Mr Duff has a rather terrible stammer. Halfway through his allotted spell he was barely past his third sentence. The consonant C was giving him particular gyp. At one point he tried to say, 'European C-C-C-'. It was too much for one Continental nearby, who impatiently shouted: 'Convention!' Mr Duff's chest collapsed with a sigh and he rallied himself for the next word.

The debate, like the air in the gleaming Paul-Henri Spaak building, was controlled to perfect moderation. No smoking, please. Disagreement also not preferred. Passionate denunciation? Devastating putdown? That is not the European way.

Chairman Giscard sat on a platform decorated with a large, blue 'E'. To his right sat two vice-chairmen: a vast-tummied Belgian, Jean-Luc Dehaene, and little Giuliano Amato of Italy. Signor Amato, being the height of a golf bag, looked like M. Dehaene's *déjeuner.* To Giscard's left was former Whitehall mandarin Sir John Kerr, the brains behind much of the Convention. The egregious Kerr resembled a solicitor at the proving of an unjust will. Time being of the essence, the Convention wasted its first 55 minutes discussing extra meetings. Erwin Teufel, a German with wire-rimmed glasses, was appalled. 'Some of us have full diaries!' Must have got his holidays booked, I'd say.

For much of the first hour M. Dehaene sucked on his molars, extracting the last morsels of breakfast *saucisse*. If it takes some neck to be a senior Euro-politician, corpulent M. Dehaene has the equipment. He must take a size 22 collar.

Yesterday's agenda concerned the creation of a new European president and foreign minister. The big countries were quite keen. The smaller ones worried they'd never see any of the action. While smart-jacketed waiters dispensed coffee and TV camera crews barged around the floor of the chamber, a Slovenian argued that 'simple majoritarianism would be a recipe for administrative deficit'.

Several delegates dwelt on the great histories of their nations. Others spoke about 'European values of democracy', only to find that the digital clock on the wall was catching up with them.

Contributions came from a former East German ice-maiden; from a smooth Peter Hain; and from a shouting John Bruton (Ireland), who perhaps did not realise that speeches were being amplified. The translators winced through their earphones. By now M. Dehaene was bowling down one of the aisles, possibly in search of sustenance. People leapt from their chairs to greet him. 'Jean-Luc!' Much clapping of backs and juddering of jowls.

Stoutness was all around. A German called Brok, blessed with a cigar-stained voice and a thick, yellow Asterix moustache, was so rotund that his shirt buttons were as deep-set as the studs on a London clubland chair. At the back of the chamber, plump wads of draft resolutions were being dispensed. Some '*conventionnels*' had such tall piles of paperwork on their desks that they were practically hidden from view.

'Monsieur Voggenhuber!' murmured Giscard, doing his best to maintain a show of interest in the slew of three-minute homilies. We turned to a square-shouldered Austrian. Chum Voggenhuber wore no tie. He is a Green. In fact he proved a red-blooded performer, attacking the lack of parliamentary power in the proposed new Europe. Giscard and friends gazed in another direction.

A Danish ex-Communist, Jens-Peter Bonde, also made a neat attack on the lack of democracy. 'There will be no direct link between our votes and our laws,' he said. But he appeared embarrassed and ended his remarks by mumbling: 'Thanks, even if there's nothing to thank me for.' Why sound apologetic? Why presume that it is wrong to utter criticism of this undemocratic con trick?

In this almost comically totalitarian format there was no questioning of arguments, no opportunity to intervene. I turned to my Benelux neighbour in the press gallery and asked: 'So when's the vote?' 'Vote? Please. What is this vote?' I tried to explain. 'No, no,' said the Beneluxer. 'No vote.' 'Come off it,' I said. 'You even get a vote in the Eurovision Song Contest.' But he was right. The *'conventionnels'* had no vote. All they got to do, if called, was speak for three minutes and otherwise drink coffee, gaze adoringly at Giscard and run up some good expenses. It will be left to Giscard and his Soviet-style 'Praesidium' to decide on the constitution presented for rubberstamping later this summer. Anything said yesterday was of utter inconsequence.

16th May 2003

Margaret Beckett's new hairdo

'COQUETTISH' might be too strong. 'Pageboy' does not quite fit the bill. Think of early Lady Diana meets Sir Bobby Charlton. It is part-bobbed, pulled sharp to one side of the fringe, and sits just above the ears. The new style will take a bit of bedding in but it is bold and, word of the moment, modern. Well done, Margo!

In my limited experience, when women change their hairdos they are trying to tell you something. What is Mrs B seeking to impart? It is no great secret that Mr Blair regards her without enormous enthusiasm. She is Old Labour, unflashy, a bit historic. But she is also reliable, brainy, and more loyal to her party than many in this Cabinet. Some haircuts say, 'howdy'. Others, 'goodbye'. This one? 'You should have made me Leader of the House again, rather than appoint that smooth South African Hain. Don't write me off yet, Tony.'

24th June 2003

Margaret Beckett eventually (albeit briefly) became Foreign Secretary.

The spin doctor with a gold elephant-topped swizzle stick

HIS Majesty Okyenhene Osagyefuo Amoacia Ofori Panin the First, a tribal king from Ghana, visited the Commons yesterday. He chose a good day. The Right Hon. James Gordon Brown, Chancellor of the Exchequer, was on parade, full of beans.

With Tony Blair in the stink, the Labour Party eating itself, Alastair Campbell in a padded cell and Third Way politics going gloosh! down the loo, this is no time for Mr Brown to look miserable. I have not seen the Chancellor quite so cheerful since, well, the last time Mr Blair was in crisis.

Let me introduce you without further delay to our Ghanaian king. He and his tribal elders presented sat at the front of the VIP gallery, swathed in bright togas that left much of their upper torsos naked. One carried a gold standard that looked like a giant swizzle stick, topped with a carved elephant. This man was the king's okyeame, or linguist. Protocol rules in Ghana stipulate that you must not talk directly to the king but approach him via his okyeame. The okyeame is effectively the king's spin doctor.

King Panin is here on a two-week official visit. So far he has met the Prince of Wales, heir to the throne, and Overseas Aid Minister Hilary Benn, heir to the great Socialist dynasty. We have tribes here too, you see.

Treasury Questions had just begun and Mr Brown was talking, or should I say shouting, about the Government's policy on gold sales. Given that Ghana is rich in gold, this topic was of interest to the king. Some months ago, Mr Brown sold a lot of Britain's gold. He did it, with that natural brilliance of any British public administrator, at almost the very hour the world gold price slumped.

Two Conservative knights, Sir Teddy Taylor and Sir Peter Tapsell, attacked what they saw as Mr Brown's costly gamble. Sir Teddy said gold prices had risen sharply since the sale and Mr Brown had lost us £400 million. Mr Brown said that 'every country' was divesting itself of gold. Sir Peter said he was wrong. The Chinese were buying, hard. My guess is that the Chinese are probably cannier in these matters than our Treasury bean-counters.

The okyeame glanced admiringly at his own gleaming piece of gold. Perhaps that's where some of our reserves went. And then Tam Dalyell (Lab, Linlithgow) wondered where Mr Brown had got some figure about his gold sale having 'reduced risk' by 30 per cent. Good question, sir. Mr Brown: 'This study is not from a PhD thesis on the internet.' Tory MPs immediately recognised this as a brutal and blunt attack on the Blairites' dodgy Iraq war dossier. 'Ooooh!' they said.

Mr Brown, enjoying himself: 'There is no question of it ever being sexed up.' Tory Hon. Members: 'Ooooh!' Mr Brown did not just smile and laugh. He positively revelled in his act of open mockery of Mr Blair's dossier. It was, furthermore, the second time this week he has done so. His Majesty, I am sure, was appalled by this cannibalism.

One other thing of note: yesterday saw the front bench debut of David Cameron (Con, Witney). Handsome boy. Charming. Moderate. Witty without overdoing it. This was the best parliamentary debut I have seen.

But by then His Ghanaian Majesty had gone, having risen at midday from his seat with a regal yawn, to leave the chamber with a flourish of bright robes and a scattering of flunkeys. It is not known if the king's itinerary will include a meeting with Miss Carole Caplin, but if we soon see Tony and Cherie in open-chested togas, and Ali Campbell with a large swizzle stick in his hands, we will be able to conclude that their encounter was a wow.

11th July 2003

The July 2003 death of David Kelly, a Government scientist who told BBC journalists his qualms about the Iraq war, leads to the Hutton Inquiry.

Plainly, he was terrified

LABOUR politicians will speak emotively, often hysterically, about the suffering of foxes ripped asunder by hounds. Their own treatment of David Kelly was far bloodier to behold. There is a fine line between scrutiny and interrogation, between the barrister and bully. I'm afraid the Foreign Affairs Committee's treatment of Mr Kelly last Tuesday crossed it.

But what of the Whitehall and Downing Street apparatchiks who threw such a fragile man into this fray? Their conduct was close to wicked.

Witness Kelly was not a political professional. He was not an Alastair Campbell, or a Tony Blair or a big, fat, swattable Lord Chancellor. He was a midge in the swarm.

Plainly he was terrified that hot afternoon in Committee Room 15. He could barely raise his voice above a whisper. The clattering air-fans were quelled to reduce the background noise but still Mr Kelly's words were little more than a murmur.

His shoulders were hunched and his hands rotated and clutched and clawed. His head bobbed, his cheeks blushed. He cleared his throat and cast his eyes beseechingly to the distant walls. These were the gestures of a man who wished desperately that the ordeal could be done and that he could escape.

Commons select committees are important bodies – never been more vital, you could argue. We should expect witnesses to tell the truth. We should expect the MPs who sit on the committees to be proud and jealous in their defence of parliamentary scrutiny.

So Andrew Mackinlay (Lab, Thurrock) was entitled to exude brisk authority as he sought answers. The paradox was that Mr Mackinlay was trying to assist Mr Kelly's position. He suspected foul play by Number 10 and he pursued the matter.

'You're chaff,' he snapped at Mr Kelly, little more than a yard from his face. 'You've been thrown up to divert our probing. Have you ever felt like the fall guy? I mean, you've been set up, haven't you?' In the intense, humid air the words came out jagged and intemperate. It sounded as though Mr Mackinlay was attacking this defenceless academic rather than people more properly accountable.

What could Kelly say? As he looked round the committee table, he knew that perhaps four of its members were Blairite stooges.

There they sat, idle puddings dependent on the patronage of the party machine. If he said anything awkward for Number 10, would they, too, start this screaming? How would 'the office' react when he got back afterwards? Mr Kelly's brow sweated. His voice faltered. His very world must have spun.

Stodgy Bill Olner (Lab, Nuneaton) asked Mr Kelly: 'Did ya use the C word?' Mr Kelly, like any normal human being, was baffled. 'The C word?' he asked. Mr Olner, sly and self-satisfied: 'Campbell.' He was surprised that Mr Kelly should not have realised this straight away. The committee's chairman, Donald Anderson, asked Mr Kelly if he felt 'used'. He put it in a way to suggest that he thought Mr Kelly was a very silly fellow. Then Mr Anderson told him to speak up. 'I accept the process that's going on,' said the unhappy wretch. Process. What a disturbing, Orwellian word.

One MP civil to Mr Kelly was Sir John Stanley (Con, Tonbridge). He told him: 'You have acted in a proper and honourable way in coming forward to your line managers.' He said Mr Kelly had been 'thrown to the wolves' by the MoD, adding: 'You were being exploited to rubbish Mr Gilligan and his source, quite clearly.' Mr Kelly replied: 'I've just found myself in this position out of my own honesty of acknowledging the fact that I had interacted with him.' Behind Mr Kelly, and to the sides, sat a thick crowd of eager spectators. The stenographers awaited his next meek syllable. The clerks regarded him with detached interest.

There was the scrum of us press boys, thirsty for spectacle, clamouring for fresh dirt. Perhaps we need to examine our own involvement, though the blame trail must always be followed with rigour, back to the very first lie.

The same Foreign Affairs Committee, when faced by Alastair Campbell, had been far less brave. No shouting then – not from the MPs, at least. No jabbing of fingers. Chairman Anderson that time had been the oleaginous hotel manager welcoming a VIP guest.

Same when Tony Blair appeared this month in front of the Liaison Committee. No one got furious with him. Whenever the PM appears, you get more scraping than in a frostbound airport car park.

David Kelly did not represent a threat to Westminster. If anything, he should have been welcomed as a whistleblower on stronger, more menacing forces. But he was sent, he was pulverised, and now he has died.

There are those who serve our system, others who seek to intimidate and undermine it. Until MPs pursue the real malefactors, the root dissemblers, we can not rest easy.

19th July 2003

From Court 73, a dispatch on some strange goings-on

PART murder trial, part public reading from an old railway timetable. What a strange, sepulchral event the Hutton Inquiry is, and all of it clocked through half-moon glasses by the benevolent, owlish figure of m'lud Hutton.

Court 73, where Alastair Campbell will present himself this morning, is a modern affair with a low, cheap ceiling, empty bookshelves, and 46 computer screens. Plasma screens shimmering royal blue, they give it a hint of NASA's Mission Control. Houston, we have a problem. Well, Tony Blair and his friends do.

The Prime Minister's chief of staff, Jonathan Powell, appeared in the witness box yesterday. He was back from holiday, tanned, stringy and having grown a beard. He reminded me of that naked rambler who is walking across Britain. Mr Powell's soft, high voice was complemented at first by tense mannerisms. He leaned forward so that his shoulder blades assumed a gaunt angularity. His eyes narrowed whenever he sensed James Dingemans QC was trying to cause him trouble.

Mr Dingemans, effectively chief prosecutor, stood at a lectern and reached for a dizzying number of ring files. These he extracted from an adjacent shelf like a shoe-shop assistant juggling boxes of brogues. Mr Powell watched his every move. The chief of staff was feline in his gestures, precise in his choice of words. 'Salient' was a favourite. He was in a higher league than plumpish, scarlet-fingernailed Ministry of Defence press officer Pam Teare from whom we heard numerous 'sort ofs' and 'ums' earlier.

There is a patrician clique at the top of Blairism. You are struck by the difference between the civil service plodders and the high-octane operatives. The likes of blousy Miss Teare bash out the draft Whitehall press releases. It is left to the Downing Street brahmins to annotate, amend, or perhaps 'sex up'. They do so in spidery handwriting with subtle menace, always using Christian names, even to their severest foes.

What was fascinating yesterday was to have these ink-scrawled documents thrown high on the plasma screens for all to read. 'Dear Geoff' this, 'Dear Richard' that, went increasingly tense but still studiedly informal letters between a top BBC man and the Defence Secretary. 'I am sorry you felt unable to be entirely frank with me,' ran another letter. Translation: you treacherous, rank dog. But let me still call you by your first name.

Slowly Mr Powell relaxed, though he had no cause to do so. Deadly Dingemans produced aces with sly unpredictability. He elicited ripe details of plottings and 'running meetings', many attended by Mr Blair.

Near the end of Mr Powell's evidence, after a confetti storm of emails and memos and darn dossiers – did 'dossiers' exist in Whitehall before ex-journalists colonised Number 10? – we learned that the PM's spokesman considered the row with the BBC to be a 'game of chicken'. There was a small gasp in the public gallery at this.

On my way to the inquiry yesterday, in a side-alley, I saw a loose sheaf of paper on the pavement. It was a lawyer's invoice. Yet the inquiry cannot quite decide if it is a judicial process. At the start of each session an usher cries 'silence, all rise' and the lawyers, though unwigged, behave as if in a court.

Mr Dingemans's questions sounded like a High Court cross-examination. We were all aware we were sitting in the great temple of Justice off the Strand. Yet no witness yesterday spoke on oath. There is no risk of perjury. And why can the TV cameras not be permitted to show proceedings? What pompous nonsense. It is face-slappingly startling to think of the Prime Minister and, today, his right-hand man giving evidence in a witness box. The nation should be allowed to watch.

19th August 2003

My own eyes were welling. High-paid lawyers hid their faces

HER sandy-fringed face gazed down on Court 73 from computer screens, its mellow smile surely photographed before any of this hideousness began.

Here was Janice Kelly, Oxfordshire housewife, floral-bloused essence of Englishness, before being caught up in a whirlpool that dragged her family into death and drama.

And here now, for the first time, we started hearing truth unsullied by positioning or careerism. David Kelly's widow testified to the Hutton Inquiry via an audio link, which meant we could not see her expression or posture. There was just the voice, exact but gentle.

Around her eyes, in that still photograph, there played some laughter lines. In recent weeks, however, she cannot have had much levity in her life. Nor was there any in her husband's fraught final month. Just worry; such intense, soul-gnawing worry that simply to hear it described gave one a knot of acid anxiety.

Judge Hutton and James Dingemans, QC, could not have been more gentlemanly. The kindness they showed to her and other family relations was of an old-fashioned, understated sort, as was the very British stoicism shown by the Kelly family. 'You'll have to keep your voice up a wee bit,' Mr Dingemans whispered to Mrs Kelly at the start.

Every time Lord Hutton spoke to her down the line his old face creased with charity. In the end it was the kindness that got to her. It was only when thanking Lord Hutton with her final sentences that she sounded close to tears.

Throughout the session Mr Dingemans addressed his questions to the empty witness box, a box of tissues by its chair. She was in fact in a nearby room, we later heard. Her husband, she said, had become a workaholic. He was often away from home. By the standards of touchy-feely modernity it was not the most demonstrative of marriages. He would do his business travelling at weekends to reduce the call on his working hours.

Her methodical, dignified voice firming, she remembered first the years in Eynsham when the children had been small and then a pretty house in Kingston Bagpuize. This is Inspector Morse country. Listening to her evidence you felt that many of the scenes could have come staight from one of those TV murder mysteries. She talked of her local history society, of his visits to the Hind's Head pub where he played cribbage, of cups of coffee on the lawn and the occasional pint of ale (before his religious beliefs deterred him).

The mundane details were what I found hard to bear – the

glass of water and sandwich that had been his last lunch, and Dr Kelly's lacklustre digging in the vegetable patch as, perhaps, he pondered suicide. In the midst of his stress he went out to the unkempt paddock and for seven hours – seven hours! – sat on his ancient motor mower, vibrating and hot through the day. Something formidable must have driven him forward, on into this gnarled undergrowth of politics.

On the evening a newspaper reporter came lurking at their gate she and her husband had been in the garden. 'I moved a bit closer with the hosepipe,' she said, explaining how she strained to hear the men's words. References to the press were not positive, we'd better come clean and say. Journalists were described in terms of fear, almost like some secret police.

Husband spoke to wife little about his attraction to the Bah'ai faith. She knew that it comforted him and that seems to have been good enough. This was a marriage of fond familiarity but not of insistent curiosity. His daughter Rachel did not probe him about difficulties at work. 'I felt that I had intruded,' she said sadly. For so private a man the scrutiny of London committee men must have been fiendish to bear.

As Mrs Kelly spoke, the mood in the court was utterly silent and at times stunned, such as when she curtly concluded that he had been treated 'like a fly, really', or when she claimed that Whitehall had assured him his name would be kept quiet.

The day of his examination by the Foreign Affairs Committee had been their 36th wedding anniversary, she disclosed, not once fishing for sympathy or outrage. 'I was thinking about him all day.' By now I confess that my own eyes were welling. I saw some of the high-paid lawyers glare hard at their fingernails, while others churched their hands and hid their faces. One of the stenographers chewed gum as she kept pace with Mrs Kelly's words but that was the only movement in the court. The rest was silence. Dead, doleful silence.

2nd September 2003

Why it wasn't awight on the night – Michael Barrymore's one-man show

LONDON'S West End has brought us numerous tragedies over the years, but this week the curtain rose on an ordeal of all-too-horrific self-delusion. Audiences were subjected to the spectacle of Britain's onetime favourite comedian stumbling to his artistic demise.

'LIVE! ON STAGE,' cried the billboards outside Wyndham's Theatre. 'MICHAEL BARRYMORE.' And there, alongside, was a giant, confident photograph of the man who, for 15 years, had only to step in front of a television camera for millions to tune in and laugh until tears coursed down their cheeks.

Now this great talent could be experienced live. Past the chande-liered foyer to the darkened stalls, a recovering alcoholic in his early 50s stood in front of a patchily filled auditorium, shaking badly and struggling for breath. 'I'm awight!' he gasped his old trademark greeting. Alas, that was something he most certainly was not.

It has been more than two years since a man died at Barrymore's Essex home. The body of Stuart Lubbock, 31, was examined by pathologists and found to have suffered severe internal injuries. How he came to receive those injuries has never been explained.

That death put a halt to Barrymore's television career. There had been drink and drugs problems in the Barrymore melodrama before, as well as endless discussion about his marital problems and his hunger for rough company. Some blamed the press, and Fleet Street certainly gorged itself on his story. But so did Barrymore, milking his notoriety.

The drums rolled. The West End lights dipped. And there he was! Something about this lanky chancer still dazzles certain innocents. A couple of stout matrons in the front row leapt to their feet and applauded his entrance. One of the women thumped her husband, urging him to join her in the standing ovation. He declined.

Barrymore's eyes, spangled by the lights, darted left and right. He had barely been on stage three minutes, but already, maybe, he sensed the audience was not with him.

Apart from a few middle-aged groupies, the crowd was proving more resilient to his allure. Beads of sweat formed on his brow. He licked his lips and strands of spit formed in his mouth. He tried some jokes. They were so old that some members of the audience were miming the punchlines before Barrymore was even halfway through them.

Barrymore pulled a face and moved his neck in and out, turkey-lurkey style. One or two admirers chuckled and the woman with the reluctant husband fired off her camera flash. The rest of the audience managed to contain its mirth.

In his heyday, Barrymore was a sure-fire TV hit. Advertisers loved him. Audiences lapped it up. His gameshow, *Strike It Lucky*, ran for nine series. There were Royal Variety Performances in front of the Queen. His programmes *My Kind of People*, *Barrymore* and *Kids Say the Funniest Things* followed. He was even drafted into a Spice Girls film. But the drugs stories had started to interfere with his image, so much that it was hard to take him simply as the likeable japester. Barrymore had developed too much hinterland.

To be the Bruce Forsyth or the Les Dawson of your generation, you mustn't have too much baggage. Television dropped Barrymore because he became too complicated. Viewers could no longer take him on the two-dimensional level required for small-screen success.

Stage performing makes different demands. A star must alter his act to the wishes of that night's audience. There are no commercial breaks to allow a pause. The musical clarions and canned merriment of the TV package are not there to cover awkward moments. Michael Barrymore started to discover this all too glaringly on Tuesday night. He was losing it, fast.

A backstage assistant was summoned to bring on some prop. As he returned to the wings, I saw the man lift a sardonic eyebrow to a member of the band. Barrymore was telling the audience they should shape up. To inject an element of fear, he embarked on some 'comic' abuse, struggling down into the pit of the auditorium to select a few targets.

He alighted, first, on a 30-something, smart-casual, black man, and mocked him about his origins (Barrymore appeared reluctant to believe he could have come from Brighton). There were some astonishing remarks about how 'well hung' black men are. Barrymore told us it was because they attach heavy yams to their sexual organs.

That hinterland of Stuart Lubbock started to lurk into the mind. Barrymore was keen to present himself as an innocent, fresh talent. But once he started telling unfunny jokes about men's sexual organs, it was hard not to remember his troubled past.

A woman called Debs, from Essex, was about the only person to laugh. She did so in a strange, sealion-at-feeding-time manner. Barrymore was delighted. He swooped and hauled Debs up on stage. Soon he had her on his lap for a love song and was trying to unclip her heavy-burdened bra. It was amusing for about 15 seconds – and then awkward to watch. Barrymore subjected the blushing Debs to some five minutes of sexual ridicule.

Next to be selected for humiliation was a middle-aged woman. Barrymore pinched her handbag and emptied the contents on to the stage. Big, big mistake. The woman was appalled and softly begged him to stop as she tried to retrieve her belongings. Barrymore had by now started to mock her humdrum posses-sions – the purse, the tablets, old sweet wrappers, female toiletries, that sort of thing. He lifted them up to the audience and tried to make them complicit in this intrusion. The theatregoers, almost as one, recoiled from his bullying. No woman likes to have her handbag invaded, least of all by a flailing comedian – a performer, moreover, who has repeatedly complained about intrusion into his own privacy.

Barrymore's support act was a pleasant New Zealand singer called Suzanne Prentice. Barrymore upstaged and mocked her, forcing her to simulate oral sex on him after he shoved her microphone down his crotch. She squirmed, as did many of us watching. Finally, in desperation, and by now wearing a pink leotard, he did some of his trademark silly walks. A few embarrassed titters rose from the stalls but then they stopped.

18th September 2003

The show closed a few days later.

The retired US general proved wobbly under fire

SPORT was to be had in a sun-dusted committee room yesterday. Five top bankers (three of them North American wiseguys) were satisfyingly mugged by Labour MPs. Matt Barrett, that mustachioed gringo who is paid millions to run Barclays, came disastrously unstuck. He had a Gerald Ratner moment and said he'd never run up big debts on credit cards himself. Heavens, no. Far too expensive!

Labour stalwarts piled in, arms flailing, voices clashing. The chairman, John McFall (Lab, Dumbarton), struggled to keep order.

A skinny bloke who runs the Royal Bank of Scotland, name of Goodwin, got stroppy. This was a schoolboy error. It just encouraged the MPs to rip him apart all the more. We even had a retired US Marine Corps general on parade. He, too, swallowed a whole buncha lead.

Let's catch our breath a moment and describe the setting. It was one of the swanky new committee rooms in Portcullis House. The topic under investigation: credit card charges. Sunlight illuminated the arena. A good day for a firing squad. There sat the bankers, a row of captured partisans. Mr Barrett was their unofficial leader, grey-fringed but with raven eyebrows possibly borrowed for the day from Dame Elizabeth Taylor. Mr Barrett, plump and tanned, has the look of one of those casting-couch plutocrats of Hollywood's pioneer days. A drinking buddy of Howard Hughes. A first-class passenger on one of the great ocean liners of the Twenties.

Beside him, lean-fingered and frog-faced, sat General Charles Krulak, chief executive officer – yessir! – of some banking outfit called MBNA Europe. MBNA? More Borrowers, Nice Accounts, perhaps. The general proved wobbly under fire. After a few questions from the Labour MPs his pale hands were shaking.

The most vigorous of the interrogators was George Mudie (Lab, Leeds E), who, like his colleagues, was outraged by the interest rates banks charge on credit cards. 'You should be ashamed of yourselves,' cried Mr Mudie. Mr Rudie, more like! More than once the bankers argued it was a free country and bank customers could decide for themselves if they wanted to borrow. More than once MPs replied that bank brochures were so complicated that borrowers often didn't understand the financial gloop they were entering.

The only Englishman among the bankers was James Crosby, a plain-vowelled chap from the Halifax Bank of Scotland (HBOS). I hope it's not my nationalist pride, but he seemed the most open of these red-clawed capitalists.

Cleverest of the bank supremos, undoubtedly, was Eric Daniels, head of Lloyds TSB. He barely said a word. Instead, he just sipped water from a plastic beaker, very, very slowly. 'You're the quiet one, Mr Daniels, let's hear from you,' said Mr McFall. Mr Daniels uttered a few sparse syllables and then retreated back into his shell.

Persecution of moneylenders is a pastime known to populist leaders since the Dark Ages. Mr Mudie and his fellow tilters were not doing anything particularly new. But these days the usurers tend to hide inside tall glass buildings and behind small print. They are seldom subjected to the fist-tightened scrutiny they received yesterday.

Mr Barrett said 50 per cent of all credit card holders do not borrow at all. 'But half do,' deduced James Plaskitt (Lab, Warwick). Mr Barrett, with a happy sigh: 'Yes!' The best moment was when Mr McFall invited the bankers to say what they would consider too high an interest rate. Five deep gulps plopped on to the floor. Too high an interest rate? Could there possibly be such a thing? Note to stockbrokers: sell banks.

17th October 2003

Iain Duncan Smith was a notable Conservative leader but chiefly for what he was not: he was not Michael Portillo, he was not a Europhile, he was not a touchy-feely moderniser, and he was not a success. In late 2003 IDS yields to the inevitable and quits.

On a day of high drama

ONE minute to seven, down came the blade and schloop! off fell his leadership, lopped into the gutter. The crowd in the Commons committee corridor reacted without cheers. Nor was there weeping. Just ruefulness, the whispered check of statistics, then a slow dispersal of the guilt-ridden throng into the wet Westminster night.

Iain Duncan Smith's last day as leader was the stuff of sheet-thrashing nightmares. He must have known he was doomed yet he had to maintain a toothpaste advert gaiety.

After a morning of TV interviews and underpant tightening there was PMQs to face. He entered the Commons at 11.55 a.m., to a few Labour cries of 'Bye-bye!' Chris Bryant (Lab, Rhondda) led these chants, waving in mockery. His purpose was to gloat at IDS's lack of popularity, but I can tell you the selfsame Mr Bryant is no pinup among colleagues.

Dunkers did quite well. After half an hour Mr Speaker called time and IDS left the chamber, alone. The condemned man ate a miserable lunch – sandwiches. Could no one have rustled him up a T-bone steak? He spent the time talking to Tory MPs and thinking through the speech he had to make at 2.30 to his colleagues in Committee Room 14.

Desmond Swayne (New Forest W) touched down. Major Swayne, a serving Territorial Army officer with the Royal Mercian and Lancastrian Yeomanry, had flown in from Iraq. Peacekeeping in Basra is nothing compared with the atrocities in the Tory Party of late. Had bullets been whizzing past his nose in Iraq? 'Just one mortar attack!' he barked. 'I slept through it.'

The committee room corridor is about 300 yards long, wood-lined, narrow, decorated in the Pugin manner. By 2.15 some 200 gawpers had gathered. 'It's like a sort of gladiatorial thing,' said IDS when he arrived. Was he confident? 'Never been anything else,' he said, and with that last untruth disappeared into the room.

We heard three deep rumbles. Nicholas Soames's tummy? Actually not. It was Tory MPs thumping their tables. For 26 minutes, IDS begged for clemency. Outside, barrel-chested policemen struggled to keep the corridor open to passing traffic. IDS's two glamorous assistants, both called Annabel, stood with doe eyes and shivery vulnerability. A single man's heart could have cracked, I swear.

At 2.57 came another rumble, a long 'un. Then the door opened and who should bound forth first but Mr Soames. Ah-ha! Some MPs said IDS had spoken like a veritable Cicero. Others were a good deal less complimentary.

David Davis lingered, lifting one foot to a bench and giving his groin muscles a good stretch. He punched his right fist into his left palm and looked hungry.

Gary Streeter (SW Devon) managed to express his preference (via telephone) all the way from Pyongyang, where he is on manoeuvres. He thus became the first person to have voted in North Korea for several decades.

Peter Luff (Mid Worcs) skittled up and announced: 'I'm Andrew Murrison's popsy.' Mr Murrison (Westbury), is married with five daughters, so this declaration had Fleet Street's earthier aces ripping off their pen tops. Interest faded when it was made clear that Mr Luff had in fact said 'proxy'.

They gathered for the final say-so from 6.45 onwards, many heads down. At 6.59 came the result. Numerous Labour MPs in the corridor looked satisfyingly depressed. 'Finally,' said IDS minutes later, 'my thanks to Betsy and my family.' Couldn't have said that myself without blubbing, but he did it just fine, wonderful in defeat. Betsy was beside him, of course, arm locked hard on to her man. She looked happier than for many days.

30th October 2003

Happily, Iain Duncan Smith's political career recovered. Today this thoroughly decent man sits in David Cameron's Cabinet as Pensions Secretary. Back in 2003, meanwhile, the Tories need yet another new leader.

Oh boy! Could this baby use some blusher

GET that man into the sun, soonest. Michael Howard, pale as a bridesmaid's veil, made a stonker of a leadership declaration yesterday. Great delivery. Terrific location (London's mod-con Saatchi Gallery).

But, boy, could this baby use some blusher. You never saw anything quite as white since Cleopatra's bath milk. There's more colour in an Icelander's bikini line.

The Saatchi Gallery is black poloneck territory, as Blairite as it is possible to get without actually entering Lord Levy's strongroom. As Mr Howard walked towards his mid-afternoon announcement, held in a room overlooking the Thames, he walked past signs for the new 'art' show by the cheap-shock Chapman Brothers.

Exhibits included 'Hell', 'Exquisite Corpse' and some sculpture called 'Two Faced Schmuck' (well, the last word is actually a lot ruder, but let's keep the party clean).

Before Mr Howard arrived the room had filled with Conservative MPs desperate to suck up to – sorry, I mean support – their likely new boss. The smiles were Miss World standard. Total delight. Few sights are funnier than a room full of politicians worried sick about their careers.

Bernard Jenkin, who had been IDS's main man, positioned himself right near the podium positively spangled with pleasure. Liam Fox brimmed forth bonhomie. Damian Green beamed like a little girl who had just won a Pony Club rosette. Even Lord Lamont was there, casting an eye over the numerous young honeys helping to stage-manage the event.

The ability of the Tory to produce slinky Miss Pennysqueezes is one of the minor miracles of production mechanics. You can see how Steve Norris veered off virtue's path.

For all my cynicism about the MPs' motives, the whooping and applause that greeted Mr Howard's arrival suggested real relief and some genuine affection. They have all been through such a horrid time in the last few weeks that they are almost weepy with gratitude that it is ending. Candidate Howard spoke about his immigrant background, his grammar schooling (no posh Fettesian, he), and his determination not simply to be 'hip or cool'. To say that in the Saatchi Gallery takes some nerve.

'We will always tell the truth,' said the same Michael Howard who once dodged Jeremy Paxman's questions. 'Most of you know I'm a lawyer but I won't argue a lawyer's case,' he said. At least this suggested he is aware of his courtroom-style shortcomings.

The camera lenses fluttered and whirred without cease. London's wiseguy set may be more prepared to give this shrewd, established London lawyer a fair toss of the coin than they were with young Hague or outsider IDS.

31st October 2003

Hale and hearty

FIRST glimpse in the cross-hairs yesterday of Lady Justice Hale, the beady-eyed old Nanny Goat who has just been made the first female Law Lord. She stepped along to a Commons committee to talk about the proposed Supreme Court.

Lawyers love the idea of a swanky Supreme Court. Think of all that pomp. The loot. The grandeur. Modernisers like it, too, because it means they'll be able to mould the new thing into their preferred image. The subject is attracting interest from the worst type of bossy-boot special interest lobbyists.

Lady Hale is a busy thing. She entered the room with the most enormous briefcase. It was more like the sort of suitcase you see Indian families dragging across the platform at Bangalore railway station. She put it down with a grunt, unclipped its combination lock, and extracted a vast file of documents.

Ski-jump nose, a mop of grey-black hair, lightly whiskered chin, paisley scarf, quite bad teeth, and a trendy pair of spectacles. Lady Hale (Girton, Cambridge) is the English lady lawyer at her most singular – Miss Marple crossed with Rumpole. Much of the time she clipped a pitying smile to her narrow lips. When her Michael Foot fringe slid across her high brow she grabbed hold of it with one hand and yanked it out of the way.

The committee was thrilled to see her. The long wait for a woman to make the top rank of judges has made her a pinup in progressive circles. 'Lady Hale!' gasped the committee chairman, Alan Beith. 'We're delighted!' She bestowed upon him a fishy eye that seemed to say, 'I should hope so too!'

She only spoke for about 15 minutes before the committee adjourned for three Commons votes and your correspondent pottered off to file this despatch. In that time, however, a few things became clear.

She was fantastically patronising to the MPs. Labour's Clive Soley (Ealing) struggled to comprehend a chewy point she was making about the remit of a Supreme Court. 'I obviously haven't made myself clear,' she said, an eyebrow darting roofwards. Mr Soley, decently: 'I'm a bad student.' Lady Hale, eyebrow by now flattening with disappointment: 'That's not for me to judge. Your peers will judge you on that.' She licked her lips, looked away, and smiled disdainfully at some other poor wretch.

19th November 2003

A photograph of a Labour MP appears on a gay web-site. Once this would have killed a political career. But this is New Britain. What does the Rhondda think?

How gay is my valley?

BIG Hooky Price only had one wobbly tooth in his head and when he saw the photograph of his local MP yesterday he almost swallowed that last precious pearl. 'God help us!' gasped retired window cleaner Hooky. And then, as the colour drained from his cheeks, he summoned the landlord of the Gelli Galed tavern. 'John, a whisky, quickly!'

Welcome to the Rhondda, most historic of Labour's parliamentary seats, home to retired coal miners, pulpit-bashing ministers and muscular-forearmed housewives. The same Rhondda whose MP, Chris Bryant, has just been caught disporting himself in his underpants on a gay web-site. Yesterday the Valleys did not quite know what to make of it. The *Rhondda Leader* newspaper reprinted the photograph of Mr Bryant from the *Mail on Sunday* and brought readers up to speed with the scandal – or as much of it as they felt able to print in a family journal.

'Free sausage roll for every reader,' read an innocent advert alongside the picture of Mr Bryant in his smalls. The first thing that greets you when you enter the constituency's main town of

Porth is a large sign saying: 'Come back to God! Jesus said, I am the way, the truth and the life.'

The quotation is one that Mr Bryant, himself a former clergyman, would have no trouble in attributing to St John. The Rhondda is well known for its rugby forwards, its male voice choirs and a certain melancholy stolidity – gloominess if you like – of its citizenry. Gay pride San Francisco this most certainly is not.

'And him a former church minister!' exclaimed Patricia Powell, 69. 'It's shocking. That's what.' Mrs Powell was out shopping with her friend Sandra Heafield, 60. The ladies had not yet seen the photograph of Mr Bryant and so I unfolded a photocopy and passed it to them (feeling, as I did so, like a vendor of grubby postcards).

Their noses wrinkled. Then came gurgles of laughter. Then outrage. 'He should resign at once!' declared Labour voter Mrs Heafield. 'It's not good for the image of this area. If he had been wearing boxer shorts he might have been more presentable, but it's not nice. Not nice at all.' Would she be voting Labour in future? 'No!'

At the Porth Meat Emporium it was sausage week. Here, people were a little more reticent. A young butcher in the doorway said he had never heard of Mr Bryant. He was not alone. Several locals, presented with the name of their MP, suddenly denied any knowledge of the man. The less said, the better.

A couple of lads kicked a car tyre outside the Play the Game video store and two ladies, Les Dawson look-alikes magnificent in their bonnets, lingered for a chat by a gift shop called Desire.

Outside a pet shop, Valleys accents lilted and fell. 'We seem to breed them here,' muttered one elderly fellow as he pointed out that the former Welsh Secretary, Ron 'Moment of Madness' Davies, who was forced to resign after a lurid incident on Clapham Common, represented the neighbouring seat of Caerphilly. 'Do you think they know each other?'

A walk to the top of the majestic hills above Porth offered

striking, rain-damp vistas: slate-coloured houses, winding, dog-fouled streets and a dank horizon. This is a landscape that broods. Yesterday it matched the mood of many Rhondda voters.

Julia Pritchard, 35, a carer for the elderly, said she was 'disgusted' by her MP's antics. The mother-of-one added: 'I don't like it and I don't like him. He's a waste of time and there's no way he should keep the seat.' Not everyone was of this view. Examiner Mervyn Richard, 80, said: 'Good luck to him, I suppose.' Some folk disliked Mr Bryant for being English. Others were offended that he had once been a Conservative. But it was those dreadful Y-fronts that really caused offence, so for expert advice I went to the Ystrad Launderette on the Tonypandy Road. The proprie-tress, an 81-year-old sweetie who preferred to keep her name out of the public prints, had seen a few underpants in her four decades in business. But even she, casting a seasoned eye over the photo-graph of our hero, found it hard to restrain her dismay. 'Horrible!' she said.

It didn't matter that Mr Bryant was gay. Almost everyone agreed on that. A man was entitled to choose. But someone in the public eye had a duty not to besmirch the name of the Valleys, Rhondda and most of all Wales. Could Labour ever lose Rhondda? With a majority of 16,000 it does seem unlikely but Plaid Cymru has made gains recently in local elections. The Bryant underpants are big news as far as the Nationalists are concerned.

Hooky Price and his drinking buddies at the Gelli Galed had not one good word for Mr Bryant. 'He's an Englishman,' said Dai, a retired factory worker. 'Been on TV. On that *Newsnight.*' Lots of heads shook in disapproval. In the corner of the room blared the racing from Southwell. Hooky's dog Milo, a talented ratcatcher, heard the name 'Tony Blair' and started to bark like some Dylan Thomas troll.

'I would put Bryant up against a wall and have him shot,' said Hooky. 'You know the only good thing to come out of England? The road to Wales! Vote for Bryant? No fear. I'd have him sacked.' And with that, he stared forlornly at the word 'love' tattooed on to his right knuckle, lifted it to the light, and gave a troubled frown. 'Don't think it sends out the wrong signal, do you?'

4th December 2003

The photograph hoo-hah does not exactly help the undoubtedly eloquent and bright Chris Bryant. He will languish many more years on the back benches. But he does finally become a minister in 2008 – and rather a good one at that.

His smile to the PM was a tangled Hornby railway track of teeth

JUST before lunch the career of Tory MP Michael Mates, sometime Colonel, full-time pudding, transcended double-cream ecstasy.

The Foreign Secretary announced that Mr Mates would be a member of the Butler Inquiry. Satisfaction syruped across Mr Mates's chops. And now we learned that Mr Mates had been made a Privy Counsellor. At this the old buffer's leylandii eyebrows jumped with plump delight. A Privy Counsellor! It means this bushy bore, this authoritarian mouthpiece of sebaceous loyalty to the System, becomes a 'Right Hon.'. Despite his friendship with the fugitive financier Asil Nadir he'll now get to kiss the Sovereign's hands. From minor public school to the Privy Council in one generation. Wear gloves, Your Majesty.

Mr Mates's pink little mouth noodle-sucked with pleasure and he turned to colleagues – almost before they could congratulate him – to say, no, really they were too kind, most generous. That other chocolate truffle of self-pleasure, Sir Patrick Cormack (Con, S Staffs), offered rotund hear-hears and a pudgy palm. Onetime Eton headboy James Arbuthnot (Con, Hants NE) scooted across the bench on his bottom to convey warmest felicitations. Mr Mates near shuddered with delight.

The day had begun with a 9 a.m. appearance by Tony Blair in front of the House's most senior Members: the Liaison Committee. Mr Blair would have a rougher time from a Nuneaton knitting bee. And who should be on it but our good friend Mr Mates, whose smile to the PM was a tangled Hornby railway track of teeth and grovelling lip.

We also heard, dear oh dear, from Dennis Turner (Lab, Wolverhampton S), a two-stroke moped in the middle of the Isle of Man TT. He took exception to some very light criticisms of Mr Blair and up shot his hand. Ignored by the chairman, Mr Turner none the less shouted a half-brained defence of the Prime Minister. Quivering with gratitude, he told Mr Blair: 'We're proud of the way you conducted yourself! Let history be your judge!' The room reacted in the only way possible. It laughed.

Mr Blair may be distrusted more than ever. Here in Westminster he has never seemed more powerful. The cogs of patronage grind. Sycophants are in sucky Heaven.

4th February 2004

Dennis Turner is now a Labour peer.

A beard the size of a rampant clematis

WE were only 15 minutes into yesterday's meeting of Synod at Church House, just over the road from the Palace of Westminster, when a wigged clerk shouted the word: 'Divide!' A schism so early? We all know the C of E has its niggles, but this was impressive.

I had come to Synod to see how, compared to the Commons, they order their debates. The previous day there had been discussion of that traditional Anglican concern, homosexuality.

After a week in which three bishops, to astonishment and great dollops of apoplexy, voted in the House of Lords for transsexual rights, it was a blessed relief to open the agenda and find no mention of gays.

'Blessed' is a very Synod word. Several speakers used it. They frequently referred, also, to God and Jesus Christ, which was not what one had braced oneself to expect at all. Then there was the member who cried: 'Finally, a quick word about rubrics.' Magnificent.

Synod meets in the round, which was also the word for the purple-clad tummy of a prominent prelate lounging on one of the curved front benches. In a box near the 'Madam Chairman' (a briskly efficient lay member in bulletproof tartan) sat the Archbishops of Canterbury and York. They looked like a couple of blokes squeezed into a motorbike sidecar.

In a fullish House several wimples, bald patches, crucifixes, and beards were to be seen. The best beard, by a very long and rather yellowing strand, belonged to the Very Rev. Archimandrite Ephrem Lash, of Chorlton-cum-Hardy, an ecumenical observer from the Orthodox churches.

Father Ephrem made a speech about liturgical matters, referring to his uncle Bill who had been Bishop of Bombay, and explaining how he had been called to the priesthood in a first-class railway carriage somewhere between London and Manchester. By the look of him it could have happened any time before the Reformation.

When he sat down his fellow beardwearer, Rowan Williams, Archbishop of Canterbury, roared with laughter and applauded, holding his hands up close to his chest and clapping with swift, feather-soft movements.

Laughter was frequent. When MPs laugh in the Commons it is normally because an opponent, or better still a colleague, has come the most frightful cropper. Here at Synod they laughed in encouragement, with one another. Almost every speaker deployed humour and self-deprecation. The speeches were generally brief, well-composed, and delivered with clarity. The only exception to clarity was Father Ephrem, whose beard (the size of a rampant clematis) got in the way. Andreas Whittam Smith, from the Church Commissioners, was also a little tricky to hear because he got his microphone snagged in his coat.

Mr Whittam Smith tried to introduce more efficient methods to the Church's accounts. Synod listened politely, but very plainly wanted nothing to do with them. Motion not so much defeated as excommunicated.

13th February 2004

Welcomed to the strains of Handel and Sir Elton John

TO the brass band parp of Handel and Elton John, some English reserve and a dusting of farce, the Royal Family yesterday took delivery of 19 proud new subjects.

The first British Citizenship Ceremony, held in a cavernous town hall in north London, proved a happy and smart occasion. It was a day for pumped chests, glamorous saris and the occasional tear. People from as far afield as Somalia, New Zealand and Nepal, plus a good contingent from the Indian subcontinent, made solemn vows 'to bear true allegiance to Her Majesty the Queen, Her Heirs and Successors according to law'.

Part marriage, part civic confirmation, the 15-minute ceremony was nicely judged. It was friendly without being informal, not over the top, thank goodness, yet sufficiently moving. An Afghan family who fled the Taliban, a Polish housewife, an Antipodean couple – these, and others, were plainly thrilled to be made full members of 'the British family'.

The Afghans' children, tiny Hasib Sharifi in his best suit and big sister Munilla with a pink garland in her hair, were the dearest little things. Hasib's eyes bulged in wonder at the chains of office worn by His (slightly soapy) Worship, the Mayor of Brent.

Welcome to the land of milk, honey and civic worthies, you two.

A brass quintet set the mood by playing that old Henry VIII tune, 'Pastime with Good Company', along with Sir Elton's 'Can You Feel the Love Tonight' from *The Lion King*. To give things an even more indisputably British feel, we also heard the *Four Weddings and a Funeral* theme tune. I believe it is by Wet Wet Wet (obviously a nod to our weather).

A line of pot plants had been arranged on the stage. A note on the programme advised that 'only the first verse of the National Anthem' would be sung. Oh, and that our sponsors for the day were Moet & Chandon and the Wembley Plaza Hotel. No British function is complete without a minor cockup, and we duly got one. To the left of the stage hung a big Union Jack . Opposite: the blue flag of Europe, which had been placed above a dated portrait of the Queen. Fate put things right. The Euro flag, which had attracted some genteel whistles and boos, started to fall to pieces. A bloke with 'Events Management' written on his back and the ever-requisite walkie-talkie in his paw had to lumber up on stage to sort out the problem.

He only half-succeeded and for the rest of the event the blue flag of Brussels drooped in a decidedly loose, lacklustre manner. Cue cheers from the chipper audience.

Prince Charles and David Blunkett arrived, the Prince having rolled through the dodgy streets of north-west London in his Bentley. A policeman hovered nearby to make sure nothing untoward happened to its hubcaps. Actually, that's unfair. Brent, a borough where 130 languages are spoken, was *en fête*. Its Town Hall, where the ceremony was held, has surely not looked so good since the Festival of Britain. The floors had been given a good scrub and flowers had been placed in the loos.

'Being British is something of a blessing and a privilege for us all,' said Prince Charles, adding that old line about how to be British is 'to have won first prize in the lottery of life'. Mr Blunkett beamed.

Looking at the new-minted Brits, who were by now clutching a certificate and (I know you're envious) a bronze medallion from the

Borough of Brent, Prince Charles firmly told them: 'You belong here and are welcome.' At that, a choir of about 50 schoolchildren burst into 'God Save the Queen' and around the auditorium hundreds of chins – this old hack's included – wanted to wobble.

27th February 2004

George Foulkes? Now there's a plump target. A more blatant sucker-upper you never found. Bluff George once saw me in a Commons corridor, pinned a great smile to his face, and cried, 'Ah, there's the wee shit.' The sentiment is entirely mutual, sweetheart.

A nearby dentist would've had a glimpse of his molars

OFTEN in politics the people who appear mean are in practice not so spiky as you think (e.g. Ian Paisley, John Redwood). It's the ones who radiate bonhomie you need to watch.

George Foulkes (Lab, Carrick, Cumnock & Doon Valley) is a model of bluff good humour. Before him, like a wave riding on to an East Anglian shore, he pushes a ginger-beer froth of merriment. Mr Foulkes has deep-rivet dimples, a gappy smile and one of those voices that seems moistened by chuckles.

In the Commons Mr Foulkes habitually begins with the words, 'May I congratulate the Hon. Member?' or, more characteristically, 'May I congratulate my Rt Hon. Friend, the Minister?' This is not to say he always sucks up to his seniors. He sucks up to his juniors, too, if only on the reliable principle that one day they will soon become seniors.

In Mr Foulkes's porker-pink fingers, promotion has time and again proved elusive. He has held office but seldom for long. 'Good old George', champion of the Commonwealth, a man who declares himself interested in the Netherlands and Canada, embodies the word 'gregarious'. 'Convivial', too. There are few greater stalwarts at the bar. What a fellow!

But in recent weeks Mr Foulkes has become a stooge for Tony Blair. It started to become obvious soon after the Hutton Report, when Mr Blair had been reinstalled as a Prime Minister at the peak of his patronage powers. Whenever the Government wanted for support, up sprang Brother Foulkes, from his habitual seat at the back of the House. At Prime Minister's Question Time the boom of his Banffshire voice could be heard decrying Tories, Lib Dems, and most of all those fellow Scots from the SNP.

In recent days Mr Foulkes has busied himself with blackening the name of a Labour colleague: Clare Short (Birmingham Ladywood). He was at it again yesterday. After accusing the former Cabinet Minister of changing her account of the UN bugging row 'from day to day', he declared that Miss Short had been 'irresponsible to a very, very great degree'. His chest barrelled to its full extent and his head was thrown back. Any nearby dentist would have had a good glimpse of his molars.

This is the same Clare Short, please note, who until recently was a glass-clinking friend of Mr Foulkes. This is the same Clare Short whose departure from government was last summer deplored by a certain, bluff Labour MP. Hansard for 12th May 2003. 'Mr George Foulkes: We have lost a redoubtable Secretary of State for International Development. I served as her deputy for four years and she will be missed.' This is the same Clare Short who, on 6th November 1996, was praised for her 'dynamism'. 'We ain't seen nothing yet!' said one G. Foulkes.

But that was when she was still useful to Mr Foulkes. That was before Mr Foulkes announced that he would not be standing at the next general election. And that was when the apparently jovial George Foulkes may have set his heart on securing himself a seat in Tony Blair's crony-rich House of Lords. If a little light treachery towards an old friend and colleague is needed to effect that plump goal, so be it.

3rd March 2004

A half-competent dawdling along in life's middle lane

SOME of you may have felt the air over your wallets quiver yesterday just before lunch. If so, it was because an MP was trying to extract yet more money out of the taxpayer. Meet Eric Illsley, professional Yorkshireman and Labour Member for Barnsley Central. Mr Illsley is one of those half-competents who dawdle along in life's middle lane, seldom overtaking anything but staring in indignation at anyone who dares open the throttle and roar past.

Mr Illsley lumbered to his feet during Questions to the Leader of the House. He swayed on his soles and blurted out his question from the rearmost bench, not quite sticking his thumbs in the pockets of a bulging bulldog waistcoat but still conveying an air of municipal entitlement. When, he plumply demanded, would the Government change MPs' expense account rules and allow them to claim for 'personal digital assistants'?

Any expression that includes 'digit' makes me feel slightly faint. But Mr Illsley was insistent. He moaned that MPs had experienced 'a huge growth in electronic mail' and that there were terrible 'demands on Members' time'. These personal digital assistants – by which I gather that he meant computer gadgets – were essential. They would enable MPs to 'access' their email from far and wide.

Phil Woolas, deputy Leader of the Hourse, invited Mr Illsley to make a written application to the Senior Salaries Review Board. There was every suggestion that he could succeed in his request. Mr Woolas joked that both Mr Illsley and the Leader of the House were 'technophiles'. Maybe they are. But they are also expenses-philes, moolahphiles. And you pay.

17th March 2004

In May 2010, the same Eric Illsley faced three charges of false accounting relating to his parliamentary expenses. Much though we gallery reporters described the greed of MPs, the Establishment and its broadcasters paid little heed. Even in early 2009, shortly before the Telegraph *broke its expenses story, I appeared on* Radio Four's Any Questions *and mentioned MPs' food allowances and the blindness of Speaker Martin to the moral drift on expenses. Although broadcast live in the Friday-night edition of the programme, this was cut from the repeated edition of the story on Saturday, for fear of causing legal offence!*

This sketch has sustained a flesh wound

BULLETS pinged during a select committee meeting just after breakfast. With regret, I must report that this sketch sustained a flesh wound.

The Editor of the *Daily Mail* was up in front of MPs to discuss Government communications (i.e. spin doctors and the way they treat public information at your expense). Labour's Tony Wright, chairman of the Public Administration Committee, was angry that the *Mail* had sometimes been jauntily dubious about these characters. And then this column swallowed lead. Mr Wright accused me of depicting current British politics as a 'cesspit'. It occurs 'every day', he said. Funny thing being hit, you know. At first there was no pain. It was only when I looked that I saw the gaping hole in my writing arm and the slow seepage of (blueish) blood.

Of course the man is right. How dare I criticise our elected tribunes? Disgraceful. In the light of Mr Wright's remarks yesterday this column is to conduct an internal review, to be chaired by someone with marital links to 10 Downing Street. Meanwhile, normal service will be discontinued and a more civic-minded approach taken, as I trust will now become evident.

At 11.30 a.m. the Commons, forum for the country's greatest talents, gathered for the start of the day's proceedings in the august chamber. On the agenda: Trade Questions with the Secretary of State, Patricia Hewitt. Can there have been a single soul in SW1 who was not looking forward to hearing what fresh nuggets of philosophical brilliance might drop from Miss Hewitt's full-bowed lips? There can not!

If there was a smallish number of MPs on parade this had nothing to do with the fact that it was a Thursday, and people had sloped off early to their homes in the provinces. Even to suspect such a thing is to connive in the wretched cynicism which so disagreeably corrupts the minds of our citizenry. Fie and damnation on those who peddle such filth.

Miss Hewitt, stylish in a grey trouser suit, her voice a sweet lyre from the Gods, surveyed the throng. Questioned by the penetrating Opposition spokesman James Arbuthnot about water services, she was the model of concise and memorable clarity. Also interested in water matters was a Labour MP called Julia Drown (Swindon S), but only a facetious schoolboy would make light of her name. Miss Drown was a torrent of good sense.

Mr Arbuthnot's low-key approach to Commons debates will be misinterpreted by agents of unrest and other fifth columnists as a sign that he is indolent, a dud battery. No! Let the world be assured that here is a workhorse of the people, one who has devoted his best years to public service. A knighthood is the least he deserves.

Dashing Sir Robert Smith, a Lib Dem baronet, urged the brilliant minister Stephen Timms to ' incentivise oil exploration'. Only a sour rat could think this translated as 'give another bung to the already rich oil companies'. Sir Robert also urged handsome Mr Timms to 'unlock the key' to the oilfields. Only the snide will find the metaphor muddled.

Further impressive contributions came from Ministers Smith, Sutcliffe, O'Brien and Griffiths. How the country manages with so few Ministers, how the turbines of industry can churn with such slim representation, is nothing less than a wonder.

All this was watched, as ever, by the Socratic figure of the Speaker of the Commons, Michael Martin. How fortunate the House is to possess this snowy-haired Solomon. Alleluia!

There, Mr Wright. Is that more to your liking?

26th March 2004

When, years later, Parliament's full, stinky, cesspit-scented corruption was disclosed by the Daily *Telegraph, the same Tony Wright said that the exposé had been inevitable.*

Sisterly solidarity for a fallen heroine

NOT since Norman Lamont warbled '*je ne regrette rien*' in his bath has there been such blithe disregard in the face of so much evidence. Beverley Hughes was making her resignation statement to the Commons after being found to have misled the House on immigration practices. Yesterday she presented herself as a Mary Queen of Scots *de nos jours*. Here was a woman wronged, a high-principled angel whose white wings had been singed merely by fate and ill fortune. Oh, and by the wicked media.

Dead Woman Walking, she entered the Chamber at 12.27 p.m., the Labour benches by then already abulge with Blairite braves. Practically every female Labour MP had scurried there to show sisterly solidarity with their fallen heroine. I hadn't seen that many women in the same place since the first day of the pots and pans sale at Debenhams. It could have been the ticket office scene before a Jason Donovan concert.

Angela Eagle (Wallasey) scowled at the press gallery and pointed accusingly at individual journalists. Not wishing to seem rude, I waved a pudgy little pinkie back. Hazel Blears, a Home Office Minister, escorted Miss Hughes to the scaffold and even sat beside her former colleague, clucking in tandem with Miss Hughes's now-redundant aide, Barry Gardiner.

'Personal statement,' sang old Gorbals Mick as the clock's minute hand thudded down to signal 12.30. Up stood Miss

Hughes, accompanied by a swell of sympathetic hurrahs from Labour. It was Bradman's last innings, the last flight of Concorde and Mother Teresa's funeral rolled into one. Gawd bless yer, Bev!

Around the Government front bench there was standing room only, such was the throng. Perhaps every true believer in the Blairite Cabinet was in attendance. Miss Hughes had chosen an olive-green suit, setting off her russet hair and a ghostly complexion. Behind her, in camera shot, was a doughnut of doughty dames. If you thought the Vikings were impressive when they saw off their vanquished warriors, it was nothing to this.

Harriet Harman looked bereft. Margaret Hodge gulped. Miss Hughes's Mancunian voice began faint but soon gathered strength. She had been 'honest and direct', she insisted. She was 'confident' she had acted properly. She was 'proud'. She would also, you sensed, like a job back as soon as possible.

Pride was there, certainly. It was there in the fury this governing claque showed towards the parliamentary system. It was there when they clapped her back as she sat down at 12.36. And it was there as she left the chamber, having her hand squeezed and her shoulder touched by the fingertips of the true and firm. Phyllis Starkey (Milton Keynes SW) stomped out ahead of her, bowlegged and bossy as she cleared a gangway.

When a minister has told untruths to Parliament, is there really so much to celebrate?

2nd April 2004

Beverley Hughes returned as a minister after the 2005 general election. She stood down as an MP in 2010. Meanwhile, with London full of talk about poisonous sarin attacks, a dramatic moment in the Commons …

They zoomed in like hornets

CLINT Eastwood would have been proud of our lads yesterday. The attacker hurled his cursed missile, its purple residue copped the Prime Minister between the shoulder blades, and several Hon. Members exclaimed: 'Oh!' But Tony Blair, one cool gringo, stayed his ground. Up in the press gallery plenty of us flinched (your correspondent had to be scraped off the floor and later needed several strong ones). Onlookers gasped. The House of Commons doorkeepers, after freezing momentarily, then sprang into action. They zoomed in on the assailant like a hive of hornets Stukadiving towards a horse's rump.

But our elected representatives showed the most marvellous British phlegm in the face of this scurvy assault. Some slowly rose to their feet and dusted the mess off their shoulder pads. Others lifted a creaky eyebrow. Gordon Brown looked no more inconvenienced than if his limousine had just run over a mouse.

Mr Blair himself remained standing, an expression of mild, amused surprise on his face. It was, I tell you, a relief to see the old ham was all right.

One can think of countries where, had this happened, burly security personnel with earphones and bulging holsters would within seconds have flattened the PM.

Not here. Mr Blair did not scream, or jump, or hit the deck. Just stood there. He and Michael Howard had just been going at each other like a couple of bodychecking wrestlers across the despatch box. It was a vintage Prime Minister's Questions. Then came the attack. The first thing Mr Blair and Mr Howard each did, within seconds, was to check that the other man was unharmed. Inside himself Mr Blair was understandably shocked. He took off his spectacles and I saw that his hands were shaking a little. But he was grinning and immediately he and Mr Howard exchanged cheerful good wishes across the despatch box table.

Speaker Mick leapt to the occasion like a spring trout. The moment the attacker started to bawl out his message – so much for that useless security glass! – he announced that the sitting of the House was suspended.

The Conservative benches executed a masterly retreat. I suppose they have some experience of this sort of thing. While Labour and Lib Dem MPs were standing round in a daze, the Tories' Chief Whip, David Maclean, stomped his shepherd's crook on the floor and ordered his men to vacate the chamber. Almost as one they stood to attention, right-turned, and filed out. Exit the Opposition, like a military band departing the Edinburgh Tattoo.

John Reid, Health Secretary, had inhaled a goodish amount of the powdery smoke that had been thrown down from on high. He coughed a little but choked it down eventually. He has inhaled worse things in his life, I'd say.

By now the attacker, or what was left of him after the initial impact from the various doorkeepers, had been escorted from the scene of the crime. In these matters I think it best to operate on the Moroccan restaurant kitchen principle. One does not really want to know too much what went on behind the scenes.

After the Cabinet had shuffled out, using the double swing doors behind the Speaker's Chair, a purple haze still hung over the chamber. It was at this moment that many of us remembered all those news stories about the danger of sarin attack and poison powders. Several minutes later the realisation set in that this could all too easily have been a disaster. Anyone for counselling?

20th May 2004

Bowing out

PEOPLE have stopped bowing to the Speaker. Custom demands that when an MP enters the chamber he or she show deference to the Chair. This, in the form of a bow, has been done for centuries. Until now.

I have kept watch this week and am sorry to report that the

non-bowers include Cabinet Ministers, a Tory knight and many Scottish Labourites – just the sort who are always telling us Sassenachs to show more respect to Gorbals Mick. Names? Well, why not? The following were some of the offenders: Peter Hain (Leader of the House), Hilary Armstrong (Labour Chief Whip), wee Ernie Ross (Lab, Dundee W), Brian Donohoe (Lab, Cunninghame S), Jim Murphy (Lab, Eastwood), John McFall (Lab, Dumbarton), Geoffrey Clifton-Brown (Con, Cotswold), Underpant Man Chris Bryant (Lab, Rhondda), Hugh Bayley (Lab, City of York). There are many more.

Mr Bayley, an Old Haileyburian, should know better. Ditto Mr Bryant, who went to Cheltenham. Mr Clifton-Brown counts a celebrated Speaker in his lineage.

This column likes to be constructive, as you all know, so let us note some MPs who bow with gusto. Gisela Stuart (Lab, Edgbaston) does not quite click her heels like Nicholas Soames (Con, Mid Sussex), but she is playfully correct, something suggestive in her eyes as they stay fixed on the Speaker throughout her bow.

Sir Robert Smith (Lib Dem, Aberdeenshire W) throws down his untidy fringe with all the floppy panache expected in a baronet. David Trimble (UUP, Upper Bann) is brisk, almost military. With that he proceeds to his seat with a sharp-toed little gait not unlike that of a Fifties typist.

Yesterday we had Environment Questions, which brought handsome, gay Ben Bradshaw to the despatch box. Mr Bradshaw, formerly of the Foreign Office, is currently becalmed as Minister for Fishing. He is also the minister for bee-keeping. David Cameron (Con, Witney), about whom there is a distinct buzz, complained that silly rules were preventing the import of queen bees from Hawaii.

Mr Bradshaw dropped momentarily into the character of the late Kenneth Williams. He said there were always alternative sources for bees. For instance, 'Slovenia and Greece produce very fine queens'.

25th June 2004

To raise charity funds, lots of Labour women wore hats to Prime Minister's Questions. Diana Organ (Forest of Dean) shimmered beneath a lacy black fedora. Joan Ryan, a Whip, had opted for rose-covered straw. Helen Jones (Warrington N) wore a small, 1920s-style, pink bonnet. It, like its owner, had the air of Miss Jemima Puddleduck waddling to market. And then one's eye rested on the unmissable form of Candy Atherton (Falmouth & Camborne). The Commons possesses few citizens more stolid than the bespectacled Miss Atherton. She is best known, politically, as an opponent of cruelty to animals. Opposition to hunting is her obsession. Miss Atherton's hat was not only vast but was also covered in swirling, black and white fur. From the far side of the chamber came a loud 'gooooood God!' Nicholas Soames (Con, Mid Sussex) had just copped Miss Atherton's pelted sombrero. Mr Soames: 'It's a dead badger!'

1st July 2004

The great hunt invasion

JUST as I was completing a rather fine doodle, despairing at an almost empty hunting debate, five lean lads in white tee-shirts and black trousies came jogging into the chamber. Houston, we had lift-off!

Some of the quintet made for the Mace and danced about the Commons table like bare-soled sunbathers on a hot beach. It was as though they could not quite believe their luck in having penetrated the police cordon. Other members of the boarding party stopped to have a word with the goggle-eyed Minister, Alun Michael, and his sidekick Elliot Morley. Did Mr Morley, who would have towered above the protester, jump to his boat-like feet to give him a bit of what-for? No. He quavered there, quite the wet lettuce, face turning as pink as cheap nougat.

It would be imprecise to say that the House's doorkeepers,

men in black stockings and braided tailcoats, reacted with the speed of cougars. Their response was rather more languid, like television viewers rising to twiddle the knob to improve a squiffy picture.

The deputy Serjeant-at-Arms, sword clanking at his side, was among the first to engage the invaders. Now I don't know how many of you have tried to arrest a fellow while a ceremonial sword is dangling from your belt, but it ain't as easy as it looks. Within seconds the poor deputy Sarge-at-Arms was flat on his bottom.

Deputy Speaker Sylvia Heal trimly suspended the House. Her tone was one of schoolmarmy disappointment. Down on the floor of the chamber, however, the entertainment was only just starting. Something approaching a tug-of-war had developed, doorkeepers holding on to protesters, protesters holding on to furniture, one another, and anything else to hand. The scene was worthy of ITV's wrestling bouts on Saturday afternoons of old. Hello, grapple fans.

Battle waged for what seemed like a good couple of minutes. 'There's no democracy!' one of the hunt lads cried. Looking at the desultory number of Members who had turned up for this peace-rupturing debate, it wasn't such a bad point to make. I had counted just 19 Labour backbenchers in the House. Outside, a riot was in full flow and smoke bombs were exploding, yet inside the banning brigade could not be bothered to listen to the arguments.

'You've mucked up pensions! You've mucked up everything!' shouted one of the protesters, as he shrugged a doorkeeper's mitt off his collar and came high-thighing round the chamber again in circles. Doorkeepers scampered after him. It was Obelix the Gaul being chased by Roman soldiers.

'This is peaceful!' the protesters hollered. By now the tug-of-war had become a human rope ladder, a daisy-chain of heavies and protesters. Clare Ward (Lab, Watford) shrieked at the intruders – 'Out! Out!', she cried, Lady Macbeth in miniature. A Labour puffball called Miller (Ellesmere Port and Neston) shouted at the Conservatives: 'So much for your friends! They've ruined you!' One hunt bloke was hopping on a single foot as he was dragged out by three doorkeepers. The human rope ladder was edging to the exit but as the protesters were being hauled away they tried to continue conducting a conversation, little pinkies at an angle, with the shrivelling Mr Michael.

Sir Patrick Cormack, a pro-hunt Tory, was the only parliamentarian brave enough to try to manhandle the intruders himself. 'I hope you go to prison!' he boomed, getting one of them in an armlock.

Oh, I know one should deplore this intrusion. I know we should speak high-minded words about terrorism and the sanctity of Parliament. But the thing was too comical. What a week for the guardhouse goons. What a refreshing geyser of excitement, spraying all over Westminster at its worst.

16th September 2004

Party conferences are always a feast of oratory. Much of it terrible!

'Look at 'em! How can I not lose with a team like that?'

THREE moments capture day one of the Labour conference. The party's chairman, circa 4ft 11in Ian McCartney, cries, 'Comrades, together, let's walk tall!' John Prescott attacks the 'contorted faces' of fox hunters, at which very moment he pulls his own wet fish of a face into an expression as screwed-up as a wrung flannel. And then the party's new General Secretary, a career functionary whose appointment had just gone through on the nod, complains about the 'political elite'.

Here inside the concrete-ringed 'secure zone' it is hard not to be struck by the elitism. Helicopters fly up and down the beach at

100ft and there are hundreds of police, all narrowing their eyes in case a post box turns out to contain an Al-Qaeda man – or, worse, a member of the Ledbury Hunt.

To get to my hotel room I first had to stand in a strange metal box to be squirted with jets of high-velocity vapour. The security guards would not say what the squirter was for but I later heard that it is a new device which can detect if a person has been handling Semtex or sarin. Not guilty. But I did touch some of my wife's cooking over the weekend.

Delegates entered the hall to find a set with purple, yellow and more candy pink than Sir Elton John's smalls drawer. In the middle of it all is a vast screen featuring an enormous blob. The conference chairman is a raspy trade unionist, Mary Turner, who has a Dot Cotton voice and seemed yesterday to be wearing someone else's false teeth, so often did she fumble her words.

A couple celebrating their 50th wedding anniversary were given a bouquet by Mr McCartney. The bunch of flowers was bigger than him. As he carried them across the stage it looked as though an entire autumn border had learned how to waddle.

After some clipped words from the conference agenda supremo – a robotic nightmare called Margaret Wheeler, who can surely stun a water buffalo from 100 yards with just one curl of her lean upper lip – we reached Mr McCartney's speech. Wee Ian has a Scots accent as thick as school porridge. Given the recent slump in foreign language skills in Blair's Britain, it was a relief to be handed the text of his remarks.

He wanted Labour to govern for an entire generation. Looking round the hall it was noticeable that 'New' Labour has been dropped. All the branding is back to plain 'Labour'. Mr McCartney screeched for about 15 minutes and then shut up. After his 'let's walk tall' conclusion he returned to his chair at the platform table, where his head barely poked above the surface. Marvellous comedy.

The Prescott speech, too, was a minor classic. He gassed on about 'own homership' (home ownership). We learned about 'fist time buyers' and 'squalor in the sums' (slums, I think) before he gestured to his lined-up ministerial team and said admiringly, 'Look at 'em! How can I not lose with a team like that?' It took him a second or two to work out that he meant the exact opposite, at which point he hit his forehead.

A few yards away Tony Blair watched and somehow managed not to weep.

27th September 2004

An acid remark about Liverpool in the editorial column of the Spectator *causes problems for the magazine's editor, Boris Johnson MP.*

In pursuit of the Blond Pimpernel

DRIZZLE drifted down on the old badlands of Toxteth. A car pulled up at the Inglenook pub. Its engine was kept running as several men climbed in, to be sped through Liverpool's rain-greased streets to an undeclared destination.

This furtive, sub-Le Carré scene was the Conservatives' idea yesterday of how to launch Boris Johnson's 'public' apology to the people of Merseyside after his *Spectator* editorial accusing Liverpudlians of emotional incontinence over the death of Iraq hostage Kenneth Bigley.

On arriving the previous night he had booked in to the Alicia Hotel, a businessmen's £90-a-night job, under the assumed name of Birkenshaw. An alias? With that mop of blond hair? He might as well have used the pseudonym Kermit the Frog. 'Hello Boris,' shouted a passer-by. Mr Birkenshaw, indeed!

The Henley MP, Shadow Arts Minister, newspaper pundit, magazine editor, gameshow host, mumbler, bumbler and eyebrow wriggler, had come to 'meet the people'. He was allegedly bent on the most open and contrite confession. We expected a walkabout, a soliloquy, maybe a barefoot walk to Anfield. The Clouseaus of

Conservative Central Office had a different idea. With their hamfisted attempts to 'control' the event they ensured that this entire episode became a farce. These so-called professional handlers ordained that Mr Johnson's itinerary throughout the morning be kept secret, on 'security grounds'.

The mood of Liverpudlians, or at least those who had heard of Boris, was certainly not violent. On such a rainy day, people were not in much mood to stop for a chat, let alone a riot. 'A wet day for a wet man,' said my cabbie, dropping me off at BBC Radio Merseyside, where rumour had it Mr Johnson would be making his first appearance.

Soaked reporters stood outside the door. 'Wossup?' shouted the driver of a blue Ford, whose door handle had just been stolen. We explained that Boris Johnson was in town. 'Where is he then?' continued the man. Everyone shrugged.

A bus swooshed through a puddle, covering a pedestrian in rainwater. Someone tried to hail a red-and-white car, thinking it was a taxi. It was actually a blood donation wagon. Janet Dacombe turned up. Mrs Dacombe, 48, lost a son at Alder Hey hospital some years ago. She, more than most, understands the community spirit of Liverpool – the spirit so controversially attacked by Mr Johnson's *Spectator*. 'I'm very, very, very annoyed,' she said, waving a pink brolly. 'Boris Johnson has been a total idiot. Has he never had a trauma himself? Has he even lost a cat or a rabbit? I rang his office several times and they said they'd get back to me. They never did. It's very discourteous. I'm putting in an official complaint to Tony Howard.' She presumably meant Michael.

An hour passed and there was still no sign of our penitent. Was he at Liverpool's cathedrals, on his knees? No. A meeting with the two bishops had been offered, along with the Lord Mayor and the leader of the city council. Liverpool was trying its best to be hospitable. The Tories turned the dignitaries down, however. They wanted the last word on the itinerary.

I managed to contact Boris on his mobile telephone. He was

finishing off a newspaper column. Where the heck was he? 'I don't know where I am,' he blustered. 'Can't talk, man. Gotta go!' Click, brrrrrrrrr, went the receiver. Some soapy-handed Tory HQ Herbert called Eustice, charged with organising the event from London, refused to return calls.

Suddenly we got wind that Boris was about to appear at the Liverpool Institute for Performing Arts a mile away. The posse galloped there, by foot and by carriage, coattails flying, puddles splashing. A security guard mulishly refused to say where the Blond Pimpernel could be found. Someone noticed him on a CCTV screen. 'Round the back!' The circus set off at another canter. And there he was, the rare beast. Mr Birkenshaw, I presume.

'Er, ahem, yah,' he said. A Tory minder tried to step in. 'Two minutes, guys,' he screeched, 'then we'll take a rain check.' 'Shaddup!' said the press corps, as one. The minder shrank back. 'Er, ahem, well,' said Boris, grey-suited arms swinging at his side. 'Yep.' More grunts. A crease of two slightly worried eyes. 'We got our facts wrong.'

It was now midday. How many 'real' people had he met, as opposed to party handlers? 'Er, one,' he said proudly. And what had this voter's message been? 'He said "Welcome to Liverpool" and "Never mind the bollocks"'. *Tempus fugit*, and he had to dash to a display by the institute's students – teenagers in leotards, performing to the theme tune for *Reservoir Dogs*. He spoke to two 19-year-olds, Fred Jones from Newport and Aram Horrell from Grimsby. That tally of Liverpudlians was still, worryingly, just one.

Next, like starlings, we swooped back to Radio Merseyside where Mr Johnson was interviewed by Roger Phillips, the Alan Partridge of Liverpool (though better). One of Kenneth Bigley's brothers came on the line. 'You're a self-centred, pompous twit,' said Paul Bigley. 'Get out of public life.' Not a happy moment.

Boris took the punishment like a man. And finally, now that he was finally engaging with the people he had come to meet, he started to work his unique charm. 'I'm here to say sorry,' he said, at last. And the deep, smart, familiar voice at last sounded genuinely crestfallen, even a little emotional. The worst of the disaster had passed and Boris had survived – but no thanks to his Tory friends.

21st October 2004

Had he tried to become mayor of Liverpool, Boris Johnson might have struggled. Instead he sought the mayoralty of London in 2008 and, much to the Left's surprise, won.

Patricia's tale

AFTER lunch in Soho I returned to the Commons to find a message from a woman we shall call Patricia. I recognised her as an MP's secretary who had tried to contact me in the summer, when she left a message saying she was unhappy about her boss's expenses claims. In the summer she had second thoughts about telling me any more.

Yesterday she was sufficiently upset to disclose a few more details. 'Patricia', middle-aged, works part-time for an English MP, although she does not particularly support his political party. She has always seen herself as an office professional, discreet and capable. For a few years now her employer has been paying his wife a salary of about £30,000 from his parliamentary allowance. The wife has not been seen in the constituency office more than a couple of times in the past four years. 'The other day we learned that she had been given a £4,450 bonus,' said Patricia yesterday.

'That money is being paid by the taxpayer, but all of us in the office know she does nothing to earn it. She doesn't look after his diary. She doesn't answer his letters. She doesn't do his accounts, because no one does. We're always being chased for late bills.'

The MP's wife does not even answer his telephone at home. 'It's always on the answering machine,' said Patricia.

She thought about reporting the matter to Mr Speaker. Then she read that Speaker Martin has a few issues of his own regarding expenses. She thought, next, about going to Parliament's Fees Office, and rang it anonymously. She was told she would have to go public. Hmmmn. Could get messy. She doesn't want to make life difficult, not at her stage in life. And it doesn't quite seem a police matter. So she took the matter to the MP's Chief Whip. Nothing has been done.

So there she is, working for a man who is raiding the public purse. There she is, a law-abiding subject of the Crown, expected to connive in apparent fraud. Yet she can go to no one, because in modern Britain there is no trustworthy, friendly official she can approach without bringing hell and fury all about her.

4th November 2004

The generalissimo looked like Stephen Byers's big brother

AN early rendezvous at Committee Room 14 where the Pakistani president, General Pervez Musharraf, addressed MPs and peers. Nobody was meant to know about it. Must-know basis, Carruthers. Walls have ears and all that.

Our parliamentarians like nothing better than a head of state's visit. It makes them feel jolly important. 'Mr President!' cried that old tortoise Donald Anderson (Lab, Swansea E). 'Welcome to Parliament! We greet you as a man of courage!' Maybe not as a democrat, though. Soldier Musharraf seized power in 1999. He is, to use the technical term, a dictator.

The generalissimo sat in a big throne chair. Centre parting. Grey at the temples. 'Tache. He looks a bit like Stephen Byers's big brother. 'Our ties are historic and vibrant,' said Mr Anderson.

This was certainly true of the tie worn by Dame Gerald Kaufman (Lab, Gorton), which was bright orange and red and yellow. It was as lurid as a chapati in a nuclear reactor.

Surrounded by senior members of his entourage, Gen. Musharraf thanked 'the Honourable Mister Donald Anderson' for his introduction, noted that the room had attracted a 'luminous gathering' (pull the other one, matey), and proceeded to speak for the next half-hour.

He did so from his throne. It is unusual to see someone make a speech from a sedentary position. It was a bit like watching Michael Buerk read the old Nine O'Clock News. And yet the tyrant had a certain magnetism. He was strangely transfixing.

Having praised Westminster as 'the birthplace of democracy', this important ally of the West proceeded to explain why democracy had become so 'dysfunctional' in his own country that he had felt no option but to extinguish it in a coup. 'When I took over the country,' he said casually, like a man describing the eradication of duck weed from the bottom of his garden, 'our economy was in a state of collapse. Our country was a ship which was rudderless, floating about on a year-to-year basis.' He referred to himself, repeatedly, as Pakistan's 'chief executive'.

Someone had obviously taken the General to one side and had taught him how to speak fluent Blairite. He talked of 'empowering' the poor and the women of Pakistan. He spoke of 'positive indicators', of his political 'strategies', and of his 'holistic' approach to solving political problems. Before long he was praising ethnic minorities and espousing a doctrine of 'enlightened moderation'. It could almost have been a Labour Party political broadcast.

To his left sat the Pakistani High Commissioner, an elegant woman with a twinkle in her eye. In the large audience were parked such sultans of pomp as Sir John Stanley (Con, Tonbridge), the Lib Dem peer Shirley Williams and Lorna Fitzsimons (Lab, Rochdale), who had a grey fur wrap round her neck and an upon-end hairdo that could well have been the result of direct connection to the socket for an electric kettle.

Musharraf gave us a lecture about the dangers of political corruption. He described how a National Accountability Bureau had been created in Pakistan to 'put the fear of God into the powerful' and reduce 'nepotism and favouritism'. His audience heard him in silence. It will never catch on in Blair's Britain, I tell you.

And then the climax. Up creaked Tom Cox (Lab, Tooting), a nut-brown Labour old-timer who positively shouted that Gen. Musharraf had 'brought respect back to Pakistan'. What a groveller old Cox was. A quite magnificent display of brown-nosing concluded with him saying of the elegant High Commissioner: 'She is always available.' What? Don't tell David Blunkett.

8th December 2004

I've been Prezza-d!

GO find John Prescott, they said. 'He's somewhere in the Midlands.' Before the tape recorder self-destructed I was told to locate the deputy Prime Minister on his 'Prescott Express' campaign bus.

He has been on the road all election but has been refusing to tell anyone of his whereabouts. The idea: to watch this so-called politician of the people meet voters. Could he persuade them that Labour is the party of trust and transparency?

In any general election it is the duty of the press to have a gander at men seeking high office. They tax us and take us to war and bulldoze our green fields. The least we should do is inspect their wares before an election.

Calls to the Prescott Express, seeking information from his sidekick Bev Priest, met with a hint of suppressed laughter. 'You want to find out where he is today?' said a male voice. 'Ha! I'm sure you would! Brrrrrrrrr.' Line dead.

Labour in London refused to disclose Prezza's itinerary. When Our Hero visited Cornwall on Monday the locals were given just ten minutes' advance notice. Getting a radar fix on the Prescott Express was not going to be easy.

I took to the streets of Birmingham. Obvious first stop: the HP sauce factory in Aston. No joy. Next: the Chung Ying Cantonese restaurant, one of the best in the area. Big John loves a Chinese. But a waiter said no, 'no booking for anyone called Prescott'. And yesterday's special sweet and sour prawns, too. On the 8.40 a.m. Virgin express from London I had earlier spied Nick Raynsford MP, Local Government Minister and one of the world's leading simultanous translators of Prescottspeak. But Mr Raynsford wore a carefree smile. It was not the expression of a man about to spend the day with Two Jags. Sure enough, he failed to alight at Birmingham New Street and headed further north.

I found central Birmingham plunged in darkness. A power cut. Aha! As surely as seagulls chase a cross-Channel ferry, so does chaos pursue Thumper Prescott. Like Doctor Who, I could sense the Force was nearby. But where?

The tourist information stand had its hands full. I stopped a couple in the station concourse. 'John Prescott? Good God, we hope not,' they said. The Birmingham Hippodrome was advertising *The Rat Pack*, but no boxing matches or slapstick comedy. BBC West Midlands' well-informed Ed Doolan was saying nowt about a Prescott visit. The local Tories were unsighted. Not even the Countryside Alliance, whose pro-hunting farm lads have been great Prescott baiters in recent days, could offer any information.

Time for some deduction, Watson. Which Birmingham seat is Labour most desperate to hold? Answer: middle-class Edgbaston. The MP, German-born Gisela Stuart, is photogenic and in danger of losing to the Tories' distinctly Brummie candidate Deirdre Alden.

At 12.10 p.m. two police cars went haring down the Hagley Road, towards Edgbaston. 'Follow those jam butties!' I cried to my valiant driver. 'Yessssir!' he yelled. We were soon in Bartley Green, poorest ward in Edgbaston. Quite a few 'vote Labour' posters were to be seen. But at the Jiggins Lane Chippy there was no sign of any Jaguar in the car park.

A school seemed a likely place for a Prescott visit. At Newman College the food and beverage manager had heard nothing. He had not been asked to order in any extra pies, put it like that. Had I tried the Bartley Green Technology College? Bingo! Two men in bulky raincoats stood outside its gates. 'Are you by any chance police officers?' I enquired. One, head like a battering ram, replied gruffly: 'And are you by any chance a j-ee-ourr-nalist?' By God, they're sharp these Plods.

Two women were wearing soggy red rosettes. Then I spotted the normally genial Gisela Stuart. 'Vat are *you* doing here?' she demanded. I was told to skedaddle. Refused.

At 1.30 p.m., to cheers from ten rain-lashed Labour diehards, the Prescott Express hove into view. Out came Buster Gusset himself. He scowled at poor Mrs Stuart, ignored the party faithful, and then spotted me with my anorak and drenched notebook. Whoosh! One kettle, fully boiled. 'Fascist!' he shouted. 'It's the fascist! Look! That's what the fascist *Daily Mail* looks like!' He was now stomping towards the school. I was elbowed in the ribs by a muscular woman. 'Are you a Labour official?' I wheezed. 'Certainly not!' she said, really insulted. 'I'm a police officer!'

By now Mr Prescott was on the far side of a high fence, meeting selected children. Pretty Miss Priest (built like Jason Leonard) firmly banned me from the publicly funded premises. And that, dear readers, is the way things look from the frontline of democracy.

27th April 2005

Prescott was not the only one hiding.

It was Greta Garbo himself!

TONY Blair and his coterie continued yesterday to treat the general election as a game of hide-and-seek – with the voters, and us Biro chewers, as 'it'.

Mr Blair helicoptered secretively to Gloucester, Telford, Manchester and Huddersfield. Save for a few trusted broadcasters, no observers were permitted to know his itinerary. Happily, a source close to Mr Blair succumbed to a crisp fiver. At breakfast I learned that 'Tony' was likely to visit Shropshire. Three hours later I was in Wolverhampton. Nearby Labour marginal? The Wrekin, whose socialist MP is public school-educated Peter Bradley. His views on land reform have brought him the nickname 'the Mugabe of the Midlands'.

Local taxi knowledge brought me, trousers flapping, to All Saints Church Hall in Wellington, near Telford. Mr Blair's visit had not been advertised. Some 50 Labour members crouched inside the hall on stiff chairs, meekly awaiting their epiphany. The only way to tell an 'event' was imminent was the uncommon number of plainclothes cops with shiny shoes, bald pates shaped like dolphin heads, and radio devices sprouting from their ears.

At 11.20 a.m. chopper blades were heard overhead. It was Greta Garbo himself! Has an elected Premier ever been so shy of the great unwashed? A longish wait ensued while, well, Lord knows what Mr Blair was up to. Doing his hair? Unpeeling Gordon Brown's fingers from his windpipe? A few ancient Tory protesters turned up, having seen all the cops and hobbled along to quaver a few genteel slogans. They were permitted no closer than some railings 50 yards away, where another posse of state troopers kept guard.

These law-abiding Tories were dismayed at being kept so far from their own church hall. One can note that the bishop of this diocese, Lichfield, recently attacked journalists for not taking a more positive approach to politicians. Maybe His Grace now understands the lengths to which Mr Blair goes to cottonwool himself from the electorate.

Special Branch had spotted a young man lounging on the grass 20 yards from the hall. This turned out to be Otis Ferry, Shropshire-based son of rock star Bryan Ferry and campaigner for hunting. Special Branch man flashed a warrant card. Otis, 22, was invited to sling his hook. A proud Englishman, he declined, and instead came over to tell us: 'Why am I not allowed to sit on this grass next to the church? Can it be that our cotton-clad Prime Minister is afraid?'

A Daimler swept into view and reversed, at speed, to within a few yards of the hall's doorway. Out stepped Mr Blair, to fling his jacket over his shoulder like some male model and walk towards the cameras. 'Stop smiling!' shouted Otis. 'Go back to the city, you greasy ...' At this point he ran out of ideas. Mind you, he was surrounded by Special Branch square-shoulders at the time.

Mr Blair fled inside to make a speech. His beetling retinue and approved press followers piled after him. The only reporter denied entry? Muggins. Last pea on the plate again. A Labour official with the name of Hopi Sen told me to 'go and talk to your friend instead'. He meant Otis (whom I had never met before). Tempting though this was, I was in Telford to try to witness the claims and promises of a man running for our highest elected office. Should critics of Mr Blair not be permitted to hear his words?

He spoke for perhaps seven minutes. You may have seen TV news pictures of a rapturous crowd. All of them were party loyalists. Once the event was over Alastair Campbell sauntered out of the hall. At the sight of him a lone anti-war protester, sporting a CND badge, went nuclear. 'Another man with blood on his hands!' cried Rachel Whittaker, 31, self-employed. 'Would you send your children to war, Mr Campbell?' Campbell scarpered.

Now things started getting lively. The local Tory candidate, a stout fellow called Pritchard, turned up with a blue rosette to demand Mr Blair's views about a local hospital closure. (He also, later, claimed that Labour supporters have quietly told him they'll buy him a few pints if he topples Mr Bradley.) Anti-war protester Ms Whittaker was by now sustaining some heavy flak. Like Custer, she was surrounded by Labour activists. Some called her a 'bloody witch'. Mr Pritchard was called 'a lunatic' and 'evil man'. Otis, meanwhile, was written off as 'a rude bugger who needs a good slapping'. Whoaa!

Amid all this I found a knot of exceedingly cheerful Labour chaps, all of them *Daily Mail* readers. Typical were Les Tait and Eric Dabbs, retired. These gents expressed surprise that their newspaper should have been excluded from the speech. 'Where's the sense in that?' they asked. Where indeed? But this is no longer, I'm afraid, the Labour Party of Bevan or Foot or Callaghan. This is now a high-mannered, sneering, sleek elite which cares nothing for the common man and is scornful of scrutiny.

4th May 2005

What has this baldie got that the others haven't?

SOME bald little man was perched on the Government bench at Health Questions. At first no one near me had a clue who he was. Could he really be a minister? 'Who on earth is that bloke?' we all asked. Someone said he looked like an undertaker. Another wondered if he was merely a familiar face who had shaved off his beard or had a sex change.

Shrugs all round. Then he started answering a question, so we deduced that he must be a genuine minister. But what was his name?

Eventually one of the doorkeepers, who have booklets with photographs of all the House's newcomers (it's a bit like a police station's directory of local child molesters), came to our rescue. He disclosed that the anonymous minister was Liam Byrne, new Minister for Care Services. Which helped us not one jot. Liam Byrne? Who he? I have had some of my best men on to this mystery and can report that Mr Byrne has been a Birmingham MP less than a year. He arrived after a by-election at which Labour nearly lost a once-safe seat.

During his first 11 months at Westminster he proceeded to do nothing to make himself memorable to the grunting wildebeest of the press gallery. He is a graduate of Manchester University and attended Harvard for an MBA. He worked for Andersen's (one of those management consultancies) and N.M. Rothschild before he started a computerish company called eGS – the small 'e' is *de rigueur* for this type of thing – with the aid of money from venture capitalists. It would seem that Mr Byrne is something of an author. His literary output includes the volumes *Local Government Transformed*, *Information Age Government* and *New Strategies for Full Employment*. He is proud to have co-edited, in addition, a snappy little bestseller called *Reinventing Government Again*. That is now enough of a *curriculum vitae*, apparently, to become a health minister.

Does it matter that Mr Byrne has so little experience in the Commons? Does it matter that his exposure to the electorate has been so limited? Not to New Labour. The fellow was once a management consultant advising the Blairites on how to organise their command structures and worked, furthermore, for the same Andersen outfit which once employed his new boss Patricia Hewitt, Secretary of State. Give him a job!

He certainly looked very much at home on the Government front bench. There was no sign of nerves. He spoke his answers, such as they were, in a voice of smooth assurance, his fast, modulated tones calling to mind one of those local council telephonists who has been on an anger management course. He was fluent in the required jargon. He burbled effortlessly about 'best practice' and 'strategy' and that type of thing.

But is it fair on many Labour backbenchers that Mr Byrne should be given a juicy job so quickly? What about the stalwart Lindsay Hoyle (Chorley), who asked him a question yesterday, and has been loyally doing his stuff for his constituents since 1st

May 1997? Why has the admirable Mr Hoyle never been promoted? What about Chris Bryant (Rhondda), so fluent and bold, but given little more than a toenail job as a ministerial aide? Surely that episode with the underpants can no longer be held against him? What has baldie Byrne got over these guys?

Finally, I saw no sign yesterday of Alan Williams – the new Father of the House. Not a sausage. If anyone spots him, can they please point him in the direction of London SW1?

15th June 2005

Liam Byrne's baffling rise continued and he was Treasury Chief Secretary – the nation's most influential bean-counter – when Labour lost power in 2010. It was Byrne who left a letter to his successor, telling him there was no money left.

Heath remembered

LADY Thatcher, smart in darkest blue (but not quite black), made sure she was in the House of Lords for the tributes to Sir Edward Heath. Her hair was whipped up into a tidy bonnet, her posture was upright, her powdering flawless. She even smiled when she heard a story about how, at a late-1980s dinner party with the Lib Dem peer Lord McNally, Sir Edward had spent much of the time denouncing Thatcherism.

She did not speak, but she was already on record as saying that Sir Edward was 'a giant' and 'the first modern Tory leader'. Would Sir Edward have behaved with similar grace had he outlived his successor as Conservative leader?

Parliament did its stuff for the old boy. John Gummer (Con, Suffolk Coastal) disclosed that, 'Sir Edward did for me what he was unable to do for himself – he found me a wife.' Sir Stuart Bell (Lab, Middlesbrough) once noticed that Sir Edward was wearing a colourful tie. 'I can tell that's a Hermès tie,' said Sir Stuart, 'because I do legal work for them.' Heath, deadpan: 'I always wondered why they were so expensive.'

19th July 2005

With the Tories looking for their fifth leader since 1997, the first sighting of Cameroon-ism ...

The good news: two full heads of hair

ONE radiated the worthy stolidity of a Rotary Club meeting, the other was twinkly and Chanel-scented – more a gala gathering at a BMW showroom for the unveiling of the new 5-series Cabriolet.

David Davis and David – Dave! – Cameron launched their bids for the Conservative leadership within an hour of each other in London yesterday morning. The events were held little more than 200 yards from each other but they were also a good generation apart, and maybe a planet or two. The good news for Tories is that both men have a full head of hair. The bad news is that it is hard to see one lot working happily with the other.

Mr Davis loped into a traditional, wood-lined Westminster room which had been filled with supporters who could have come from almost any point of the Thatcher and Major years. There were few women. One man wore a turban. The rest were white blokes in dark suits. At the door we were greeted by the watery stare of Whips. 'Changing Britain, Improving Life' said the posters. A succession of Conservative MPs stepped up to declare their support. 'Opportunity for all,' intoned David Willetts. 'Strategy,' gulped Julie Kirkbride. 'I believe,' said Shailesh Vara, as though reciting the Creed. Was it my imagination or did they look frightened, like Middle East hostages making a filmed confession?

Mr Davis spoke briefly, holding his hands in front of him as though they contained a bowling ball. He is not fluent or mannerly. Given his experience of front-bench politics, he is a lamentably unthrilling performer. But maybe that will make people warm to him.

It was a quick canter up Whitehall to the Cameron beano. This was held in a Georgian rotunda whose walls had been draped and uplit to resemble a classy pavilion, all whites and pale blues. From the speakers there dribbled relaxing, fishtank music of the type they play on long-haul aeroplanes to send you to sleep.

Strawberry smoothies and chocolate brownies were handed round and the air filled with sophisticated chunter. Smoothies! That's Mr Cameron, all right, strawberry-cheeked and bum-fluffy, as smooth as toothpaste. If the Davis lot were a brotherhood forged by rough experience, Cameron's lean lovelies were more like co-members of a gym, or parents before a prep-school play, waiting for a performance they just *knew* was going to be marvellous.

At first there were just a few public-school MPs, fussing around the stage to check everything was in place. Then the drawling Hugh Grant look-alikes with their Joannas and Mintys started turning up, the women with amazing legs and tanned ankles and chesty Diane von Furstenburg frocks. Boris Johnson MP was to be found under a thicket of blond hair, gazing, gulping, eyes spinning like the wheels of a Porsche on black ice.

George Osborne, Shadow Chancellor, said a few words about his friend 'Dave'. Oliver Letwin added an effective little intro, as did a token Asian and a token rustic (a woman from Mr Cameron's Witney constituency who had Little Britain vowels). When Dave spoke – for ages – he was assured, artful, eerily Blairite. He did without notes or lectern, all the better to show off his long inside legs which he positioned in a wide, crotchy stance. If the chin is a little shiny and his face reminiscent of the young Willie Whitelaw I'm sure the style advisers can work on it.

He impressed yesterday. Did better than even his allies can

have hoped. The Davis launch was an Ariane space rocket job. The Cameron one was NASA.

30th September 2005

Five sets of buttocks clenched like vices

FOR one terrifying moment I thought he was going to burst into song. Michael Howard, near the end of his farewell speech, strolled to the front of the stage with an aw-shucks grin and a rueful flick of his elbow. Mike Yarwood used to do the same thing at the end of his TV programmes with the words, 'and this is me' – before delivering a final song which was invariably the weakest part of the show.

'Hold yer heads up high,' said Mr Howard, a slight check in his flu-thickened voice. To my left an old woman sponged at a mascara-smeared eye. 'Be strong and of good courage,' said parting Mike, and around the hall sorrowful smiles wilted. 'Unite behind a new leader. Fight for a better Britain. Go for it ...' And at this point, Earthlings, we lost the signal from Planet Howard. The screen filled with snow, the sound descended into electronic fuzz and we must accept, gulp gulp, that we will never again have contact with the small, insulated pod of Mr Howard's leadership of the Conservative Party.

Actually, he took his leave with dignity. A decent man. This was never going to be an easy speech. All that needed saying was 'er, see you then, and thanks for having me', but somehow he had to spin that out for half an hour and in an upbeat manner that would send the representatives tootling home in cheerful mood.

Mr Howard said that he had decided to name the person he hoped would become Leader of the Opposition. 'It's Gordon Brown!' he said. The five leadership contenders were seated near the front of the hall, doing their best to appear relaxed but failing. Five sets of buttocks were clenched as tight as workbench vices.

Sandra Howard was also near the stage, fringe newly tweaked and beautified. Beforehand she had appeared in a video in which she said, 'Michael's not going to be allowed to retire – I won't have him in the house all day.' Yet Mrs Howard looked at one with life. It can't have been undiluted pleasure these past two years. At one point yesterday her husband quietly said he couldn't have done any of it without her, and as he looked down towards her his eyes formed two round puddles of immense affection.

Repeatedly he told Tory MPs not to squabble once the new man has been chosen. 'Whoever you choose to succeed me I shall support to the utmost of my ability.' This won a strong murmur of agreement from the hall. There should be 'no bitterness and backbiting'. 'We're not and we never have been a nasty party,' said the man under whose leadership Howard Flight was treated to much the same fate as poor Gloucester in *King Lear*.

The old wolf made his adieu. Akela's time is done. The pack will not stare at his bones for long. Now is the time for some sharp-fanged fighting until the new top dog is declared. Howl at the moon. Draw close your young. Bloodshed beckons.

7th October 2005

Peter Mandelson is no longer an MP but he has not disappeared entirely.

A soft-soled schmoozer, a spouter of nothings

TO be in the presence of Peter Mandelson is an oddly intoxicating thing. It is to inhale the presence of a great diva, to stand in proximity to a Tibetan lama, to clink cocktail glasses with the late Jackie O.

Mr Mandelson, sometime MP for Hartlepool, is these days an unelected tribune of 470 million European Union souls. Trade Commissioner Mandelson is a soft-soled schmoozer, a spouter of seamless nothings, a shadowy figure of silken, sugared insouciance. In truth he may be contemptible but in the flesh he is magnificently sleek and unshakeable.

Mr Mandelson shimmered into Westminster yesterday to appear before the European Scrutiny Committee, a second-division outfit chaired by a Labour MP called Hood. Mr Mandelson, invited to discuss the European Commission's 'work programme', appeared at the end of the corridor shortly before the appointed hour, accompanied by various aides. Seeing a scrum of reporters he tried to avoid us by entering the Members' entrance to the committee room. He was rebuffed. So he had to wander past us, trailing in his wake the faint scent of men's grooming unguents. As he eased past us he said how delighted he was to see us all. First lie of the day!

His file of papers was separated by stiff canary-yellow squares of cardboard. A gold-topped fountain pen was languidly extracted from the jacket of his pinstripe suit. With it he made feline notes.

A hush fell. It could have been the start of divine service. Then Mr Mandelson spotted a political journalist of his acquaintance. 'Hallo Toby,' he said softly, slowly, closing his eyes and then opening them again. Silence resumed.

He told Mr Hood that it was 'nice' to be in Westminster. 'Nice to come back to a national parliament to which I'm not accountable but to which I am answerable,' he said with a puckering smile. I'm not sure I really know what the difference between those two is, but maybe 'answerable' means you do not have to tell the truth.

Mr Mandelson started to talk about the 'benchmark of change' Brussels could create for the continent. He spoke about 'the delivery of strategy' and of 'decoupling' and LDCs (least developed countries). Puzzlement all round.

It was some time before anyone got stuck in. That distinction fell to Lindsay Hoyle (Lab, Chorley), who mentioned the recent 'bra wars' trade dispute with China and told Mr Mandelson he hoped there would be no difficulty buying pants next year. Mr Mandelson: 'I can assure you, Mr Hoyle, there is no chance of you losing your pants while I remain Commissioner.' The only other MP to distinguish himself was Michael Gove (Con, Surrey Heath), a new boy who spoke with clarity and had Mr Mandelson in a momentary stew when he asked about agricultural subsidies. Recognising dangerous ground, Mr Mandelson leaned back in his chair and affected relaxation.

The day's other big excitement was the Tory wives' hustings, held 50 yards up the corridor. They were having all the Conservative Party leadership hopefuls in for a chat. Some 100 women (plus one man in a raincoat) had gathered. Occasionally the doors opened and the noise was not dissimilar to that of a barn full of battery hens.

We were not told the questions the Tory leadership contenders were to be asked but I imagine they may have been: 1. Will you give my husband a front-bench job? 2. Tell us, without hesitation or conferring, the date of your wedding anniversary and your children's birthdays. 3. Do you floss?

14th October 2005

With his new wife, the Prince of Wales travels to the United States for an official visit. It nearly ends in tears.

The Admiral slid a hand behind Camilla's back … and then tried to walk her through a window

AFTER two days of stiff-bottomed American formality, Charles and Camilla's US tour broke free yesterday with a delicious moment of slapstick.

The Surgeon General of the United States, dressed in the gold braid uniform of a Vice-Admiral, greeted his royal visitors outside a medical establishment in Bethesda, Maryland. Having given a neat little bow and made a few sentences of gluey small talk,

Vice-Admiral Richard H. Carmona slipped his hand round Camilla's back. He then tried to walk her through a plate-glass window.

Maybe the camera bulbs had blinded him. Maybe it is some years since the Surgeon General last wielded a scalpel over a patient's bloated appendix (given his eyesight, one hopes so). But he simply didn't notice the disaster looming. This Vietnam veteran, Commander of the US Public Health Service, onetime member of the US Special Forces, thought he was steering the Duchess of Cornwall through an open doorway.

Prince Charles saw his new wife being hurtled towards certain disaster. He lifted a hand towards his mouth. Camilla was by now trying to put on the brakes. The Surgeon General was a man not to be deterred. No, sir! Forward they surged, ever closer to the plate glass.

Eventually the photographers let out a shout of 'noooo!' and 'wrong way, mate', and at the 11th moment Mr Carmona realised his imminent error. The Duchess came to a halt about three inches from the 8ft-high sheet of glass. It was like one of those thriller films when the runaway train finally comes to a stop within touching distance of the heroine in distress.

Charles, connoisseur of *The Goons*, hooted at the near-miss. Camilla got the giggles, too. She turned to the photographers and touched the tip of her nose – as if to say: 'One more step and this would have been squashed.' Killer Carmona was covered in embarrassment. Still, as a registered nurse he could presumably have made himself useful if the worst had come to pass.

All this happened the morning after the Waleses' big night at the White House. The Wednesday dinner thrown for them by President and Mrs Bush was measured a success, not least because the teetotal Mr Bush had stayed up past his normal bedtime of 9 p.m.. Prince Charles got away with making some political points in his speech. Nobody was rude about Camilla's dark-blue dress.

Guests had included actor Kelsey Grammer who plays Frasier on TV, the poet laureate of Texas (gulp) and Rolling Stones keyboard player Chuck Leavell. Strapping young Jenna Bush attended with her boyfriend. Vice-President Cheney's rather bow-legged daughter turned up with her girlfriend. Washington's court and social register took a deep breath and calmly noted the duo as an item: Mary Cheney and Heather Poe.

As for yesterday's trip to the National Institutes of Health, it was originally to have been a solo outing by the Duchess, publicising her charity work for osteoporosis. In the event, Prince Charles went along to hear his wife make her first overseas speech as a royal. It did not last long and was made in a small room which could hold no more than 40 people. She was nervous, tapping her notes on a table and sipping a lot of water, but all went fine. She spoke of 'this devastating disease', and recalled how generations of women fell prey to the 'dowagers' humps' of osteoporosis. She also used the phrase 'my husband and I'.

She was thanked afterwards by her host – that man Carmona again. He gave her an autographed copy of his 404-page work, *Bone Health and Osteoporosis: The Report of the Surgeon General.* Thud. 'Thank you,' said Camilla the stoic. Perhaps remembering that window, she added: 'I'll do my best to get through it.'

14th November 2005

Resuming his seat, the churchman silently wept

PETER Hain had a torrid afternoon. The Commons was debating a Bill granting on-the-run Irish terrorists their freedom. I have not known the chamber angrier or more upset.

Unionist MPs from Ulster have long had a weakness for exaggeration. It has sometimes been as though they knew no tone other than outright, pinched-face fulmination. They have so often sounded like men whose laughter muscles have atrophied from lack of use. With their joyless, diphthong-twanging voices, Unionist politicians have long been their own worst enemies.

Yesterday the mood was different. Yesterday the fury was genuine. You could tell not only from the tears one old man shed, a moment that will linger long in Westminster's memory, but also from the tremor in their voices.

This was a remarkable debate. The Rev. Ian Paisley, leader of the Democratic Unionist Party, raised his papery voice to the firmament and said that the Government wanted to 'enthrone expediency and dethrone principle'. Each word received several shakes of Mr Paisley's redoubtable larynx.

'Despicable' was the verdict of Nigel Dodds (DUP, Belfast N). 'A capitulation to Adams and McGuinness,' said Mark Francois (Con, Rayleigh). The normally cautious Sir Patrick Cormack (Con, S Staffs) physically ripped the Bill in two, threw it to the ground, and called it 'shoddy'. 'We are besmirching our reputation,' thundered Sir Patrick. Sharp criticism also came from Labour MPs Frank Field and Kate Hoey.

But the most telling moment came when the Rev. William McCrea (DUP, S Antrim) recalled seeing the shattered corpses of two of his cousins after an IRA attack. One, a girl of 21, had been engaged to marry that very day. The other, a lad of 16, was reduced to such a mess of bones and guts that his earthly remains had not been worthy of the mortuary slab, but had merely lain under a sheet on the floor.

It was the perpetrators of such deeds, said Mr McCrea, his mouth starting to widen with a low moan of bereavement, who would benefit from this appeasement. With that, the old churchman resumed his seat, silently to weep and shroud his brimful eyes. His neighbour Lady Hermon (UUP, N Down) gently placed her arm round his back and consoled him. Mr McCrea's shoulders shook with muffled grief.

Almost alone, Mr Hain stood in front of Opposition MPs while they cried bitterly that his Bill was 'shameful!' and that there had been IRA 'blackmail!' Mr Hain merely said that it was time to seek 'closure'. Mr Hain kept saying that he understood the positions of Hon. Members opposite. For almost the entire hour of his speech, there came shouts and interruptions. 'I do not do this with a spring in my step,' said Mr Hain, somehow keeping his voice level.

He took many interventions. It was Miss Hoey, eventually, who winkled out of him the admission that unless the Government had accepted this deal there could have been a return to violence by the IRA.

Past Prime Ministers, when giving a minister such a difficult debating position, might have felt moved to show their support by attending the debate and sitting on the Government front bench. Not the shallow, blame-dodging Blair. He was in Number 10, preparing for a news opportunity meeting with some polite Ulster widows. No doubt he will soon tell us that there must be 'no giving in' to Al-Qaeda terrorists, 'no quarter given' to political fanaticism. Even while the murdering dogs of Irish terrorism return to their homes, to saunter the streets without censure, free to gloat in their infamy.

24th November 2005

Following Charles Kennedy's departure in a mist of Scotch, the Lib Dems seek a new leader.

Mark Oaten's bid for glory

TRY as one does to take this Lib Dem leadership contest seriously, they are not making it easy. Yesterday Mark Oaten, the party's 'Shadow Home Secretary', summoned *tout le monde* to a grand announcement of his intention to win the great trophy.

Where Whiggish Gladstone and Lloyd George once stepped, so does this unphotogenic ex-PR man, holder of a diploma in 'International Public Relations'. Yesterday's event was held in a windy alley next to a modern hotel, of brutalist architecture, near the Department of Transport. One wall was covered in concrete. The other was composed of grey metal and window glass, through which could be seen a couple of blokes finishing a late lunch in the hotel caff. The alley, which led towards a municipal car park, was decorated with a couple of weedy trees. On the ground a small X was marked with white sticky tape, to indicate where candidate Oaten would stand. It was the sort of material the police use to mark the scene of a murder. Charlie Kennedy's?

'Not long now!' cried a young man with a scarf round his neck. 'Thirty seconds! He's comin'!' Cue the Clint Eastwood movie snake rattle and vapour-shimmers across the cactus-choked chapparal.

Mr Oaten did, indeed, walk across the urban horizon. A busy bustle. His suit jacket was flapping open to betray a small paunch and his gait suggested flattish feet. At his side was just one MP, the mercurial Lembit Opik, spotter of asteroids and fiancé of TV weather girl Sian Lloyd. Also accompanying Mr Oaten were perhaps eight young party supporters wearing wide grins. Intermittently they gave muted cheers of delight. The gallant band was completed by his wife. Mrs Oaten is a friendly-looking sort but she was yesterday the victim of a dark rumour – namely, that she works in the clog trade, importing them from Sweden.

A draught whistled down the alley but Mr Oaten was hot, hot, hot for action. Some might think the Lib Dem leadership tussle a matter for satire but the wild man of Winchester was treating it like a run for the White House. He was wearing cufflinks (uncommon for a Liberal) and a new, luridly striped tie which positively shimmered under the lights of a couple of bored TV news crews who had trundled along.

Mr Oaten started speaking about how it had been a hundred years since the Liberals were in power and how that was simply not good enough. No, sir! From what I could gather he was also, in politician's code, a little rude about his rival, the 64-year-old Sir Menzies Campbell. Every time he talked about his own 'energy' it was seen as a dig at auld Ming's decrepitude.

Trouble was, it was hard to concentrate on Mr Oaten's words. My eyes kept dancing between a large spot on his neck and his aggressively close-cropped pate. He does not have much hair, but what he has is mown as short as a Pakistani Test wicket. Then there was his voice. It is not an authoritative trumpet. Actually slightly childish. Like the late Roy Jenkins, he has difficulty saying the letter R. Nothing wrong with that, of course, but it is distracting in this television age, particularly in a politician who is hoping to lead a party of Liberals ('Libwaws', as they emerge from Mr Oaten's lips).

He delivered his spiel from memory, speaking briskly. Then he took just three questions before speeding off, pleading matters of the greatest import. By this we can perhaps deduce that he had a jigsaw puzzle to complete or some dry cleaning to collect from the laundry before closing time.

It was left to Mr Opik to Hoover up the last few questions, but most of us soon lost interest, and after four minutes the alley returned to its empty state, home to nothing more than a couple of dry leaves dancing in a mini-whirlwind.

11th January 2006

It turned out that Mr Oaten had a little too much 'energy'. Days later his campaign ended when it was reported that he had employed the services of a male prostitute.

Still flapping, the Birdman of Bognor was hit by decibels of scornful laughter

DOWN on the seafront at Bognor Regis they hold an annual event called 'the Birdman of Bognor'. This involves eccentric people, often bald men of a certain age, jumping off a jetty to see if they can fly. You may have seen it on telly.

Mad inventors spend weeks on elaborate flying machines, some involving homemade wings, others incorporating goose feathers. These frequently demand much flapping of the arms. Some manage to travel a few feet in the air but the result is never long delayed: splosh!

The Commons yesterday had its own Birdman of Bognor competition when two contenders for the Lib Dem leadership stood up at Prime Minister's Questions. Sir Menzies Campbell went first, followed by Simon Hughes. Oh dear.

Of Charles Kennedy, recently canned, there was nae sign. Mark Oaten, the Libs' third leadership contender, was also absent. He may have realised that Ming (who as acting leader got two bites at the PM) and Mr Hughes (who had an early question on the order paper) were bound to be called, while he was not. Mr Oaten had shrewdly decided to spend the half-hour session sitting in a nearby BBC studio.

Sir Ming sat in the place recently vacated by Mr Kennedy and stretched out his long, elegant legs. He is always sleekly tailored. Quite a vain old panther.

At PMQs the Conservative leader always gets a go before the Lib Dems' man. Many people, Sir Ming perhaps among them, expected David Cameron to ask Tony Blair about schools policy. Instead the Boy Wonder (wearing a too-short haircut) piously pressed the PM about Iran. This was just the sort of thing we had all expected Sir Ming to choose. Clever Mr Cameron had pinched his new rival's special subject. There was some quick shuffling of papers in Sir Ming's hands. Option B, soonest!

At seven minutes past midday Speaker Martin uttered the words 'Sir Menzies Campbell', and Ming was up. At once there came much mooing and noisy mockery from the full chamber. Everyone thinks Ming was the one who did in Charlie, you see. The heckling was along the lines of 'watch out – that man's dangerous'.

Sir Ming must have spent hours working on his questions. Like one of those Bognor Birdmen he was confident his baby could fly. Flaps? Check. Joystick? Check. Okay, ground crew, chocks away, flap, flap, flap. Soar, that bird. Go, nighthawk!

Alas, alack, it all went spectacularly, farcically, joyously wrong. Sir Ming trundled down the runway, all right. His preamble was faultless. The first of his two questions (about education) was even all right. But then disaster struck. He complained that 'one in five schools does not have a permanent head'. For about half a second the remark hovered in the air. Then the House, as one, remembered that the Lib Dems themselves at present have no 'permanent head'. Sir Ming was still flapping when he was walloped by decibels of scornful laughter. Lib Dem MPs sitting behind him looked pop-eyed with embarrassment. Some crossed their legs.

Mr Blair wittily noted that it was indeed 'hard to find a permanent head of an organisation if it is a failing organisation'. Onlookers nodded hard and pointed gleefully at the Lib Dems. More hysterical joy from them and the Tories. Grown men wiped their mirth-moistened eyes. Mr Blair chuckled. Moments later, Mr Hughes tried to rescue Lib Dem honour – and failed. The PM wondered out loud which of them he should support. Hon. Members slapped hands on knees as they laughed at the blushing Lib Dem duo. 'Where's the other one?' demanded Mr Blair, meaning Mr Oaten. More cackling merriment. I am told that by this stage Mr Oaten, in his TV studio, could be seen wearing a broad smile. What a boon to see his two rivals bobbing around in the briny shallows, their flying contraptions reduced to splinters of balsa wood and tangled rubber bands.

12th January 2006

A sad Tessa Jowell at the height of her husband's legal troubles.

A stricken pet pleading for her master's favour

FEW artists could have captured such sorrow. Tessa Jowell, on the Government bench at Prime Minister's Questions, was rueful regret made flesh and bone.

Maybe not even Michelangelo's Pietà caught quite the level of gnawing anguish, the woebegone exhaustion. Tessa, Tessa, Tessa, what torrid tales those hollow eyes told, gouged deep into a stoical façade. Not so very long ago she would have been found next to Tony Blair. Yesterday there was more of a barrier. Between her and her onetime ally sat Gordon Brown, Jack Straw, Margaret Beckett.

Mother Beckett was all shrouded in a red wrap, like a fireman with a blanket ready to douse flames. Her body was angled just slightly away from Miss Jowell. She produced a large white handkerchief and held it to her nostrils. Ring a ring a roses, a pocket full of posies. Tough old Margaret did not want to fall down with any plague.

Miss Jowell was wearing a checked jacket and pink top, fatigue marked in the drawn lines of her countenance, in a stiffness of her neck movements, in the gaunt stretch of her neck sinews. She kept casting her gaze up to the rafters. Her left index finger tapped repeatedly against a pale-blue folder she was holding over her crossed knees.

Proceedings were watched from the visitors' gallery by a Latin pop star called Shakira (very well known, I am informed). Perhaps Miss Jowell's dismal plight will inspire Miss Shakira to croon a lamenting fado. Behind the singer sat a swarthy-looking fellow with a pair of dark glasses on his forehead. Was he her manager? Or was he one of David Mills's Sicilian business associates?

Prime Minister's Question Time dripped by. For once we had a competent professional in the Chair. The Deputy Speaker, Sir Alan Haselhurst, proved himself more than up to the task of filling in for the ailing Speaker Martin.

Eventually, as we had all known it must, the bald matter of Miss Jowell's difficulties arose during the exchanges. It happened when a Conservative backbencher, name of Bacon, almost apologetically asked the Prime Minister about the Cabinet Secretary's inquiry into the Mills affair. When Mr Bacon finished his brief question Miss Jowell gave a deep, visible, soul-squashed sigh. Mr Blair's response to Mr Bacon's question was a savagely brief 15 words. They did not include any reference to Miss Jowell. There was no expression of confidence in her. There was no little jest to indicate that Downing Street was still slightly on her side.

Tony's gaze would have been so welcome. One flash of his sunny smile, no matter how brief, would have lifted her spirits. Yet she was not to be blessed. When the half-hour session of Question Time ended the Prime Minister hurried past her, moving within six inches of her deflated being. She looked up to him, a stricken pet pleading for favour from the young master, yet Mr Blair chose not to acknowledge his suffering friend. It was as sharp and surprising an example of the political cut as I have seen.

2nd March 2006

Her right eyebrow hovered flirtatiously

WATCH out, Cherie. What with Samantha Cameron and now Elspeth Campbell, Mrs Blair faces formidable opposition on both the shopping and schmoozing fronts.

Elegant Lady Campbell, eyes glinting like a pearl-encrusted killer, sat in the front row yesterday afternoon to hear her warhorse husband announced Lib Dem leader.

Sir Menzies made a formulaic speech about how the Lib Dems were going to be the party of the future. 'Modernise … brightest and best … challenge … relish …' burbled old Ming, grimacing like Chalky the schoolmaster from the *Beano*. I love the fact that when he says the word 'modernise' his shoulders give an involuntary shudder and he lifts his filmy eyes to peer through a pair of smudged spectacles. No one was particularly interested in his words but he had to say something and he managed not to hiccup, which may be an improvement on his ginger predecessor (who was present, looking dazed).

Sir Ming's wife, though, was the one to watch. Fast bowler. Erect. Nimbly attentive. She was dressed in patent-leather shoes, smart black trews, a stonkingly valuable brooch and a coat of many colours. Fashion expert that I am, I can disclose that it was by Daks and cost a pretty sum. Her grey, luxuriant hair was swept high off the forehead, as though blow-dried by the up-thrusts of a Harrier Jump Jet. She looks not unlike Ann Parkinson, fair wife of bottom-pinching Cecil.

The Libs' leadership announcement was held in a humdrum office block near the Commons. The room was filled with an untidy crew of reporters and Lib Dem parliamentarians. Lady Williams stood in the middle in a red jacket, blinking. I found myself next to a cheery, faintly beery fellow called Colin Breed, MP for SE Cornwall. He kept cracking jokes. When Charles Kennedy had entered lots of people clapped. 'Good God,' said Mr Breed. 'You don't think he's won, do you?' Lord Dholakia, presiding, shouted: 'Quiet please!' Mr Breed: 'We're already quiet.' During Sir Ming's speech many of the lights briefly went out. 'Anyone got a shilling for the meter?' cried Mr Breed. There was something infectious about his impertinence.

When the result was announced the vanquished candidates, Simon Hughes and Chris Huhne, got to make short speeches. Third-placed Mr Hughes approached the microphone. Mr Breed predicted: 'He's going to thank his mum and his auntie and the other two people who voted for him.' In fact Mr Hughes congrat-ulated ex-sprinter Sir Menzies on 'a truly Olympian victory'. Everyone groaned.

Mr Huhne, whose voice would have fast driven us mad had he won, gave a brief homily and yielded to Sir Menzies. Ming held up his hands in an odd gesture which made him resemble a ballerina about to do a twirl. 'Someone call a cab,' muttered my neighbour Breed. By now the photographers were shouting at Sir Ming to 'turn left'. He won't need much encouragement to take his party in that direction. 'Give 'im a kiss!' they yelled. This, let me stress, was directed at Elspeth, not at Mr Hughes.

3rd March 2006

Their truth is marching on, sang Tessa

YESTERDAY, it being International Women's Day, we ardent feminists piled down to a statue of Emmeline Pankhurst near the House of Lords. Tessa Jowell, or what remains of her, was there for the great occasion, too.

Conditions were atrocious. Heavy rain. Just the sort of weather that wrecks a hairdo, I tell you. But a crowd of about 60 gathered before lunch. Those in attendance included the Government Chief Whip Hilary Armstrong (where's my garlic and crucifix?), the Leader of the Lords, Lady Amos, and Harriet Harman from the Constitutional Affairs Department.

The mood was not dissimilar to a school netball team's away match, when they all give three cheers. There was a wholesome sense of optimism and pride. Only a small, discreditable part of me contrasted this to the needle-sharp bitchiness that can prevail when more than two women are in the same room. They addressed each other by Christian names except for Barbara Follett (Lab, Stevenage) who talked about colleagues as 'Sister Smith' or 'Sister Jones', or whatever.

One of the few men on parade was Huw Irranca-Davies (Lab, Ogmore). Mrs Follett, not wishing to show any prejudice, duly addressed him as ' Sister Irranca-Davies'.

I had arrived to find a man from one of the leftwing broadsheets murmuring his appreciation for some of the women's ankles. Tut. Mrs Pankhurst stared down, radiating dignity and wisdom. What would she have made of the Jowell/Mills scandal? Would she have accepted Mrs Jowell's dithery insistence that she let her husband do all the sums? Tiverton's Angela Browning, the only prominent Conservative, was holding a large bouquet which included purple peonies, cream roses, white stocks and greenery — the traditional suffragette colours. Then Meg Munn, junior Minister for Women, turned up. I am glad to say that no one was vulgar enough to ask her, on this day of equality, why she receives much less money than other ministers.

The time had come for a warble. Mrs Follett announced that the words of the 'Battle Hymn of the Republic' had been rewritten specially for the day by 'Sister Ken Follett' (her author husband). Gazes turned to a small, shivery man who was holding a guitar. Gosh he looked wet. And not just because of the rain. Up he strummed and forth fluted 60 voices. 'My eyes have seen the women in the Commons and the Lords/They have trampled out the prejudice that was so long ignored …' And so on.

Both verses ended with the line 'their truth is marching on'. Readers, I kid ye not. I was watching Mrs Jowell closely when we came to those lines and I swear, I swear, that she sang the words 'their truth is marching on', without so much as a fluttered eyebrow of self-knowledge. If you put this in an Alastair Beaton satire, the audience would say the playwright had gone too far.

Lady Crawley (Lab) had the best singing voice. A lovely, strong soprano. There being no sign of Lady Trumpington (Con), the bass line went unsung. During the rendition (dread word) many of the women looked at each other happily, lovingly. Jolly Miss Munn made a brief speech, as did Mrs Jowell. Each was cheered. 'By our deeds shall we be measured!' cried Mrs Jowell, referring to the fight for women's rights, and not, in this instance, her domestic mortgage arrangements. The Lib Dems' Sandra Gidley also spoke. Her presence was proof of sexual parity: female MPs can be every bit as dreary as their male counterparts.

The ceremony ended with Mrs Jowell, in time-honoured fashion, scuttling to her waiting ministerial Rover, pursued by a male BBC reporter who was shouting questions about her career prospects. He found his path blocked by Miss Armstrong and by chunky Claire Ward, a Whip. Scylla and Charybdis. Sensibly, with the rain closing in, the man gave up and tootled off to his lunch.

9th March 2006

Commons select committees have certain powers to call witnesses to their meetings. This way we get to see some of the elusive characters who operate behind the scenes. The sheer hopelessness of some of these important figures can be astonishing.

Birt's voice was part SatNav, part Alan Bennett …

GIVEN the meddling they have done, Lord Birt's hands are surprisingly small things. Yesterday he placed them on a Commons committee table and – at last – subjected himself to scrutiny by MPs. Those two hairy trowels, lightly liver-spotted, trembled with nerves. He is not used to having his word sharply questioned.

Lord Birt used to run the BBC, imposing barmy management structures and doing immense wreckage. Then he spent five years as 'strategic adviser' to Tony Blair, infuriating and bypassing Cabinet Ministers. It has been a life of seamless, ruinous triumph. Parliament tried long to get him to explain himself but he was never made available by Number 10.

Yesterday Tony Wright's Public Administration Committee finally had its chance to quiz this maestro of 'strategy'. The title of the meeting was Governing the Future. How very Birtist. The future is what Lord Birt considers his specialist subject. He leaves the present to the little people.

He explained, in a voice part Alan Bennett, part SatNav, that he has now 'left government'. To 'be in government' was traditionally something said of ministers. Lord Birt was only ever a prime ministerial cling-on. A boxy, humourless figure, he was dressed in a striped tie, anonymous suit and the sort of rubberised soles favoured by policemen. He has a habit of wrinkling his nose to push his spectacles up. His voice is regulation northern (now the ordained argot of the BBC) but occasionally goes off-piste. The word 'always' came out as 'olweys'. 'Confidentiality' took a lisp in the middle. Yesterday his diction became stickily short of spittle.

Asked to name his three crowning achievements in Number 10, Lord Birt said: 'I can't answer that question. No I can't.' Tory MP Iain Liddell-Grainger told him: 'You were in Downing Street for six years and what have we got out of you? Pitifully little.' He added: 'I am simply appalled that he has the gall to sit there and refuse to say what he achieved.' Mr Wright (Lab, Cannock Chase) asked him to define the word 'strategy'. Lord Birt said this was 'a much overused and often abused term'. He proceeded, for the next hour, to use it repeatedly to the point of ruination.

How did 'strategy' differ from 'policy', wondered Mr Wright, struggling to keep his tone free of hostility. Lord Birt, who had just said that strategy was 'a plan to achieve a desired outcome', explained that 'policy is a subset of strategy'. Titters could be heard at this point. Mr Wright again: 'What is forward strategy as opposed to strategy? You wouldn't have a backward strategy, would you?' Lord Birt, level, pleasantly dismayed: 'That is not a term I would use myself.' He was soon talking about 'whole-system strategies' and 'organisational solutions'. Utter balls, much of it stating the obvious, but fluent balls none the less.

We heard much about 'standard strategy methodology', the 'coherence of strategy units', 'making institutions fit for purpose' and ' growing the capability of The Centre'. The Centre? Is this some new villain in *Dr Who*? Or just a ruse by Mr Blair to screw up the civil service and give the impression of intense brain activity where there exists only short-term waffle?

There was a twang and we found that Paul Flynn (Old Lab, Newport) had snapped. Mr Flynn had looked at a Birt report and was appalled by its informal clichés. It made heavy use of lower-case simple sentences, bullet points, pie charts and repetitions. 'It's the way a good primary school teacher would address an eight-year old,' said Mr Flynn. Lord Birt began to shake. 'I wonder how much experience you have of the private sector,' he said, quietly but angrily. Mr Flynn: 'Is this really the way you communicate with a prime minister?' Lord Birt: 'It is an appropriate way to communicate with an executive.' Ah! 'Appropriate'. The telltale word of today's clerical elite.

It was left to Gordon Prentice (Lab, Pendle) to ask how Lord Birt had first met Mr Blair. Was it over a game of tennis? 'My tennis is not good enough to take on the Prime Minister,' intoned Lord Birt, pretty certain he had just recognised a joke. It transpired he had first met Mr Blair 'socially somewhere'. Another cosy little encounter. Another crony. Another tale of footling waste by a caste blind to the pointlessness of so much state activity.

21st April 2006

John Prescott – not one to close his office door – is caught having an affair. The Commons is in Heaven.

This show will run and run
(until the old fool quits public life)

WHAT a vintage week for West End comedy. Last Tuesday we had the revival of Michael Frayn's magnificent *Donleys' Years*. Now comes another must-see thigh-slapper of a farce: Questions to the Deputy Prime Minister, starring John Prescott.

This show opened in SW1 yesterday and is quite the most ludicrous thing I've seen. It combines innuendo with humiliation, hubris with slapstick. This devastating new production, which at times makes the viewer almost physically uncomfortable, had a packed House weeping with mirth.

The plot is as old as history. Rich old man succumbs to his libido and makes lubricious overtures to Mistress Lovely. Cannot see what a chump he has made of himself. Receives slow comeuppance. The show's ringmaster, played by a begowned booby called 'Mr Speaker' (sorry, but no one could be such a biased gooseberry), tried in vain to restore calm. Each time he tried to protect Mr Prescott and demanded 'order!' the howling hordes only laughed harder. Commons Leader Jack Straw, sitting next to Mr Prescott, was in severe difficulty. He kept corpsing.

What a pro Mr Prescott is. Even when he had the whole British House of Commons roaring with levity he stayed in character and kept scowling. It takes monumental concentration – or lack of knowledge – to do that. Shoulders in the public, press and VIP galleries heaved. Mr Prescott glared at them with a bulldog jaw.

The half-hour show ran just before Prime Minister's Questions. It began with a Tory MP, Rob Wilson (Reading E) asking Mr Prescott, 'what steps will he be taking to ensure that staff working under him …' At that 'under him' the whole place collapsed. A few MPs waggled their little pinkies. Mr Wilson persisted, saying, '… working under him are not subject to sexual harassment or bullying?' Mr Prescott talked about how the PM had talked to him about his 'day-to-day activities'. They loved it. Absolutely loved it.

Mr Prescott delivered a glowering soliloquy about Michael Heseltine. I have known Shakespeare's Bottom heard with greater seriousness. At its conclusion a flamboyantly coiffed Tory, Dame Michael Fabricant (Lichfield) shouted: 'Keep the door closed next time!' Mr Speaker screamed for order.

One of several Labour women was next up. Big Anne Snelgrove Swindon S) asked a volcanic Mr Prescott if he knew how 'proud' she was of him. Tory heckler: 'She'll be next!' Whooompf! Another blast of chuckles. The expressions of some onlookers only added to the pricelessness. Blairite feminist Phyllis Starkey (Lab, Milton Keynes SW) kept her arms crossed, her stare Arctic. When Mr Prescott started boasting about his 'domestic responsibilities' (he meant in Government), and earned another roar, a decent Sheffield MP called Angela C. Smith looked plain embarrassed.

Mr Speaker tried to threaten the Tories by saying he would not call them (even though the laughter was coming from all sides). They piped down for barely three seconds before frontbencher Oliver Heald attacked Mr Prescott's vast perks. Mr Prescott was by now blinking repeatedly with self-justification.

Then the *pièce de résistance*. A Labour woman, Dari Taylor (Stockton S), tried to be helpful. She asked: 'In his new role is he still going to have a hand-on in these areas?' Hands on? Not even Carry On films would have attempted such a *double entendre*. The roof nearly took off. New minister Ed Miliband must almost have drawn blood, so hard did he bite on his lip. Other Labour MPs just let rip with helpless laughter.

The wigged clerks sitting at the table in front of Mr Speaker put their heads down and doodled hard on their blotters. Anything not to catch someone's eye and do the nose trick. Warning: this show may not be suitable for youngsters or widowed aunts. But it's going to run and run. Until, as is surely inevitable, the old fool quits public life and resigns to his well-deserved obscurity.

18th May 2006

An almost crazy pleasure in offending the mainstream

THERE was an empty place on the Conservative benches. It was where Eric Forth used to sit. But the magnificent Forth died unexpectedly on Wednesday night, of cancer, aged 61, and yesterday that empty seat of his kept tugging at one's eye, gnawing at morale.

Forth regularly made a lot of mediocre people terribly cross. He was a first-class nuisance, a gadfly. A libertarian, he opposed the politician's normal cry of 'something must be done'. Eric Forth belonged to the 'something must *not* be done' school of thought.

It was always something of a surprise to find that the Member for Bromley & Chislehurst was a 'Rt Hon.' – i.e. a member of the Privy Council – because he was the very opposite of the modern Establishment. He was not clubbable. He was too bloody-minded to be a great joiner-upper. He took an almost crazy pleasure in offending mainstream opinion. Today's elite, so loaded towards the public agencies and the spending czars, hated the way Eric Forth questioned at principle some of their most closely hugged beliefs.

They automatically clothed themselves in causes such as global warming, health and safety, consumer protection, animal rights, state funding of the arts, and so on. Eric Forth would spring to his cowboy-booted feet and, in his spiky Glaswegian accent, ask: 'Why?' So many MPs today regurgitate worn phrases such as 'fuel poverty' and 'social exclusion'. Forth would pull a terrible face and tell them they were spouting clichés.

The cowboy boots were but part of an odd sartorial look. Forth, who liked Elvis Presley and Country and Western music, dressed in sharp suits with vivid ties, appalling shirts, and watch fobs whose chains hung from his waistcoat pockets like mooring ropes on a canal boat. Sometimes he would have wideboy sideburns. Recently he had grown a rather dashing goatee beard.

Eric was as unfashionable in his dress sense as he was in his boldly stated political views. Every thread of clothing seemed to shout the message, 'I'm not a conformist'. No David Cameron 'A-list' type, he. He would not even have made the Z-list of some of Mr Cameron's supporters.

Yesterday the Leader of the House, Jack Straw, spoke well in memory of the fallen Forth. Mr Straw recalled the double-act in Blair's second term when Forth, as Shadow Leader, was the opposite number of the late Robin Cook. 'Each sharpened his wit on the other,' recalled Mr Straw. Now they have both gone.

When I first started sketching the Commons, Forth was a consumer affairs minister in Mrs Thatcher's Government. She must have sent him there as a private joke. Government was never really his forte. Forth was more comfortable in Opposition. He often got things wrong. He supported apartheid South Africa. In 1988 he was silly to say that 'all' Citizens' Advice Bureaux staff were 'Trots'. His belief in low wages was distasteful. In the mid-1990s he was closer to lobbyist Ian Greer than he should have been. But for 99 per cent of the time Eric Forth was his own man. He spurned the mania for constituency surgeries, perhaps because he found the electorate tiresome, perhaps because he believed he had been sent to Westminster as a lawmaker, not as some sort of wet-palmed Nanny to help poor diddums voters grab their benefit entitlements.

The greatest service Eric Forth did, apart from making the Commons a more interesting place to attend, was to create obstructions for the interfering, money-wasting fusspots who rule our lives.

19th May 2006

Miss Ryan's eyes revolved almost in different directions

MINISTERS claim, with rising hysteria, that they are going to press ahead with ID cards. John Reid, Home Secretary, chose not to be drawn into the matter yesterday. Instead he left ID cards to the least convincing of his ministerial colleagues, Joan Ryan.

I say 'least convincing' to be kind. She is terrible. As bad as I have seen. Well-informed people at Westminster say that ID cards are never going to happen. It is suggested that Gordon Brown has put the kybosh on them, partly for money reasons, though that has never stopped him wasting Treasury billions before. Mr Brown may also feel indisposed to ID cards because they would be run by the Home Secretary, Mr Reid. Whom Mr Brown hates.

Tony Blair on Sunday came over all PMT-ish (Prime Ministerial Tension, since you ask) when asked about ID cards. He insisted, eyes blazing with defiance, that the scheme was not being dumped. So that has to be the 'line'. Ministers have to repeat Mr Blair's assertion, even though they suspect it may well be tosh. The 'line' must be defended. The 'line' is everything. Which inspiring sequence of events brings us to Miss Ryan.

Tall as a second-storey drainpipe, she clutches hold of her briefing folder rather as a toddler cuddles its security blanket or a well-chewed teddy bear. Really, one should not mock, for Parliament is a serious place and ID cards, or the ludicrous sums of money they will cost, should not be a matter for comedy. It is, however, impossible to take Miss Ryan seriously. She arrived recently at the Home Department from the Whips' Office. The great thing about being a Whip is that you never have to speak at the despatch box. Whips do not debate. They menace. They torture. But they do not speak on the floor of the Commons. If they did, backbenchers might mock them and they might lose face.

This means that Miss Ryan, who entered Parliament in 1997, has been little tested as a debater. Her quickness of wit, smoothness of delivery, the serenity of self-confidence as she stands there in front of a doubting, scornful House – all these have gone undeveloped.

David Ruffley (Con, Bury St Edmunds) asked: 'In which year will ID cards be introduced?' Mr Ruffley is brilliant at lacing his questions with rancour. He could make even a casual call to National Rail Enquiries sound like a QC's cross-examination. Miss Ryan started to bluster, waffle and throw out chaff. Eventually she stumbled across the date of 2008 and said it angrily. 'I would repeat, 2008!' she cried. The House laughed.

David Davis, Shadow Home Secretary, was soon on his suave soles. He noted that the Government, in its pro-ID cards propaganda, claimed that ID cards would save banks £504.8 million. The banks themselves say the figure is more like £37 million.

Which is right? Miss Ryan's eyes revolved almost in different directions. 'ID fraud is a growing crime,' she said. 'It costs a great deal of money. It is a scourge and an affliction to our society.' By now she was blushing so hard that her reddening skull was visible through her blonde hair. She told Mr Davis that he should explain what *his* policies were, rather than asking the Government such questions. Er. No. I don't think that's the point of Parliament at all, dear heart.

By the time Miss Ryan sat down she was quivering, visibly. Labour backbenchers looked on in quiet horror. Mr Davis chuckled. Mr Reid did not move.

18th July 2006

One of David Cameron's first acts on becoming Prime Minister in 2010 was to scrap the ID cards project.

The Strange Case of the Vanishing Labour Candidate

RAINWATER gurgles down broken gutters and all I can hear is a squelch squelch of wet soles plodding along a dog-messed pavement. Dai Davies and Trish Law, however, are brimming with laughter.

If they were a New Labour project you'd call this 47-year-old ex-electrician and his widowed colleague a Beacon of Hope, the embodiment of Things Can Only Get Better and all that. Except Dai and Trish are not New Labour now. Oh no. Definitely not.

'Been through four pairs of shoes during this campaign, I have, and three razors, and now I'm on my fifth suit,' cries stubble-chinned Dai, two shoes sploshing like a penguin's flippers as he flaps from door to door, shoving People's Voice leaflets through letter boxes. 'Get the suits for £37 from the supermarket. Very good, too, so long as you don't stand too close to the sun in them!'

There is no chance of sun today. We are on a wind-ravaged hillside near the Sirhowy Valley and the clouds have closed in for one of their south Wales huddles. The council estate houses seem to crouch into one another for shelter against the filthy weather. Then Trish spots a voter. 'Mornin'!' shouts Dai (the voter is elderly, with imperfect hearing). 'All right?' And the old man finds his hand being pumped and someone knows someone else's name and it's all suddenly more like a family gathering. This certainly doesn't feel like what it is: the frontline of a remarkable and ill-tempered by-election which has seen a heartlands rebellion against New Labour.

Welcome to Blaenau Gwent, once one of Labour's safest seats, now too close to call. When the people go to the polls on Thursday they will have a chance to tell Tony Blair what they think of him and his elite. It is hard to overstate Blaenau Gwent's Labour heritage. Nye Bevan and Michael Foot were Labour MPs in this melancholy, poverty-stricken area.

Merthyr Tydfil, crucible of the Labour Party a century ago, is just a few sodden valleys to the west. At the 2001 election Labour's Llew Smith, a bookish Leftie, had a majority of 19,313. Then he announced he didn't want to stand again and the Blairites imposed an all-female shortlist on the local party. As candidate, they jemmied in one of Cherie Blair's London friends, Maggie Jones. Peter Law, a flamboyant local councillor who had been furiously loyal to Labour for decades, was so angry that he stood as an Independent – and won. It was the most striking result of the 2005 election. Mr Law not only overturned a majority of almost 20,000 but ended the night with a 9,121 majority of his own. Maggie Jones left Wales a flattened, rejected crony. She will be sworn in to the House of Lords in a few days' time.

Peter Law did not live long to enjoy his success. His death from a brain tumour has given Labour a chance to win back this seat it so long took for granted. To do that, however, the party of

Blair must see off the spirited challenge of Dai Davies, who is standing for the Westminster seat, and mother-of-five Mrs Trish Law, who is standing for her late husband's seat in the Welsh Assembly. They and their People's Voice outfit are tiny and amateurish compared to Labour's campaigning machine, which has been 'throwing everything' at the seat, but they quite like being underdogs.

Fifty-something Mrs Law has not found the election easy. 'It's been an emotional time,' she says. 'We were married for 30 years. Peter's last words to me were "Be positive", so that's what I'm trying to remain. The people are bigger than the party. That is what Labour forgot.' Some elements of campaigning seem alien to her. She is wearing elegant black trousers and smart shoes which are getting wrecked. But many people recognise her. Peter Law was a big, big man in this area. His gentle-mannered widow has their respect.

Mr Davies, who lost his electrician's job at the local steel plant a couple of years ago (he had joined Labour as a 16-year-old), admits he hasn't any job to go to if he loses on Thursday. 'I suppose I'll still be walking the streets but picking up litter or something like that instead of electioneering,' he says. He has used all his savings to fight the campaign and is standing on a manifesto of traditional Labour socialism and trying to get Blaenau Gwent its overdue share of European poverty-relief funds.

The hearty activists at his HQ in Ebbw Vale include some of the 21 Labour members who – in an act of cack-handed vindictiveness – were thrown out of the party last year for opposing Maggie Jones. Some of these people worked hard for Labour for 40 years. Quitting their old party has been almost like a divorce. Former mayor Moira Wilcox says it has been the main topic of conversation over her kitchen table for months. The town's serving mayor, John Rogers, joined the People's Voice campaign last week. Maggie Jones's name remains a stinkeroo. In the village of Sofrydd, ex-water engineer Nick Jones, 56, says that the imposition of Lady Jones, as she will soon become, was 'disgusting, disgraceful. The Labour leadership think we live in wigwams down here. They had this seat for generations and look at the place. They ignored it.' Cyril Watts, 83, who did 44 years as a coal miner, explains that he could not bring himself to vote again for Labour. 'It's not the party I once supported.'

Labour seems aware of its image problem. There is talk that Tony Blair was asked to stay away. Labour posters do not say 'New Labour' but 'Blaenau Gwent Labour'. Gordon Brown swung by last week and the septuagenarian Labour MP Dennis Skinner, the very opposite of a Blairite, put in a brief appearance. Yesterday Owen Smith, New Labour's candidate, came out in opposition to the Trident nuclear deterrent which Gordon Brown has just endorsed.

I would have liked to ask ex-spin doctor and BBC producer Smith about that surprising decision. Indeed, there are many things I would have liked to ask him. Is it true his salary from pharmaceuticals company Pfizer is £200,000 a year (a vast amount by Blaenau Gwent standards). What does he make of his nickname 'Oily' Smith? Why has Labour been circulating posters aggressively attacking the recently widowed Mrs Law?

It would also have been good to have seen him on the campaign trail, to check what he was telling people and see how electors responded. There is a duty on politicians, surely, to present themselves openly at election time. Have Labour campaigners really – in a reference to the late and hugely popular Mr Law – been telling electors not to bother voting 'for a dead man'? I'd have liked to have asked Mr Smith.

Sadly Mr Smith would not speak to the *Daily Mail*. His aides would not even tell me his wheareabouts. A spokesman said that he did 'not have time for national newspapers'.

The Liberal Democrats and Conservatives have sent down some of their big names. David Cameron campaigned last week and, naturally, the sun shone for Wonder Boy. William Hague came and visited a butcher's shop in Ebbw Vale. Didn't buy a thing.

And yesterday I was just retreating from a chippie in the centre of slate-coloured, puddle-drenched Abertillery, where a Vicky Pollard look-alike and her layabout boyfriend were stroking their paunches, when a familiar ginger fringe came bouncing down the street. It was the former Lib Dem leader, Charles Kennedy!

Cheerful Charlie was supporting the Liberals' candidates – but maybe also reminding us all of his existence should Sir Menzies Campbell fall under a bus. I followed him down to a bus stop where a crowd of damp-haired passengers were awaiting the X15 bus to Newport. They seemed delighted to see him. But as he wandered off a woman asked me: 'Who are those people, anyway?' Very welcoming, the people of the Valleys, but national politics is not their forte.

27th June 2006

Dai Davies won. He held the seat until 2010 when it was retrieved by Labour.

Ker-ching! Another £250 for doing … practically nothing

BACK to the Lords yesterday to see how their new Speaker was faring. On Tuesday Lady Hayman, an off-the-peg Blairite and sometime militant breastfeeder, landed the £140,000-a-year sinecure. The job was done for centuries by the Lord Chancellor but Charlie Falconer cannot be fagged.

I was there just under an hour. Given that Lady Hayman will be *in situ* three hours a day (max) for perhaps 180 days a year, I reckon that in the time I was watching yesterday she ker-chinged about £250. What did she have to do? Practically nothing!

The good news: this Speaker, unlike the specimen in the Commons, wears tights. And a wig? I don't think so. Her elegant grey head of hair looks genuine. Lord Speaker Hayman, as she is properly known, has also opted for a black gown with white collar tabs, of the sort favoured by barristers.

There were fears she would do away with the daily procession to the chamber, or replace it with something less formal. Perhaps a conga line?

Happily not. At 10.59 a.m. the stentorian Principal Doorkeeper, Keith Phipps, late of the Coldstream Guards, marched stiffly into the lobby, executed one of his mustard-hot about-turns, and rasped: 'Me-lords, laydees and gen'lemen, pah-leese rise for the Lord Speaker!' Now entered Lady Hayman's little convoy. First came a rigid-spined doorkeeper, not swinging his arms (this is a peculiarity to the House of Lords although at the end of the day when the procession goes the other way, they *do* swing arms. Got that?). He was followed by the mace bearer, brandishing his implement like an enemy's fresh-severed scalp. Behind him stepped Lady Hayman, looking suitably marble-cheeked. The procession was completed by Black Rod, so practised that when he marches he looks as relaxed as a nudist strolling the beach.

This was the first time Lady Hayman's procession had taken place. Such is the genius of the British Establishment that it already has the air of a well-oiled custom, ticking to some unseen metronome of tradition.

In the lobby I bumped into Lord Weatherill, ex-Speaker of the Commons. He was pleased Lady Hayman had dressed up. 'I always felt quite comfortable in tights,' he cried. A passing tourist, picking up fag-ends, gave us a strange look. Lord Weatherill disclosed that Lord Hailsham, when Lord Chancellor, made him a proposal. 'Quintin offered me his suspender belt.' The tourist was by now, thank goodness, out of earshot. After prayers the day's business got under way in the chamber. Lady Hayman was on her Woolsack, her mien that of a Borders magistrate. She held an A4 folder on her knees and made a show of looking at it. What was inside? A copy of the day's lunch menu?

Question Time, which always opens the Lords day, began of its own accord. Lady Hayman did not say 'order!' or anything like that. Lord Bassam, the sometime Brighton squatter, made quite a good anti-Lib Dem joke. Lady Hayman kept a straight face. Lady Uddin (Lab), who has a tin ear for protocol, droned on for ages about women's rights. Lady Hayman did not tell her to belt up, as a Commons Speaker would have done.

Then there was a minor to-do when Lord Hurd and Lady O'Cathain wanted to speak at the same time. The House would have preferred to hear Lord Hurd but he, being a gent, let Lady O'C hog the moment. Lady Hayman could perhaps usefully have intervened to tell Hurd the floor was his, but that is not what the Lords have asked her to do.

A few people stopped for a chat, parking their bottoms on her Woolsack. Lady Hayman was pleased to see them. Half an hour passed. She said nothing. Then, in a brief flurry, she uttered some procedural formalities before she moved off her Woolsack and to a different seat for a committee debate.

Not bad work if you can get it.

7th July 2006

One small word

THREE times in recent weeks Tony Blair has said 'Lootenant'. The latest instance was yesterday, when answering a question about a military widow's pension. Lieutenant was pronounced 'Lootenant' instead of the British 'Leftenant'. It's a small matter, maybe, but by pronouncing the word like someone off *Star Trek* – 'good work, Lootenant Uhura' – does our transatlantic Prime Minister not increase the perception that he is an agent of America? On all those trips to Basra and Kabul to pose for photographs next to British soldiers and their officers, did he not listen hard enough to learn how to say Lieutenant? One small word can speak volumes.

29th June 2006

Old Hokey Clinton left them bored

UBUNTU? Is he one of those Third World dictators who attended Sandhurst in the 1970s and now lives in the south of France? Apparently not. Nor, as I wrongly presumed, is Ubuntu the name of Peter Mandelson's magnificently well-endowed, Swahili-speaking bearer. 'Ah, there you are Ubuntu. A large pot of chilled yoghurt for Reinaldo and me, there's a good fellow.' No. Ubuntu, we learned yesterday from ex US President Bill Clinton, is what the Labour Party needs to bear in mind if it is to win the next general election. It is a Zulu word and contains the secret to political life.

Old Hokey Clinton had come loping along to speak to delegates for, well, ages. They greeted him with excitement and listened for the first 15 minutes with wide eyes and innocent smiles. But slowly the ghastly realisation sank in that Mr Clinton's wrinkly-necked blether was not going to lead to anything truly novel or informative. The longer he went on, the more forgettable he became.

Tony Blair had introduced Mr Clinton to delegates as a 'rock star' and as one of two major influences on his politics – the other was Bob Geldof. Mr Blair's words were Bonking Bill's cue to enter. The first thing you noticed was the hair, now as white as something from a Daz ad. Then came the fingers, long and gropey. Throughout his speech he kept wagging one or other boney index finger at the audience. That bulbous bit at the end of his suntanned nose is not as inflamed by power as it used to be. He may even have lost some weight. Lookin' dang good!

But he didn't quite seem to know what to say when he reached the podium. A few hesitating words dropped from his pushed-out lower lip in a James Stewart accent. 'I like these Labour Pardy canferences,' he drawled. He pushed his groin against the lectern like a cow rubbing its flank on a tree trunk. Good burghers of Manchester, lock up your daughters. He said Labour were 'agents of change', that they should keep changing during 'this difficult and uncertain and uprooting time'. He had watched Mr Blair's speech on Tuesday and had found it 'proud but humble, hopeful but cautionary, appropriately full of gratitude, devotion and lurve'.

His left eye closed, slowly, with creamy pleasure, as he said 'lurve'.

Out in the commercial sector people pay hundreds of pounds to listen to motivational speeches from this windbag. Amazing. But we must not forget Ubuntu. It was, said Mr Clinton, an African word meaning (and he said this bit extra slowly to give it bogus weight) 'I am because you are'. In other words: stop squabbling and remember the electorate, you twits.

Bob Geldof also appeared yesterday, in a pinstripe suit, and was far better. He said that 'the reason Africa is weak is that 70 per cent of African intellectuals live outside Africa'. The obvious answer to this is that we must despatch a shipment of intellectuals at once. What an idea! Let's send them George Walden and that little de Botton fellow – and the entire BBC2 *Newsnight Review* crowd.

Unlike Mr Clinton, who spoke at about one word an hour, Mr Geldof rattled away, his fury at Africa's sorrows fuelling his tempo. He spoke of the 'pornography of poverty' and of how 90 per cent of African children go to bed hungry every night, and of the 'panic' this must cause in their parents' hearts. 'I mean,' he cried, 'what da fock is goin' on?' It is a question surely asked, in one form or another, whenever 'Ubuntu' Clinton makes a speech.

28th September 2006

David Cameron, now leader of the Tories, makes his 2006 conference speech.

A shameless caress of the female vote's G-spot

WHAT a masterly bit of greasing-up to the nation's mothers-in-law. What a shameless caress of the female-vote's G-spot. David Cameron not only talked about the importance of family and marriage, which is something no Tory leader has dared do since the trouser-dropping atrocities of the 1990s. He also coughed up the one word that all men – blokes all over the globe, but particularly of the Anglo-Saxon variety – find difficult to utter. You know. The C-word. The word that gets women going all gooey inside.

Commitment.

Up and down the land girlfriends' mums will be on the blower, saying: 'Did you hear that nice Mr Cameron? What a *good* passage about marital commitment and saying your vows at the altar.' The bachelors of Britain may take some time to forgive this brotherly betrayal. And then, to compound the offence, he turned all folksy to his demure wife Samantha, summoned a droplet of moisture to his right eye, and said, with quivery adoration and papery smile: 'Every married couple has rows.' Toothbrush down the throat time, some of us might say. But I looked up at a 50-something lady in the balcony and saw her mop her nose. Cameron may be corny but he has a horse whisperer's ability when it comes to the mares of the meadow.

The young Tory leader's main conference sermon was a long 'un. About 40 minutes in I began to think he was never going to stop, and feared I might have to send out a runner for chocolate. He may have speechwriters and strategy consultants and make-up artists on his staff but he could usefully add a decent sub-editor who can scissor out the padding.

The delegates did quite a lot of coughing in the middle. That is invariably a sign of boredom. It is all very well delivering a few slower passages for the TV bulletins, but the crowd in the hall need something either shorter or faster. He wore a red tie, black suit and an air of 'this is the serious me'.

He has developed a Bill Clinton head wobble – three quick, rightward shakes of the head when asserting or reassuring. There was also a moment when he tapped the lectern with his right index finger – it came when he 'pleaded guilty' to being a defender of British interests. This reminded me strongly of preacher Clinton.

Also interesting was the way he dared to tease Norman Tebbit. He spoke of him in the same way that Tony Blair speaks about Dennis Skinner, part in affection for a veteran hardliner yet with a faint watertint of mockery. Al Gore was treated with far more respect. This would once have been amazing but now Mr Cameron is trying to barge Labour off the centre ground. All the guy-ropes of certainty are being twanged. He even got the hall to clap gay weddings.

This good-humoured, love-bombed conference has given us plenty of laughs. Yesterday lunchtime I saw a TV crew interviewing younger delegates. The film was running when nearby a fat, middle-aged man in a pinstripe suit blew his nose as only a traditional Tory can, with much great parping and prolonged excavation and flourishing of spotted kerchief. The TV crew soundman on the listening end of the microphone almost shot out of his earphones, such was the gun-crack of nostril being sluiced. It was a moment that captured the incongruous mix of new funk with old crusty.

They gave Mr Cameron a hefty reception yesterday. They realise it is this or oblivion. He is committed. So, I'd say, are they.

5th October 2006

An evening of Beckett. That's Samuel, not Margaret.

Waiting for Godot, New Ambassadors Theatre

THINGS that dribbled through my mind while watching Sir Peter Hall's production of *Godot* (having already seen the thing in Bath last year):

1. They're taking it faster this time. More Irish, too.
2. Wish I'd gone to the loo beforehand.

3. No one next to me, or in front. Several empty seats, in fact.

4. James Laurenson, playing Vladimir, looks too prosperous/ suntanned/well-toothed for a down and out. Why does Mr Laurenson bug me so? Is it his impeccable delivery? His habit of watching a line hit its target like a fastidious marksman? He makes me feel claustrophobic.

5. Alan Dobie much better as Estragon. More authentically stinky.

6. Oops, we have our first bolter, 25 minutes in.

7. Bed. I want my bed.

8. Pretty theatre, the New Ambassadors. Two oval mirrors on the walls. It breaks the monotony to watch the action via them.

9. How much longer till the interval?

10. Lucky the slave (Richard Dormer) is dribbling impressively. How has he done that? Is he chewing something?

11. Lucky's master, Pozzo (Terence Rigby), is eating a chicken leg. Lucky, indeed! Didn't Terence Rigby used to be the dog handler in *Z-Cars*? Or *Softly Softly*? Adaptable.

12. Interval. Phew.

13. Hall has made this London version more slapstick. Does he think London audiences need something punchier? Haven't they got the staying power of a Bath crowd?

14. Oops, another person leaves.Wish all these girly voices in the audience wouldn't keep twittering with know-all laughter at moments that are at best wry.

15. Does any tramp wear a top hat these days? Why not a modern version of *Godot* with two dossers wearing baseball caps? Wouldn't tramps today drink something? British cream sherry? Carlsberg Special Brew? This *Godot* feels so dated.

As I age I fear I am losing patience with Beckett. Next door to the New Ambassadors they are still showing *The Mousetrap* (the M on the neon sign has gone out, so it looks like The Lousetrap).

This is a classic *Godot* but if you were me you'd opt for the Agatha Christie.

10th October 2006

Buster, a liability in a Union Jack waistcoat

WE had the Dog of the Year competition at Westminster yesterday. The Kennel Club and a charity called the Dogs Trust organise the annual contest. It's always worth hoofing along to see how many parliamentarians look like their pets.

Sure enough, there were two rightwing Conservatives, Andrew Rosindell (Romford) and David Amess (Southend W), both with sharp-fanged Staffordshire bull terriers. In the shaggy-fringed, waggy-tailed Cameron Conservative Party should they not be schnoodles or bichon frises?

Mr Rosindell's snappy little dog Buster was dressed in a Union Jack waistcoat and was soon involved in a fight. Like master, like dawg. The animal he attacked was black, but we'd better not pursue that line of thought. The victim was a labrador, also called Buster, owned by Westbury's Tory MP Andrew Murrison. Dr Murrison had been one of the first to turn up at the competition, having been pulled so fast along Victoria Tower Gardens by this powerful lab that he could almost have been a waterskier behind a full-throttle speedboat.

Buster the labrador is something of a political liability, one learned. The other day he spotted a constituent's child bouncing happily along the pavement on a Spacehopper. The dog ran up and bit the Spacehopper, which went 'Pop!', loudly. Result: one wailing child and one constituent determined not to vote Tory next time until an aghast Dr Murrison rapidly bought a replacement for the shrivelled, flaccid toy.

In the Kennel Club's marquee a sleek young Irish setter put his snout on the coffee table and, in an act of outrageous larceny, licked an open packet of shortbread which had been left there. I didn't have the heart to tell a stout man who moments later helped himself to the biscuits. The Irish setter was owned by the political editor of the *Sun*.

Genial Labour backbencher Derek Wyatt (Sittingbourne & Sheppey) turned up with two labradors, one of which almost killed itself recently by leaping off a 30ft bridge on to a railway line. Mr Wyatt winced when I asked him about the vet's bill.

The judging was done at the House of Lords end of Westminster and I can report that the peace of the morning kept on being disturbed by the tinkle of hundreds of bottles being loaded into a skip. 'Last night's empties from their lordships' bar,' someone explained.

David Blunkett's Sadie was nowhere to be seen but Black Rod (Lieutenant General Sir Michael Willcocks) entered his frisky black labrador Sugar. A gundog, Sugar. Maybe this politically incorrect hobby explained her failure to win. Sir Michael explained that Sugar's name had proved a bit of a problem. He was recently weekending in the country and a maid delivered early-morning coffee to his room. The dog was about to misbehave and Sir Michael, spying this from his bed, shouted sternly: 'Sugar!' The maid got the wrong end of the stick and thought she was being told off. 'It's on the tray, sir,' she quavered meekly.

The competition was won by an alsatian belonging to Eric Martlew (Lab, Carlisle). Diana Johnson (Lab, Hull N) came second. Or rather, her labrador George did. As regards human news, yesterday's Prime Minister's Questions was a draw. Tony Blair did much better than in last week's disaster. David Cameron's voice has started to alter. It sounded less echoey yesterday, cutting through the hubbub.

Much of the football stadium-style heckling of Mr Cameron was done by a pack of Labour men at the far entrance. What a bunch: Ian Cawsey (Brigg & Goole), Gerry Sutcliffe (Bradford S), Ed Balls (Normanton), Tony McNulty (Harrow E), Martin Salter (Reading W), Tommy McAvoy (Rutherglen & Hamilton W).

They could have been six Rhodesian ridgebacks, teeth in the snarl, hind legs quivering as they showed off their tight-veined reproductive equipment to the big, bad world.

19th October 2006

Why bother, Ma'am?

TOMORROW morning, to the pop of distant field guns and the crunch of guardsmen's boots, the Queen will alight from her carriage outside the Palace of Westminster. Ignoring her sciatica, she will process slowly to the Throne, crown on head, and graciously open Parliament for the legislative year.

All the Royal Household gang will be there, from the dear old Lady of the Bedchamber upwards. The obscure Cap of Maintenance (no one quite knows its origins) will be to hand, as it has been since the days of Henry VIII. The great Sword of State will be within reach should the Duke of Edinburgh feel the urge to decapitate anyone. Keeper of the Privy Purse, Gold Stick in Waiting, Garter King of Arms, Uncle Tom Cobbleigh: all these Ruritanian officers of the Royal Household will be on parade in gold braid and silken bows. It will doubtless be the usual spectacle of British pageantry.

We will potter off to lunch, thinking that we live in the finest, albeit most eccentric, kingdom in the world. And as MPs watch the royal fandango with their exaggerated air of languour and superiority, they will glow with confidence that they are the ones with real power.

They, 'Her Majesty's beloved Members of the Commons', the ones with the cheap suits and slip-on shoes, are the ones who truly run the country. Aren't they?

I'm sorry to disillusion them, but I simply cannot understand why they bother. More specifically, why does Britain still put up with this sorry excuse for an elected legislature which has been so trashed by Tony Blair and the European Union?

Officially, the State Opening symbolises the Constitutional Monarchy, that genius arrangement whereby we retain the colourful majesty of a monarch but make sure the Crown is subject to a lawmaking Commons. This was the system introduced when the Monarchy was restored after Cromwell's revolution, and for centuries it was the best political system in the world.

Parliamentary power was certainly the great idea when these traditions started. In 1642, Charles I was thrown out of the place after trying to arrest five MPs. The Commons asserted its sway. It remained that way until at least the middle of the 20th century.

The Commons was the high court of the land. It was the cockpit of our democracy.

The social cachet may have always belonged to the spangled visitors from the royal court, but it was the home team, the ones who put themselves up for election every few years, who really ran British society.

The State Opening was a celebration of monarchy bent to democratic will. The Commons, supporting the Prime Minister, was the true font of power.

No longer. In recent years, things have changed. The Crown may, to the surprise of its critics, have survived with many of its baubles intact but the Commons has seen its powers drastically reduced.

The laws and customs of this land are nowadays decided much more by outside and unchecked forces, be they European commissioners, over-mighty ministers or unelected quangos, than they are by the Hon. Members of the Lower House. MPs may never have written more letters or attended more meetings or been more busybodyish than today. They may never had been fatter in terms of clerical support staff, top-whack pensions, travelling expenses and holidays. But at the same time the Commons has lost its ability to make a decisive difference.

The elected chamber has never had more administrative rivals in the form of the European Union, government agencies, various commissions and quangos. Its occupants, in relation to the other great professions and to commerce, have never looked more plodding.

That is why tomorrow's ancient pantomime no longer represents the reality of our political system.

Our Constitutional Monarchy's ingenious balance depended on a strong Commons. Today's Commons is not up to the task. The place is stuffed with passengers. It does contain a few men and women of virtue and merit – sprinkled equally between the Labour and Opposition benches, and numbering perhaps 100 – but they are heavily outvoted by the gormless and the gutless.

The Lower House's public esteem has never been lower, in part, I admit, thanks to us piechuckers of the press, but more truthfully because so many of our MPs are time-serving Dogberrys in hock to their party hierarchy.

The sheer uselessness of many MPs has encouraged rival power centres to flourish. Mr Blair, more than any recent Prime Minister, has scorned Parliament, misleading it into an unwise war and filling the House of Lords with his paymasters and friends. His whole attitude to the Commons is tinged by contempt.

The 21st-century Commons, thanks to successive governments, is no longer the ultimate policy-making body in this country. It has lost power to European bodies, be they the European Commission or the European Court.

As in cricket and rugby, a sort of third or fourth official has entered the equation. The Commons might, like the referee on the pitch, take one view but that can swiftly be overruled by a higher arbiter.

The latest example of this concerns the buying of tobacco and alcohol from abroad. The European Court of Justice is expected next week to say that foreign excise rates must apply. The decision could cost the Treasury £10 billion.

Much as we enthusiastic boozers might cheer the prospect of cheaper hooch, an important principle is at stake. This country has a rising social problem with alcohol. Should it not be up to our elected Government to decide excise rates?

The Commons no longer has power over agricultural and trade subsidy decisions, such matters having been outsourced to Peter Mandelson and his chums in Brussels. Safety standards are now moulded to the demands of foreign regulators. 'Harmonisation', ordained by European experts, now guides many of our tax rates. In all these important areas, the Commons has been diminished.

Last week, several MPs stood up on their hind legs to demand an independent inquiry into the Iraq war. Mr Blair refused and got his parliamentary placemen to vote down the suggestion. Yet he is more than happy today to give evidence in private to a Washington DC inquiry into this disastrous war.

Meanwhile, thanks to an extradition treaty Mr Blair signed with the US, American law enforcers are roaming our land almost unchecked by their British counterparts.

The Commons was never properly informed about the true consequences of the treaty. Parliament, the supposedly all-powerful body whose sovereignty is symbolised tomorrow by the presence of the Queen, was ignored.

At Westminster select committee meetings, it is rare to walk away with the impression that the MPs were the most intelligent and influential people in the room. The people who appear before them invariably outfox their parliamentary interrogators.

This country's ruling class no longer sees the Commons as the pinnacle in public life. Far better to run one of the big charities or agencies or commissions.

You get better paid, you do not get bullied by the Whips, you are not tormented by the press about your private life and you probably have a far better chance of 'making a difference' – not to mention getting a knighthood.

Things have reached the point that it is now hard to understand why so many people still want to add the letters 'MP' after their name. It will certainly be hard to equate the dignity of tomorrow's ceremonial with the grubbiness and weakness of today's House of Commons.

Most of us can, with some enthusiasm, subscribe to the notion of *Vivat Regina*, or Long Live the Queen. But Long Live the House of Commons in its current form? Count me out.

14th November 2006

The Tories' salty man o' war was a magnificent sight …

DID you know that Dodo pads are still going strong? They were a sort of humorous desk diary popular with hippies in the 1970s and I was sent the 2007 edition by a friend the other day. Jokes include a drawing of two insects, one big, one small. The latter is captioned: 'The lesser of two weevils.' Then there's the conversation between musicians. Musician A: 'Who was that piccolo I saw you with last night?' Musician B: 'That was no piccolo – that was my fife.'

I thought of dodos because Sir Peter Tapsell (Con, Louth & Horncastle) creaked to his uprights in the Commons yesterday. Ah, Sir Peter. What a sight it is when this galleon, this salty man o' war, comes coursing through the waves. Break open the rum ration. Cue the theme tune to *The Onedin Line*. As Sir Peter rises to his feet you imagine scores of deck hands tugging on ropes and midshipmen supervising the operation to open full sails.

You imagine the Admiral of the Fleet on a distant headland, telescope held to one of his milky globes, expressing joy that Her Majesty's dreadnought Tapsell, that great old tub, veteran of the seven seas, was able to join the show with all guns blazing. Is Sir Peter a dodo? Is he one of those burnished Tory knights who are becoming extinct in the era of David Cameron? It would be easy to caricature him as such were he not so inconveniently astute in his targets and quotable in his pronouncements.

P. Tapsell was right opposing the Iraq war and right in opposing the timing of the Treasury's gold sales. Yesterday, he stood during Questions to the Minister for Women. Responsibility for this almost completely pointless area of government activity has just moved from Tessa Jowell's Culture Department to Ruth Kelly's Communities Department.

By now Sir Peter was upright, swaying slightly. He threw back his teak-coloured pate, lifted an eyebrow and launched forth with a question about Tony Blair's recent apology for British involvement in the slave trade.

'When,' he began, 'are we going to get a Pwime Ministewial apology (I should explain that Sir Peter has trouble saying the letter R) for Henry VIII's disgwaceful tweatment of his wives?' Up went a great roar of approval and mirth from all sides of the chamber.

Sir Peter licked his lips, straightened the sleeve of his Savile Row suit, and resumed his seat. Short, crisp, offbeat, funny, it had been another perfectly executed operation, another textbook barrage deep into the enemy gundecks. He had intended to satirise Mr Blair's ludicrous posing on slavery and he had succeeded.

The Minister at the despatch box was Miss Kelly herself. Poor thing. It's never easy to face Sir Peter. What could she say? That she was pleased to welcome Sir Peter to the dungareed ranks of the feminist cause? That Sir Peter, come to think of it, reminded her of Henry Tudor, if only in the matter of his girth and grandiloquence?

She decided instead to play things very dull and issue a po-faced remark that she was sure 'most members of this House would think it is the right thing to express sorrow for the slave trade'.

People say that Miss Kelly is 'well in' with Gordon Brown's camp. But will this be enough to save her ministerial career? It suddenly seems a long time since she was the Cabinet's talented youngster. If I had to say who was going to be next to join the dodo in (political) extinction I'd say it was the Kelly bird. Ancient Sir Peter looks good for several more seasons.

1st December 2006

Shilpa Shetty was watching from the gallery. I attended a press photo call for Shilpa earlier. Amazing eyebrows. They are composed almost entirely of cosmetic eyeliner and have been applied with the precision of the *trompe l'oeil* at Chatsworth.

8th February 2007

In January 2007 the police arrest Downing Street aide Ruth Turner in the course of their cash-for-honours investigations. No charges ensue, but Miss Turner does attend the Commons

RUTH Turner, the Number 10 aide who was arrested last Friday, attended Prime Minister's Questions. She sat three along from Mr Blair's chief of staff, Jonathan Powell, who plunged a thoughtful index finger deep into his left cheek.

Miss Turner is an elegant creation, delicate, demure. She radiates something of the young Cherie Booth although she is, if this can be envisaged, even more beautiful.

Her dark hair is almost feathered at the collar, she has a sweet little overbite, her black, classical suit was open an inch or two below the neck. At times of stress she leaned back her head to betray a slender, long neck.

From time to time she made discreet notes in a small, black book. Watching Mr Blair closely, she seemed rapt and pushed some hair behind her right ear.

It must be heartbreaking for Mr Blair to think of those narrow, smooth wrists, so white they could be hewn from alabaster, being clasped into the handcuffs of one of Assistant Commissioner Yates's chunky female officers.

25th January 2007

MPs are not the only ones who can lose their seats.

Damn the deckchair

MY children went skipping off to school yesterday with gaiety gurgling in their throats. The reason? As I write this I can feel it throbbing through my poor, unfortunate buttocks.

On Sunday afternoon, with the sun blazing down, I plonked myself into one of our deckchairs – and broke the wretched thing. Rrrrrrrrip! One moment I was that picture of bourgeois self-congratulation, the post-prandial father of three, roast pork joint having been cooked, a small brandy in my right hand, the Sunday newspapers in the left. Time for a spot of R and R. Middle-class man strides forth to a sun-dappled part of the garden under the willow tree. Assembles deckchair. Gives sigh of contentment. Lowers self into his garden chair. Crrrrrack! Legs akimbo, bottom suddenly on the grass, brandy all over face, to be followed by delighted cries of 'Yippee! Dad's come a cropper and gone and bust his chair!' They haven't laughed that much since I squirted tomato sauce all down my white suit at the county fair.

The deckchair is, of course, a long-standing menace in garden life. English provincial man does not, generally, face many mortal foes. The great white shark is not a threat to his wellbeing. Scorpion, malaria, tornados, killer tarantulas – although such hazards may await the adventurer who ventures east of Suez, here in England we need not worry. But the deckchair is a long-standing fiend, as generations of squashed fingers will attest.

My complaint is, however, not simply about this well-known villain of the greensward. I have a more general thesis: namely, that garden furniture itself – everything from new sunloungers to barbecue banqueting sets – is one of the great, unacknowledged, overpriced causes of misery. And we bring it on ourselves. Summer after summer we go out and spend a small fortune on love-seats and bird baths and stately home-style patio accessories.

The sums are astounding. They compare to the gross national product of a middle-ranking African country. And yet, autumn after autumn, we realise that these purchases were a complete waste of time. Every spring comes the inevitable moment when they are discovered rotting at the back of the shed and have to be thrown away. In the past few days we have been clearing out just such a garden store. At the back of it, as no doubt at the back of hundreds of thousands of sheds in Britain, we found some of last year's garden chair covers. They were covered in mouse droppings and had been half-chewed by the teeth of nest-building rodents. The covers have had to be thrown away. This was, by my reckoning, the third set we have had to discard in five years. We found a hammock which had been bought in a moment of supreme silliness and, as far as I recall, was not used once. We discovered a metal chair which had lost one of its legs, clearly the result of botched manufacture. And we found that annual horror, the sun umbrella at the end of its winter hibernation, which on being opened promptly covers its unfortunate owner in a wriggling shower of spiders and woodlice, cobwebs and dust.

Next week's May bank holiday will again see millions of families heading for the garden centres. Homeowners will wander innocently into the garden furniture section and allow themselves to be sold that most elusive of all dreams: that you can relax in comfort in your garden. Nonsense. It is only ever possible to relax in someone else's garden. There is an even worse misconception, namely that you can eat outside and enjoy it. Really? With squadrons of wasps stacking over your table to do a kamikaze nosedive into your long, refreshing drink? With ants ready to march on to plates bearing any scraps of food? Is there any expression surer to strike dread into the heart of a guest than 'al fresco dining'?

But let us return to that garden centre. You espy the brightly canopied double swing seat and you 'give it a try'. It seems well-padded, all right. It seems to carry your weight. So you pay several hundred pounds for it and take it home. It has come in the dreaded flat-pack box. Only now does suspicion start to turn in your brain. Flat-pack. Never a good idea. What shall we say? Five, six, or is it seven hours later, after much swearing and fiddling around with your blasted tool box, you manage to construct your new acquisition. Does it not feel smaller than it did in the shop? Those springs: are they meant to protrude quite so sharply? It squeaks heavily when you swing in it. When it is asked to withstand a combined freight of 20 stone of adult flesh and bone, it groans, kicks like a rodeo pony and starts to buckle. It is used one or two more times and after that, is slowly left to perish in the season's heat and downpours.

The same is true of reclining chairs. Having for once mastered the 'easy to assemble' instructions, the proud new owner must now become familiarised with the workings of the ingenious, Swedish-designed tilt mechanism. They are always Swedish-designed, in my experience. Sadists. At first, the super-duper executive tilting chair seems reluctant to cooperate. You press the recline button and four times in a row nothing happens. 'Perhaps you put it together wrongly,' says your wife accusingly. 'Did you read the instructions?' Of course you didn't. Who reads instructions? You go and make yourself a cup of tea, bring it back, try the stupid button one more time, whereupon it shoots you backwards with such hurtling velocity that you are left prone. With hot tea all down your shorts.

If the people from the Advertising Standards Authority are ever looking for something to do, they could address themselves to the pictures of smiling, middle-aged couples 'enjoying themselves' on their new garden furniture. Why, in such adverts, have the tables never been carpeted by bird droppings? Why do the adverts never show the chair arms wobbling because – as happens with every single set I have ever encountered – the washers, nuts and screws soon rust and fall from their appointed place.

I can still remember the smell of the strands of black-and-white plastic spaghetti which made up the faux wicker design of a fully reclining garden chair my father had 30 years ago. I was wondering to myself recently what happened to that. Then I remembered. It broke, sending my snoozing father careering towards Earth after lunch one day. From what I recall, we children all laughed. Perhaps that is the only true function of garden furniture. To provide slapstick entertainment for bored youngsters on Sunday afternoons.

1st May 2007

Exit Pescott

SO it's 'goodbye' from John Prescott – again. Last month the Deputy PM made what many of us thought was his farewell appearance at the despatch box. He received generous send-offs from his Tory and Lib Dem counterparts. A grateful nation said 'phew' and removed its tin helmets. Yesterday Parliament's own Les Dawson was back to give us a repeat performance. One more time, now, folks, you've been a luvverly audience. Oooh yes.

He really has finished this time. I think. He ended his 15-minute Question Time yesterday with a tremendous huff-and-puff against the 'penny scribblers of the press gallery'. As he mentioned us he looked up at the gallery with a crooked grin, a few wonky, canine teeth glinting amid all the spit-bubbled blubber of his gums. You know, I do believe the old gorilla developed a sneaking affection for us. There was love in that look. I feel sure of it. I'm touched. Just like that Tracey from the typing pool! No Prescott performance would be complete without a self-applied linguistic custard pie in the face. We duly got one.

He noted that David Cameron recently referred to him (not entirely seriously, in fact not at all seriously) as 'a cross between Ernie Bevin and Demosthenes'. Demosthenes was a fourth-century BC Athenian statesman noted for his brilliant oratory.

Trouble is, Mr Prescott did not quite get his floppy old tongue round the name of Demosthenes. He pronounced it as 'Dame

Osthenes', making it sound like a female character from a pantomime at the West Yorkshire Playhouse. The Commons collapsed in laughter.

Being Prescott, he did not click as to why they were laughing. Never does. He thought they were cheering and guffawing with him rather than at him. This therefore only encouraged him to look around feverishly with delight and lick his lips and continue all the longer with his 'jokes'. He thought he was doing well! William Hague, for the Tories, was sure that 'Dame Osthenes would be very flattered to have been singled out for praise by the Deputy Prime Minister'.

Still Mr Prescott did not seem to comprehend why MPs on all sides were wiping their eyes and shaking their heads.

When he mentioned the 'national linimum wage' it only set them all off again, great geysers of weeping, wheezy laughter shooting towards the ceiling. And still the old booby thought he was doing terrifically. His eyes sparkled with what he thought was his success. Tell ya what, chuck, I'm on a roll. Aye, a sausage roll!

21st June 2007

Gordon Brown has only just become Prime Minister but already it is obvious – to some of us, at least – that public spending has gone mad.

Do the maths

HERE is a horrible statistic: 20 million Britons suck down state money from Gordon Brown's crazily complicated tax credits. By my basic maths, that makes about a third of the population.

The 20 million figure was given to the Commons by Jane Kennedy, a Treasury Minister. What made it worse was that Miss Kennedy uttered it with pride. She was pleased that so many people have been fixed up to the drip-feed of the state by Labour.

You can see why an unprincipled politician might like this. Make people dependent on the state and they are more likely to vote for you and be in your thrall. But can it make sense for a scheme to be so enormous? What is the morality here? And what are the running costs? Are a third of us truly so poverty-stricken that we cannot make do without Nurse Kennedy's morning spoonful of malt? Might these people not be stronger and happier if Miss Kennedy and her boss Alistair Darling did not take away so much tax in the first place?

Tax credits were being discussed because an official report has found bad failings in the system. Miss Kennedy, assured but orthodox, said: 'I accept we are not where we want to be.' She later added: 'It's not a good place to be where accounts can not be signed off.' Not a good place to be: this year's accepted way of describing a balls-up.

Miss Kennedy talked of her 'customers'. Indeed, she purred about 'the tax credit customer experience', which roughly means your dealings with the tax and benefits inspector. Customers, surely, are people who buy things. Should recipients of state handouts not more accurately be called 'patients'? And there are 20 million of them in tax credits alone.

19th October 2007

The Queen could not have looked more delighted to greet the old despot

WHAT a gymkhana of hats and headgear we had on Horse Guards Parade when the king of Saudi Arabia was welcomed by the Queen. Human rights protesters may have been cross but it was an event to bring tears to the eyes of any milliner.

King Abdullah Ibn Abdul Aziz Al Saud, Custodian of the Two Holy Mosques – now there's a name to give immigration officials something to suck on – rolled up in the Queen's spare Bentley.

His Majesty was attired in a white *ghutra an iqal* (Arab topknot) above his magnificent gold-bordered robes. He was followed by a convoy of silver Mercedes from which sprang an anthill of Saudi princes, their heads covered in red-and-white teatowels fixed by circles of black rope.

The home team had risen to the challenge. Major-General William Cubitt, General Officer Commanding London District, was kitted out in a helmet topped by ostrich plumes which fluttered in the autumn breeze. Lord Vestey, Master of the Horse, was also in feathered splendour, his red uniform decorated with so much braid that he looked like something from the rope store at Chatham docks. Pull the right bit of scrambled egg on old Vestey and he toots like Thomas the Tank Engine.

The royal pavilion also boasted two fluffy tricorn hats, the military titfers of an admiral, general and Air Chief Marshal, the Metropolitan Police Commissioner in his best cap, the Queen in a claret-coloured pillar-box number, and the Duke of Edinburgh in black top hat. On the parade ground it was busbies for the 1st Battalion Welsh Guards and shiny helmets for the Household Cavalry.

Gordon Brown, looking a spare part amid this lot, was bareheaded. Ditto Foreign Office Minister Kim Howells (standing in for Foreign Secretary David Miliband, who had decided he had better things to do at home with his newly acquired American baby).

To fill time the Welsh Guards band played a medley which included the theme tunes to *Indiana Jones* and *Star Wars*. The Sergeant Major bawled at his guardsmen to get their dressing. 'Number Nine, forward, forward, forward, STOPPPPP!' The Queen arrived on the button at 12.15, the Horse Guards clock striking the quarter-hour the moment her Bentley purred on to the gravelled parade ground. Behind the Monarch's limousine chugged a Volkswagen Caravelle containing flunkeys.

Beside the royal pavilion were the away supporters' enclosures, one for guests of the Saudi ambassador, the other for all those princes. I spotted just one woman in the ambassador's box. Meanwhile Jacqui Smith, Home Secretary, was standing near the Prime Minister. She was in a chocolate trouser suit with cream piping. Mr Brown, spurning any thought of a morning coat, wore a lounge suit, lilac tie and lopsided grin.

When King Abdullah turned up at 12.20 p.m. he was sporting sunglasses and a soup-strainer moustache. The Queen could not have looked more delighted to greet the old despot. Her gaiety at these occasions is infectious. My gaze, however, was by now glued to Abdullah's impeccably neat goatee beard. What a dark colour it is for a man of his 84 years. Looks as though he has dipped his chin in a bottle of black Quink ink. Prince Charles, who had arrived with the king, moved to the sidelines and looked a touch sad. Not even his mother's merriment could lift his apparent melancholy.

After the Saudi anthem – creditably brief – and distant guns of salute, Major Benedict Ramsay of the Welsh Guards marched up, dipped his sword and spouted some Arabic. He was asking the king to inspect the Guard of Honour. Prince Philip accompanied the king, as did a Saudi military man with a faint air of Chief Inspector Jacques Clouseau of the Sûreté. Prince Philip thought he had trodden in something and looked back at where he had stepped.

The king returned the salutes of the various Gilbert and Sullivan top brass. He shook the hand of Sir Ian Blair which was covered in a white glove. Loaned by forensics? The female Lord Mayor of Westminster did an odd little gesture when presented to the king. First she touched her left breast. Then she fell into a dramatic curtsey. For a second I thought her high heel must have snapped.

Up clopped horses and carriages, complete with postilions in Regency wigs. The Queen and King Abdullah – plus interpreter – mounted steps into the Australian State Coach and were ridden away by Head Coachman Jack Hargreaves, gently clicking his tongue at horses Daniel, Stevenson, McCarthy, San Anton, Marsa and Jasper. The Duke of Edinburgh and two Saudis clambered into the Scottish State Coach (no steps for them). Prince Charles, still looking sad, had to make do with Lord Vestey and the open-topped No. 1 Semi-State Landau, plus cargo of two Arabian princes. Small talk looked to be at a premium.

And that was pretty much that. Ceremonial at its whiskery best had drawn to an end. The Prime Minister stomped off back to his work and the Band of the Welsh Guards (one of the few military bands left standing by Labour) departed to the strains of 'Cwm Rhondda'.

31st October 2007

One thing MPs really, really hate is when you report that they have fallen asleep. I can't think why they mind so much. Where is the dishonour in nodding off to Gordon Brown's voice? The country did it for years and I can think of at least one parliamentary sketchwriter who in the Commons gallery regularly closes his eyes for long passages of debate.

Eyes shut, he was at peace in his little world

BOY, that felt like a long 'un. Shortly after breakfast Gordon Brown did his first turn in front of the 'Liaison Committee', the ageing liggers, losers, placemen and palmed-off sycophants who chair select committees at the Commons.

Sorry. Deplorable manners. I meant 'Parliament's most distinguished elected Honourable Members who bring the wealth of years of experience to their doughty deliberations'. Cough.

Over in Lisbon they were limbering up for the blue-lit gameshow spectacle where all the other elected leaders of Europe were signing away our birthrights. But Mr Brown had sent a boy in shorts (Miliband Major, Form VIb) and had stayed in London for the morning to spend time with the decrepits and dead beetles of the Liaison Committee. Macavity strikes again! The PM spoke for two and a half hours. I lasted two hours before I could bear no more and bolted for the exits, a hanky held to my mouth to muffle the long, Hitchcock-film scream. Others fell asleep or scarpered long before that. This really was an ordeal of ennui, long, sandy passages of wilderness blown dry by the insistent mistral of Mr Brown's voice.

The meeting began at 9 a.m.. At 9.12 we had our first casualty. Sir Patrick Cormack (Con, S Staffs) is plainly not a morning man. I was sitting just to Sir Patrick's right and from my position in the slips I watched in fascinated horror as his right eyelid struggled against the forces of tedium.

Mr Brown was saying something about 'vah-lue for money', his foggy accent enveloping all. Sir Patrick's eyelid crept downwards. Momentarily it was repulsed by some fading instinct of duty, a deep-set animal fear of letting the side down. Sir Patrick rallied briefly.

But then the crafty eyelid resumed its heavy, downwards progress. Simultaneously his jaw slackened and his head stretched backwards. The Cormack system was closing down. Shrrrrrrp. Eyes now completely shut. Sir Patrick was at peace in his own little world. Lucky blighter. Michael Jack (Con, Fylde) tried to liven things up by beating up Mr Brown about the Government's 'efficiency savings' (efficiency! that's a laugh!). Mr Brown was soon launched back into that jowly monotone.

On the far side of the room an MP called Hywel Francis yawned. The reference books tell me that Mr Francis (Lab, Aberavon) has been at Westminster since 2001. I must confess I have never seen or heard of him before. Mr Brown ignored some antsy questions from Edward Leigh (Con, Gainsborough), flicking idly through a document while Mr Leigh spoke. The Prime Minister leaned back, sucked on his lips and threw his gaze to a distant horizon. Contempt. Stubbornness.

At 9.32, while Mr Brown was using a dead metaphor about 'a wake-up call on global warming', Keith Vaz (Lab, Leicester E) ate a yawn, chewing it at least 15 times. Nanny will be pleased by such assiduous mastication. By 9.37 the yawn had made its way round to Sir Stuart Bell (Lab, Middlesbrough) who half-heartedly tried to cover his mouth with one hand. Sir George Young, Bt (Con, NW Hants), clutched his dome of a head, possibly to stop it rolling off the table.

Mr Brown was soon claiming that he did not believe in 'top-down Government' – as blatant a lie as I have heard from him. My notebook records: '9.41, man in 2nd row of public seats, pink tie, marvellously asleep'. He was not the only one.

At 9.43 one of Mr Brown's Downing Street aides, a bald, camp creature, also lost the battle. Eyes shut. Another snoozer! Mohammed Sarwar (Lab, Glasgow C) clutched a cup of coffee and looked as though he might bite anyone who tried to take it off him. John Whittingdale (Con, Maldon & East Chelmsford) inspected the ceiling like a tourist at St Peter's. Mr Francis rallied briefly to ask a couple of questions and then lapsed back into hibernation. By now we had lost Andrew Miller (Lab, Ellesmere Port & Neston) who later awoke at 10.42 with a start, smacked his lips and took a deep slug of water.

Gordon Brown? Boredom Brown, more like.

14th December 2007

Cirque du Soleil, Royal Albert Hall

SIGH, it's that time of year again: the Cirque du Soleil is back. The Canadian circus-cum-marketing-roadshow has a number of shows which slowly tour the world in vast lorries.

This one is called Varekai, which apparently means 'wherever' in the Romany language. It might as well stand for 'whatever' or even 'same old tosh'.

As ever there is plenty of trapeze work, juggling, vaguely surreal clowns doing Gallic humour and high-floaty vocals in an improvised, indistinct non-language. It's a bit like listening to music underwater, or to singers who have been given too much local anaesthetic.

Because it visits so many countries the Cirque, with modern Canadian wetness, chooses to operate in a fusion culture which won't offend anyone (well, that's the idea). South Americanish pan pipes one moment – God, how I hate pan pipes – yield to a South African township beat and then some gipsy violin music, all overlaid with that non-ethnic-specific caterwauling. On stage, some pretty decent traditional circus artistes do their stuff, but to suit the Cirque ambience they have been dolled up for some sub-Tolkien netherworld which demands painted bodysuits, glorified bath hats and much stretching of necks in the 'look at me!' fashion.

The promotional bumf claims Varekai is 'an extraordinary world, deep within the forest, at the summit of a volcano' and that 'this production pays tribute to the nomadic soul and to the infinite passion of those whose quest takes them along the path to Varekai'. Utter cobblers.

You would never know it from proceedings on stage, which convey no clear narrative owing to the incomprehensible nature of the singers' words.

The good bits include two blokes who flip each other to and fro on their backs; a balletic turn on the trapeze by Mark Halasi, who enacts the flight of Icarus; some fast Georgian dancing by men with a lot of zeds in their surnames; one of the clowns' routines in which Steven Bishop tries to sing 'Ne Me Quitte Pas' while chasing his spotlight; and an astonishingly double-jointed rubber woman, name of Irina Naumenko, whose contortions make you want to cross your legs.

Children aged four to ten will probably be wowed. Any remotely educated or inquisitive adult will go away feeling starved of intellectual stimulation. Programmes this year are a rapacious £9. The interval is 25 minutes long, presumably to give punters even more time to empty their wallets at the Varekai souvenir stand.

11th January 2008

Mr Conway just had the misfortune to be caught

PLEASE don't call it downright theft. No, no. The man is a member of our political elite and you know how saintly they are. But a long-serving Conservative MP came to the Commons yesterday to utter his 'unreserved' apologies for bunging his son an annual £11,773 Westminster research salary plus juicy bonuses of about £10,000. The son was at that time a teenage student. In distant Newcastle.

Derek Conway (Old Bexley & Sidcup) made his personal statement at 3.33 p.m., just after Culture Questions. The Standards and Privileges Committee had just found that he had 'misused' public funds. Mr Conway did his best to remove the smile from his face. 'I unreservedly apologise for my administrative shortcomings,' said Mr Conway. Administrative shortcomings? Is that what they call it these days?

Conservative MPs, rather than avoid the tainted Conway, chose to 'doughnut' around him in support. Roger Gale (N Thanet) sat on one side of him. Mark Field (Cities of London & Westminster) arranged his long limbs on the other side. As soon as Mr Conway finished his brief statement he had his hand shaken heartily by Nigel Evans (Con, Ribble Valley). Damian Green, Shadow Immigration Minister, also chose to sit just next to Mr Conway to boost his morale. The Labour benches, meanwhile, offered no disapproval of Mr Conway's misbehaviour. There was no evidence of disgust anywhere.

This Conway is no gauche blow-in. He is a member of the Chairman's Panel, which means he gets to supervise some parliamentary debates. Chairman's Panel members are the House's prefects, if you like. Mr Conway was recently talked of as a future Speaker, presumably on the grounds that anyone would be an improvement on the truculent, baffled incumbent.

Mr Conway was MP for Shrewsbury & Atcham from 1983–97 and in 2001 he inherited Ted Heath's old seat. He led David Davis's campaign for the Tory leadership. He was a councillor in the North-East of England. A quarter of a century ago he was a luminary of that temple to ethical rectitude, the North of England Development Council.

The Standards and Privileges Committee, a cross-party body run by Establishment steadies, was, by its own measures, pretty rude about the way he employed his son. The arrangement was 'at the least an improper use of parliamentary allowances, at worst a serious diversion of public funds'. A 'serious diversion of public funds'? Would that be a euphemism? MPs did not yesterday vote on the matter but it seems likely that Mr Conway will serve a ten-day suspension from the Commons and will be asked to pay back a few thousand quid.

At which point any lay observer might ask: why is this matter not being referred to the police? Why is the Tory Party not thinking about deselecting Mr Conway? And why has the Speaker not chucked him off the Chairman's Panel? Well, murmurs the cynic, that's because Mr Conway simply had the misfortune to be caught. Maybe he is not the only one.

29th January 2008

Derek Conway was kicked out of the Tory Party but, rather than resign as a man of principle, chose to remain in the Commons until the 2010 general election.

His chair sighed as it received its burden

YURY Viktorovich Fedotov, Russian ambassador, came to Parliament for a chinwag. Well, 'chinwag' is perhaps not quite the term. The ambassador's jaw moved. His jowls juddered. The Fedotov larynx operated and grunts emerged through his pursed lips. Not one of life's thigh-slappers. The fact that he was there was, however, of note – a sign of cooperation with the deluded, imperialist-minded British authorities. But cooperation has its limits and Meester Fedotov brought a blunt message of real politik.

He was appearing in front of a Lords committee looking at EU–Russian relations. The session was chaired by Lord Roper, a Lib Dem who peers at life through 1970s spectacles, their lenses imperfectly polished. Tall, wide Mr Fedotov plonked himself down. His red-upholstered chair gave a faint sigh as it received its burden. Beside him sat one Andrey Pritsepov from the Russian embassy. This lean, dark-haired Pritsepov remained motionless and silent.

The ambassador is a testament to his country's diet of dark stews and potato cakes. Sitting behind him I was transfixed by the bulging middle seam of his suit jacket. Would the thread manage to contain the ambassador's magisterial bulk? The back of Mr Fedotov's close-cropped head was ridged by flesh. From time to time a surprisingly feminine right hand made economical gesticulations or pushed his Andropov-style glasses up his nose. A petite hooter. Mr Pritsepov said nothing.

The ambassador grandly said he did not mind if the proceedings were televised. He then announced that Europe without Russia was not Europe. 'Ees no secret we seek close relayshuns.' He added that, 'Ees well known fakt that Russis ees number-one supplier of energy to Europe.' Lady Symons, formerly a Labour minister, vouchsafed some pleasantries and fluttered four lacquered eyelashes. She spoke in a throaty whisper.

She pushed back her shoulders, accentuating her cavernous embonpoint. 'Ees very good question, Lady Sandbag,' said the ambassador, agog. Lord Crickhowell, once a Tory Cabinet minister, was given a couple of overs. He suggested that it suited Russia to have a fractured Europe. The ambassador implausibly said Russia would prefer a stronger Europe. 'But when thees day weel come we're gonna see.' A joke! His shoulders heaved and the thread held – just. The committee tinkled with polite laughter. Mr Pritsepov moved not a muscle.

Lord Anderson, a former Labour MP with a scruffy shirt collar, raised Russia's mistreatment of the British Council. The ambassador replied that Breetish Council would only be treated better when London eased up on the Litvinenko investigation and on visa requirements for Russians. Lord Chidgey waffled at length. No one really listened but Lady Symons watched the ambassador over her half-moon specs, as though transfixed. She fondled her left earring. From nearby kitchens came an aroma of frying meat.

Labour's Lord Truscott, who wears a Chekhovian goatee, blurted a few words of fluent Russian. Hansard's stenographer froze. Mr Pritsepov's right cheek twitched. Lord Crickhowell rasped that it was 'difficult to understand' why cultural relations should be damaged by the Litvinenko case (translation: this is outrageous). Lady Symons said the ambassador's answer had 'at least been helpful in so far as it was very stark. One couldn't misunderstand what you're saying.' Translation: well, that's a poke in the eye! Mother Russia's finest sat with his thighs thrust apart. He could have been a clod of earth cut from the Steppes, still damp on the shovel. He blinked.

Lady Symons smiled, slowly, until her lips were apart. 'Eees a matter of kind of goowill from both sides,' said the ambassador eventually. She'd done it! She'd melted the Siberian icecap! The session ended with a cordial apology from Mr Fedotov that Mr Pritsepov had not said a word. I wonder if he ever does.

8th February 2008

An outbreak of locusts

AMID much stamping of little booties (or should that be sandals?) almost the entire contingent of Liberal Democrat MPs stomped out of the Commons chamber yesterday teatime.

Tools down. It's a walkout. The Libs were furious about a ruling by the Speaker, who had declined to let one of their amendments be called on the Lisbon Treaty. (Clegg's little heroes are mostly pro this constitutional treaty, by the way. They thought the Speaker was going to cooperate.) Such, readers, is the lack of respect for Mr Speaker nowadays that even the mild-mannered Libs are prepared to ignore his rulings. In the past they would not have dared to rebel like this. But now that he is so discredited his name carries little clout.

Speaker Martin himself was not in the chamber at 4.40 p.m. when the prison riot started. Who knows where he was? Settling down with a buttered crumpet in his grace and favour mansion, perhaps. Or maybe he and Mrs Mick were at that very moment in the back of a cab – stick it on our account, driver – bowling along to Fortnum & Mason for a tea of cucumber sandwiches and tipsy cake. The Chair was occupied instead by one of the Deputy Speakers, Sir Michael Lord, who called for order. He was ignored.

The Liberal benches were almost full, unlike the rest of the chamber. Ed Davey, their foreign affairs man, tried to make a point of order asking the Chair to reconsider its ruling on the amendment. Sir Michael regretted that was not possible.

Mr Davey got back to his feet. Sir Michael asked him to sit down. Mr Davey, still standing, said: 'We are being gagged.' Sir Michael was still on his feet, so we had a spaghetti western stand-off. Sir Michael shot Mr Davey a Paddington stare. Mr Davey returned towards his bench at a crouch.

Nick Clegg, leader of this small band of desperadoes, had a point of order. 'I share my Hon. Friend's dismay,' he began. Sir Michael raised his arm to indicate a command for silence. 'I have made the situation quite clear,' he said, his voice a bit crackly with 'flu and maybe a few trembles of anger. Mr Clegg shook his head. Lots of Liberal voices tutted and moaned. Sir Michael coped as well as anyone could have done but it was like trying to control an outbreak of locusts from a school science laboratory. Every time he trapped one pest another hopper appeared from nowhere.

Simon Hughes, Lib Dem president, sprang to his heels. He

complained that he had been to see the clerks many times and had not been given satisfaction. I hope that sentence is not open to misinterpretation. 'Many times!' squawked several Lib Dems, nodding like fishwives. 'Tell me what we have to do to get an amendment accepted,' urged Mr Hughes. 'Many times!' continued the fishwives. Sir Michael, hands now shaking, called for order. Norman Baker (Lib Dem, Lewes) was standing. So was Mr Davey. 'This is an outrage!' cried Mr Davey.

Sir Michael said he was in danger of being impertinent to the Chair. Mr Davey showed no remorse. Julia Goldsworthy (Lib Dem, Falmouth) was on her pins too, piping: 'This is outrageous!' Sir Michael explained repeatedly that the decision on the amendment had been made not by him but by Speaker Martin. He really hammered that point home. The Speaker's name had no effect on the ongoing mayhem.

Sir Michael said if Mr Davey persisted in arguing with the Speaker he would become 'extremely annoyed'. Various voices gave a mocking, high-pitched: 'Wooooooo!' Sir Michael was now turning grey with rage and told Mr Davey that 'stronger measures will have to be taken'. Mr Davey refused to sit down, the tips of his shirt collar starting to bend upwards like old toast.

'OOOOOORDER!!!!!' yelled Sir Michael. I have never heard it shouted so loudly in the Commons. For a second or two it cowed the Lib Dems. What a nasty shouty man, Cedric.

But then the locusts started hopping again. 'Mr Speaker has made the selection and it is not open to question,' said Sir Michael. 'Yes it is!' chorused about 50 Lib Dems. 'I have had enough,' said Sir Michael. He told the Minister, Jim Murphy, to start the debate. 'Noooo!' squealed the Lib Dems.

Mr Davey was now thrown out of the Commons for the day. Mr Murphy started droning away with his prepared speech but the Lib Dem benches were in uproar, several of them standing and speaking. Mr Clegg decided he'd had enough and left the chamber and the locusts, as one, followed him.

'The order of this House is every bit as important as any matter they are trying to raise,' said Sir Michael. He is right. And we will not have proper order in our elected House until we have a new Speaker.

27th February 2008

France's President Sarkozy and his smouldering wife are in town. The day after a royal banquet at Windsor Castle – where Gordon Brown managed to get lost on arrival – Monsieur le President and his entourage are invited to Arsenal's football ground.

The Anglo-French farce

NORMAL British and French Government activity was suspended yesterday to enable two preening premiers to pose on the pitch at Arsenal's football ground.

In one of the more ludicrous stunts it has been my privilege to chase after on your behalf, the circus of modern politics descended on the Emirates Stadium, north London.

Summits are best held at central Government addresses in dignified, sober surroundings. The choice of yesterday's venue said it all about this Anglo-French fandango.

Gordon Brown managed not to get lost. Given his Frank Spenceresque performance on Wednesday night that, readers, was progress. But then Gormless Gordon was given a simultaneous translation earplug which duly appeared to go wrong. The man is fast turning into a walking comedy routine.

Arsenal had been chosen because it has a French manager and several French players. Teamwork. On the ball. Doing well in Europe. Geddit? To hammer home that this Anglo-French junket was Something Special (even though it lasted barely 36 hours), various ministers from London and Paris had been spooned into the operation. Numerous 'bilaterals' were taking place in hidden meeting rooms at the swanky stadium. Jacqui Smith, David Miliband, Jack Straw, John Hutton: all were on parade, as were their French counterparts. The visiting team looked a good deal more sleek. Dear Jacqui was at her dumpiest. The French contingent included a languid gent who looked like something out of the 1950s and an angular-limbed, heavily made-up lady who would not have been out of place behind the smellies counter at Selfridges.

The Brown–Sarkozy photo call on the pitch was a laughable nonsense. There must have been about 200 journalists on the premises. Were we allowed out into the fresh air to watch the PM and Monsieur le President? We were not. One vast stadium, capable of seating some 60,000 fans. But 'no room for you lot', ruled a Downing Street flunkey.

Then a Hitlerian little figure turned up to make life even more difficult for the massed scribes of Britain and France. We were told we could not even watch Messrs Brown and Sarkozy – tiny figures, about 200 yards away – through the windows of the Emirates reception hall. These were covered in blinds. When some of us tried to lift the blinds to see what was going on, the little Hitler, who answered to the name of Terry, started shouting at the top of his weedy voice about how his 'guvnor' forbade such behaviour. He came round, slapping down the blinds.

We reached the main event: the Brown–Sarkozy press conference. The two leaders arrived. Jacqui Smith and the British ministers leapt to their feet. The French stayed seated. Jacqui and Co. sheepishly sat down again. Beside M. Sarkozy stood a French naval figure with much gold braid, guarding a heavy briefcase (which presumably contained France's nuclear button). Earphones were issued to enable everyone to listen to simultaneous translations. M. Sarkozy managed to get his earpiece to work perfectly. Mr Brown had less success.

He started to fiddle with the controls, frowning and smiling at the same time. It was clear that the thing wasn't giving him the live feed because he kept grinning at the most inappropriate times.

There was an awful lot of stuff – again – about how Britain should be more involved in Europe. Then a man from *Figaro* asked if M. Sarkozy had been upstaged by his wife Carla. Whoosh! Off he flew into a tirade which contained a passage about how Mme Sarkozy was a woman of *'conviction, humanité, sensibilité'*. He later waded into the press lot to continue his row with the *homme* from *Figaro*, while Mr Brown watched in amazement.

The French have now gone home and we can all calm down. What a relief.

28th March 2008

Let gush the geysers of state extravagance

NO one seems to have told the House of Commons that there is a Western financial crisis which could bring the capitalist system tumbling to Ground Zero.

MPs yesterday gaily demanded more public spending here, more Government intervention there. Turn those Treasury taps to full blast. Let gush the geysers of state extravagance for tomorrow we may lose our seats.

I apologise if the following sketch sounds anguished but no one seems to be facing up to just how bad things could become. At every turn yesterday Hon. Members seemed to have no grasp of what might happen if budgets need to be tightened. If the West goes into bank-collapse hell, European Governments will simply not be able to splurge as they have been doing in recent years.

Is it not time ministers – and, equally, their Conservative opponents – woke up to this horrible likelihood? Is it not time that a responsible politician stood up on his or her hind legs and said 'let's just hold our spending plans until we see what's round the corner on Wall Street'?

Yesterday in the Commons we had Health Questions. I don't

think there was a single set of exchanges which did not include Labour boasting about 'investment' in health facilities or some dire demand from backbench MPs of all sides for more healthcare spending by Whitehall. The subjects being discussed were worthy. They included things like cancer clinics, GPs' opening hours, NHS dentistry, looking after the old, organ donation and medical apprenticeships. Few people would happily slash spending on such areas. But what happens if the money is simply not there in future? Are our elected politicians mature enough to face a recession?

Andrew Rosindell (Con, Romford), who styles himself a Right-winger, complained that only 70 per cent of women are regularly screened for cancer. He felt the Government was 'letting the women of this country down'. Myself, I'd have thought 70 per cent was a pretty good achievement for cancer screening but Mr Rosindell had to go and make an overstated political point. Tony Lloyd (Lab, Manchester C) wanted reconstructive surgery offered to all breast cancer patients. A fine ideal. But how is it to be paid for? We moved to the treatment of drug offenders. Everyone struck sympathetic poses. No one said the unutterable and suggested that if NHS budgets are squeezed it should surely be people who become ill through no fault of their own – rather than self-harming drug addicts – who come at the top of the spending pile.

The reason for this? Any politician who questions public spending is attacked by opponents and by the media as a hard-heart and an uncaring brute. We will not get honest politics until that attitude changes.

Phil Willis (Lib Dem, Harrogate) argued that patients should never be discharged from hospital unless they have 24-hour care available at home. What if there is simply not the money to pay for such a scheme? What if patients do not want to be detained? Meanwhile, another Lib Dem, Gregory Mulholland (Leeds NW), had some statistics which showed that the turnover of staff in old people's homes led to £151 million being spent on agency temps and a further £20 million being spent on job adverts.

The public spending hose is snaking out of control, sprinkling largesse in every direction. How much longer can this continue, if there is indeed a Wall Street crash, before the country goes bust? At one point in the debates yesterday the Health Secretary, Alan Johnson, uttered the words: 'All areas must receive an increase in funding.'

No one picked him up on this. They are all such blinkered nags, our MPs, able to see only in one direction, that they do not wonder how such rosy optimism can come true if our economy follows America and staggers into recession.

Where are the pessimists in our politics? Where are the bearded Elijahs, covered in dust and shaking their gnarled staffs at the storm-bleak horizon?

19th March 2008

The Brown Government is less than a year old but is having to rely on the Whips to maintain party discipline.

Keenly observing the pondlife, ten Whips

SUCH is the Brown regime's unease that the Commons was yesterday riddled with spies from the Whips' office.

The Whips are Westminster's enforcers, the torturers, the persuasion-by-menace brigade. When an MP rebels against the party line the Whips (of both main parties) will sidle up and enquire, with palpably fake smile, after the health of their family pets, or even younger children. 'Wouldn't want anything unfortunate to happen to Tiddles would we? Now why don't you just forget your silly ideas and vote as we suggest?' Yes, O Whip. Whatever you say, O Whip.

During Treasury Questions there were no fewer than ten

Whips in the chamber. Ten! Normally it is just one duty Whip on the Government bench, taking a quiet note of who says what, in which tone of voice. For the files. Just so we know, you see? The Whips are Parliament's speed cameras. Yesterday we had more than half the Commons Whips out on parade, dotted round the Labour benches.

When you added their number to the ministers and 'PPS' aides who were sitting behind them, they easily outnumbered the other Labour MPs who had turned up to question Alistair Darling and his ministers.

Burly Tommy McAvoy, who would have found handy employment in the thumbscrewing days of the Borgias, stood at the far end of the House with his arms crossed. Labour backbenchers could not have possibly missed his formidable bulk. By standing in such a prominent place Mr McAvoy was effectively saying, 'We're listening to every single word you say, pondlife.'

Frank Roy, another rotund Scots Whip with one of those laughably nasty goatee beards (he looks like the baddie in *Toy Story*), was perched in a little box seat near big Tommy. Liz Blackman was also down that end, eyes narrowed. If she had been a cat her tail would have been swishing from side to side. Miss Blackman is a great adornment of the Whips' office. Cruelty on two slim pins.

In the middle of the Labour benches another Whip, Hull North's Diana Johnson, had inserted herself. Watching, waiting. That's what Whips do. Down by the Speaker's Chair there was another little nest of Whips: slow-to-stir Bob Blizzard, a wispy creature called Tony Cunningham, Pavlovian-trained Steven McCabe and dumpy Siobhain McDonagh whose sister used to run the Labour Party for Tony Blair. Sadiq Khan, an intellectual Whip, was sitting a yard or so along the bench, smouldering nicely. Essex glamourpuss Alison Seabeck was flitting about, glasses up on the top of her hairdo. Miss Seabeck is the Jackie O of the Whips' office. Used to be a lifeguard. Knows when it is worth giving the kiss of life to a backbencher's political career – and when to press down on that career's windpipe. Hard. Until the gurgling stops and the limbs fall still.

This was an extraordinary turnout by the heavies. It was the Whipping equivalent of a police line with shields and batons before a Countryside Alliance demonstration in London. Mr Darling and his Treasury ministers certainly need the protection. The Chancellor was subdued for much of the hour session. His ministerial team offers him little help. Contemptuous Yvette Cooper is a major vote loser. Angela Eagle is the poor man's Thora Hird. Jane Kennedy lacks the ability to reverse out of a cul-de-sac.

An odd week in Westminster ended with a din of music and amplified shouting from an open-topped bus going round Parliament Square. At the front of the top deck, craning forward, was a familiar-looking exotic with moustachings and dark glasses.

Then I recognised the voice. It was George Galloway MP, campaigning for his Respect Party in the coming elections. What a racket! And lest there be any legal misunderstanding let me stress I mean 'racket' in the sense of noise.

24th April 2008

From his doughnut mouth came a Herbert Lom laugh

WHAT a fandango when the Dalai Lama dropped by yesterday morning. His Holiness became the first living deity (we've had plenty of devils) to talk to the Commons Foreign Affairs Select Committee.

Given that he is the exiled spiritual leader of a Tibet oppressed by Communist China, Mr Lama, if we can call him that, seemed pretty cheerful.

One could also call him Kundun ('O Presence') or Yeshe Norbu ('Wish-fulfilling Jewel'). Not that he seemed much hung up on formalities.

I have never seen a select committee witness so chucklesome and twinkly.

On arrival our purple-robed visitor and his small delegation of monks was greeted by Nick Clegg and some Liberal Democrats.

One group of orange-clad, sandal-wearing, powerless peaceniks embraces another.

Lembit Opik (Lib Dem, Pluto) bowed. The Buddhist visitors bowed back. Mr Opik bowed again. You need a match referee to call time on these occasions or the bowing will go on until the midday prayer bell.

Refreshed by his top-level talks with global player Mr Clegg (please, do try to take this seriously) the Dalai Lama floated upstairs to the Foreign Affairs Committee.

A large crowd had gathered and the police were in best bibs, doing rather more 'Stand back!' and 'Make way!' than was strictly necessary. The genial old monk, slowly moving past the throng, kept stopping to clutch hands and bow and do his little '*namaste*' greeting of pressed palms. Commons staff started to return the compliment. He may on one level only be a dispossessed political figure from a distant mountain kingdom, but he's a shrewd bird and knows that a little oriental mystique goes a long way in the religiously untutored West.

This small, infectiously smiley figure has been pulling off the same trick for decades – even longer than the Queen. Mike Gapes, Labour chairman of the committee, hurtled out of a side door and went into a bow so deep he could have been a collapsible drinks trolley. 'Welcome!' he boomed, like some courtier from *The King and I*.

The thought may also have bubbled through Mr Gapes's head: 'Hah! This should put one over Keith Vaz at the Home Affairs Committee.' Publicity-crazed Mr Vaz will certainly need to pull off something big to match Mr Gapes's coup. While the committee room settled I took the chance to ask the Lama what he had in a little gym kitbag he was clutching.

He pulled out a sun visor, a glasses case and, after determined rummaging, a sweetie. I think it was a Werther's Original. He said he quite often carries some bread in his bag, too. How comforting to think that it is not only Winnie-the-Pooh who occasionally succumbs to the need for 'a little something' between elevenses and lunch.

A Commons flunkey delivered a ceremonial water jug to the witness table. Then Andrew Mackinlay (Lab, Thurrock) accidentally struck his foot against a metal table leg and it gave off the 'plonnnng!' of a temple gong. The Lama started to speak about the suffering of Tibet. He described the 'rural terror' of life under the Chinese and of an 80-year-old monk having his leg broken by torturers. He thought it possible Peking might let him back into Tibet soon.

If we're going to be brutally honest, much of what he said was incomprehensible. His English had bursts of intelligible stuff followed by grunts and high-pitched squeaks before his mouth formed a doughnut shape and he gave a Herbert Lom laugh. Panic flittered across the eyes of the reporters from Hansard, particularly when he started to list various Tibetan provinces. Gordon Brown may want to take a good interpreter along when he meets him today.

The living god was watched closely by the former Lib Dem Lama, Sir Menzies Campbell. How Sir Ming must yearn for reincarnation. Other MPs kept nodding with encouragement, even when His Holiness was at his most bafflingly cryptic. Forget soundbites. The Dalai Lama showed yesterday that nothing works so well in foreign affairs as a spot of robed, radiant incoherence.

25th April 2008

Herman Munster rose like a giraffe from his waterhole

SHORTLY before 3.30 p.m. a roar erupted in the Commons chamber. The Minister at the despatch box at the time was dear old Stephen Timms, the circa 7ft Herman Munster look-alike who is number two or three at the Department of Work and Pensions. He was talking with his customary earnestness about some detail of the welfare state.

For one brief second Mr Timms, hearing that hoot of pleasure, looked up from his notes with delighted surprise. Me? Is this applause for me? Why, thank you, Cupcake. This has made my day. He could have been a giraffe rising from the waterhole, slurpy water dripping from its lopsided lips, two topknots forming a sweet frown. Acclaim? For me? Well, well! Then, as quickly as the delicious possibility had entered his mind, it evaporated. Underloved Mr Timms realised the roar was not for him. Poooof.

Another bubble bursts. Another dream is snapped at this theatre of the cruel we call politics.

The roar was for the victor of Crewe and Nantwich, Edward Timpson (Con). He arrived at 3.27 p.m. to stand by the Serjeant-at-Arms's seat before stepping forward to swear allegiance to the Crown. This was the first sitting day at the Commons since Labour's defeat in the Crewe by-election a week and a half ago. Mr Timpson was flanked by his Cheshire constituency neighbour George Osborne (Tatton) and Angela Browning (Tiverton). Mrs Browning fought Crewe for the Tories in 1987. On that occasion the town fought back but now, for the time being, it is a Conservative seat.

Once Mr Timms and Co. had finished Work and Pensions Questions it was time for Mr Timpson and his outriders to approach the Commons Table. Speaker Martin summoned 'all new Members desiring to take their seats' and the packed Tory benches again went wild with happiness. Order Papers were waved. The Labour benches were nearly empty but a few Government supporters had done the decent thing and remained in place.

'Cobbler!' shouted David Taylor (Lab, NW Leics). Mr Timpson, you see, comes from a family which runs a chain of heel bars. Quite a few members of that family – who had to endure class-war vilification during the by-election campaign – seemed to be present for the event. The new Hon. Member's demure wife was in the downstairs gallery, accompanied by what looked like a beaming Dad. Upstairs were further people with 'proud relations' written all over them. As Mr Timpson inched past the Labour benches, Lindsay Hoyle (Lab, Chorley) bawled: 'He looks well heeled!' Stephen Pound (Lab, Ealing N): 'Don't get comfortable. You won't be staying!' All this was in good heart. Less cheerful was a remark from the direction of Dennis Skinner (Lab, Bolsover). 'Where's yer top hat?' snarled a distinctive voice. From the gallery it was not easy to hear what was now said but having interviewed various MPs I understand that 'verbals' were exchanged between Mr Skinner and Mr Osborne, with Mr Skinner allegedly enquiring if Mr Osborne kept his policies 'up his nose' (he has a thing about Mr Osborne's snorting habits) and Mr Osborne suggesting that Mr Skinner hold his flubbery old tongue. Somebody, again near Mr Skinner, was heard to mutter something about 'another toff'.

Conservative toughs, who no longer fear Mr Skinner, hit back. 'It'll be Bolsover next!' yelled a Tory heckler, suggesting Mr Skinner's seat might also turn Tory. Dream on. 'Time you retired!' squawked a female voice, aware that 76-year-old Mr Skinner is not what he was. Another Conservative, not 100 feet from Mike Penning (Hemel Hempstead), told Mr Skinner to cheer up because '*Countdown*'s starting soon'. The TV show *Countdown* is popular with the elderly, you see. Old Skinner, head turned away, looked furious.

We close with the news that one suave Etonian Tory, formerly in the Shadow Cabinet, has welcomed Mr Timpson's arrival with the remark: 'I really must talk to that young man – the heel of one of my shoes is a bit loose.'

3rd June 2008

Mother Margot arrived with two oblong-headed grunts

ONE of the top autocrats from the European Commission stepped a toe in Westminster yesterday.

Name: Margot Wallström, vice-president and head of the EC's 'institutional relations and communication strategy'. Quite a piece of work. Tory MP David Heathcoat-Amory asked with light jocularity: 'Given that you're in charge of communication, what do you think the Irish voters are trying to communicate to you?' (The unspoken answer to this question, given Ireland's referendum result on the Lisbon Treaty, is 'bog off!'). Glacial Ms Wallström, a Swede, did not find Mr Heathcoat-Amory's question amusing. These are irksome days for the Euro elite. She gave Heathcoat a Paddington stare and said she was 'interviewing' the Irish 'to better understand' why they gave the treaty such a fantastic raspberry.

Mother Margot arrived at the Commons European Scrutiny Committee with an entourage of two comically oblong-headed Scandinavian grunts, a little British sidekick with curly hair and specs, plus a mouse-like press aide. The Brit, Patrick Costello, did much frowning during the session, as though keen to give the impression that everyone except his boss was talking rubbish. Quite the reverse was true.

Ms Wallström, not overfreighted by gaiety, used to toil in the telly business (as a TV station executive, that is, rather than fixing aerials). She was also a Minister for Women, Culture and Social Affairs in Stockholm. Photogenic though she may be in an Abba blonde sort of way, she speaks in a metallic monotone. After noting that some other countries had ratified Lisbon, she said: 'The Irish "no" is an answer but it is not a solution.' I'm afraid that one made me bark with laughter.

Lindsay Hoyle (Lab, Chorley), a Eurosceptic, could not contain himself. 'So, a "yes" means "yes", a "no" has to mean "yes"!' he said. Sarcasm entering his soul, Mr Hoyle added: ' Why not go back to the people who said " yes" and ask them to have another go?' The oblong-head to her right was Reijo Kemppinen, a former Finnish journalist who now runs the European Commission in London. He used to work for the BBC. During yesterday's session Mr Kemppinen kept tearing pieces of A4 into smaller strips of paper. And tearing them into even smaller pieces. He'd make some shrink a useful case study.

The MPs did not distinguish themselves. At one point so few of them were present that the meeting, shambolically, fell out of quorum. Mr Kemppinen smirked, perhaps interpreting it as a sign of weakness by British Eurosceptics that they could not even muster enough interest to quiz Ms Wallström.

From time to time Mr Kemppinen scribbled a few words on one of his notelets. Some of these were passed to Ms Wallström. Others were torn into tiny squares and left in a little pile in front of Mr Kemppinen. When the meeting broke up and the EC crowd had left the room, a Fleet Street colleague and I scooped up the litter left by Mr Kemppinen. Using jigsaw techniques we managed to reassemble a couple of the notes he had scribbled.

One read: '*WE* did not lose one single referendum.' (This may suggest that the EC considers itself blameless re: Ireland.) The other, a peach, reads: 'Yes is yes but no is unfortunate.'

24th June 2008

A Clegg conference speech

MOCK Cameron, attack Cameron – but ape him, copy him, do the Cameron cha-cha-cha. That was the approach of Lib Dem leader Nick Clegg when he gave a conference speech which could easily have been the work of a Cameron tribute band.

Mr Clegg pooh-poohed Cameron's Conservatives as 'Blue Labour' – yet he himself was in blue tie, against a blue background, looking every inch the Cameroon.

He deplored the way 'David Cameron and his cronies have tried to take over every comforting, soft-focus word in the dictionary', yet Mr Clegg's own speech was a patchwork quilt of soapy selling, mashed potato buzzwords and moist-eyed thespishness.

There were some badly oversweetened passages, pure hokum, when he gave us sob stories from voters he said he had met. We heard about 'Angie, a middle-aged mum, who was finding it hard to sleep'. A few minutes reading Lib Dem policy papers should put that right, dear. And we were told about an encounter he had with a pensioner called Joan. 'I could see the anxiety on her face,' claimed Mr Clegg. Maybe it was the experience of meeting a Lib Dem politician that alarmed her.

After calling Labour 'zombies' – thus is the currency of political abuse inflated – he laid into Cameron's 'born-to-rule conceit'. Yet this is the same bum-fluffed Clegglet who went to public school, worked in Brussels (for Leon Brittan, of all people) and strolled into leadership after roughly five minutes at Westminster.

None of this marvellously blatant hypocrisy should prevent us noting that Mr Clegg delivered his speech with poise and the requisite fakery. The speech was certainly modern, a good deal more modern than the party itself. He doesn't really look like a Lib Dem.

Advertising agents say there is no point advertising a brand's image until you have addressed the basic design of the product itself. Has Mr Clegg done that? He strolled the stage, using a side lectern only as a stand for his water glass. He did not quite memorise his speech, Cameron-style. There were three prompt screens a few rows back in the stalls. But he walked around the place like one of those sales evangelists on a daytime TV shopping channel.

He even pioneered a presentation gimmick when he threw the occasional phrase over the back of his shoulders. For instance, 'one year ago David Miliband was telling reporters he wasn't interested in being Prime Minister' – pause, backwards look over the shoulder – 'oh, right, David!' It is hard to imagine Gordon Brown attempting, or wishing to attempt, such slangy, sardonic notes in his Labour conference speech next week. That is why Mr Brown now feels such a dated figure.

Actually, it's hard to imagine any Cabinet minister delivering quite such an informal, conversational speech. Mr Clegg certainly achieved an intimacy with the hall yesterday. He pulled in quite a few references to his wife Miriam and her pregnancy. She was wearing remarkably high heels for a woman in such a condition.

The snags with this speech were twofold. First, when he said that the Lib Dems were 'headed for Government' I don't suppose many of them really believed him. All this guff about 'my Shadow Cabinet' and how 'we are a powerful party, growing stronger' was at odds with the opinion polls which suggest that the Lib Dems are about as popular as vinegared herring rollmops.

Second, he has not yet worked out the contradictions in calling for 'less Government' while at the same time bawling out for more redistribution. You surely either believe in a bigger state or a smaller state. You can't boast about liberalism while demanding state action every time someone is born with a social problem.

The creaky delegates, plenty of them with wall eyes and strange limps, reacted warmly to the speech. They know that Mr Clegg looks the part and sounds the part. That, in itself, is a great advantage. But it may not be enough to stop them being walloped in the next election.

18th September 2008

They duly were walloped at the next election – and yet made it into Government – a case of your sketchwriter being half-right. Better than normal!

Some of us, leaving the hall after David Miliband's speech, conceded that it was an improvement on the stinker he made to the conference last year. 'Yes,' said a colleague on Another Paper.

'But that's like being told you're a better violinist than Abu Hamza.' – Labour Party conference.

23rd September 2008

Mr Peter Mandelson, restored to Westminster, becomes a peer of the realm

OH the smirk! Peter Mandelson was dolled up in ermine and introduced to the House of Lords yesterday afternoon. His hair was so neat that the parting looked like a zip. He had entered the chamber at 2.37 p.m., face and shoulders immobile under those robes. Shuffle, shimmer, shimmy, in he glided, as though auditioning for a role in *The Mikado*. He must have had his bottom almost completely clenched to have moved so seamlessly – or maybe he had some castors attached to his shoes.

At this point in proceedings his lean lips were still drawn primly together, pressing against one another, determined to betray no emotion. Such composure, for the rest of us, was a harder task. To see this Cabinet twice-reject, this Brussels blow-in, this greased porker made a lord – and not, ourselves, to squeal with disgust? But barracking and loud raspberries from the galleries are not permitted, or there would have been scenes of Hogarthian retching.

The little line of grandees accompanying him included not only military man Black Rod, jaw like a tugboat on the Solent, but also a gold-braided flunkey holding a wand high in the air. Imagine Sir John Barbirolli about to launch into some Mahler with the Halle. The House stilled. One person coughed. On the Woolsack was Lady Hayman, the overpaid and pointless Lords Speaker. She crossed two slender pins.

Then we caught sight of the candidate's two supporters. First came Jim Callaghan's glacial daughter Lady Jay (boo hiss), followed by rotund Lord Falconer (hooray, if only for comedy value). Fatty Falconer! We haven't seen much of him in the House of Lords since he was booted out as Lord Chancellor. He looked careworn – a hint of mould at the crusts – but at least his propeller is still somehow churning through life's briny swell.

The House was full, as it often is at the start of the day. They get paid for turning up, of course, but there was genuine wonderment. We have had appalling Eurocrats before in the House but none with such a record of disgrace and devilment.

Easily the jolliest person on the premises was Lord Strathclyde, leader of the Tories, chubby cheeks dimpled like two deep-set tummy buttons. The elevation of Mr Mandelson to the peerage may be a wonderful present to the Upper House's Conservatives. A peek into the robing room showed the about-to-be-ennobled Mandelson touching the side of his hair, patting his fur-edged robes and stretching his neck. The Lords byways were a nest of Blairites. In the lobby outside there loitered and joked Tony Blair's sometime Downing Street aide Phil Bassett (husband of ex-Defence Minister Lady Symons).

Up in the galleries sat Roger Liddle, a long-term Mandelson colleague. The tense, sad face of Tessa Jowell also stared down from on high, ghostlike, drawn. Will it ever be Lady Jowell? What a worry that Italian court case involving her husband must be.

Came the big moment. A nation paused. Pregnant was the air. Squire Mandelson was walked at ceremonial pace to the Opposition despatch box where the oaths are sworn. He was greeted by a beaky, wigged clerk who proceed to read out a magnificently twirly Letters Patent from the Queen. This royal proclamation began with a thunderclap: 'Elizabeth the Second! By the grace of Gord of the United Kingdom of Great Britain and Northern Ireland and of Our other Realms and Territories, Queen, Head of the Commonwealth, Defender of the Faith.' Oooh. The show-off.

Everyone watched the smooth figure standing in the centre of the chamber. He clasped before him those infamous hands. Not an inchlet did he stir as he stood, poised, wreathed by a cologne cloud of delight. A once noble House's brew was being poisoned by hemlock.

Drip, drip, drip.

We heard him described in Her Majesty's clarion message as 'our right trusty and well-beloved counsellor, Peter Benjamin Mandelson'. Trusty? It's not the same thing as trusted. Then came his title. The poor Queen had been forced to write that Mandelson would have – and it was at this point that he smirked, gloatingly, radiant in his triumph – 'the state, degree, style, dignity, title and honour of Baron Mandelson of Foy in the County of Herefordshire and Hartlepool in the County of Durham'.

And yes, it really is Foy, not Fey, lovely, tiny Foy near my very own digs, found on a tiny spit of land where swans drink the Wye and puffballs bowl down the empty lanes. Poor Foy to have acquired a baron of such medieval villainy.

14th October 2008

We've saved the world! – A slip of the tongue that left Mr Brown sitting very uncomfortably

ANY scriptwriter knows that 'man accidentally puts foot in bucket of whitewash' is only half a laugh. 'Man then has difficulty kicking same bucket off foot' is every bit as comical, particularly if the man becomes increasingly batey. Laurel and Hardy built their careers on this theory and it explains why Gordon Brown's error at Prime Minister's Questions was quite such a gem.

A momentary lapse in concentration made the Prime Minister claim to have 'saved the world'. It occurred in his first answer to David Cameron while Mr Brown was roaring away about recapitalisation of the banks. 'We not only saved the world …' said Mr Brown. At which point, in a cartoon, there would have been a screech of brakes, followed by a poised nanosecond of silence. 'Er, saved the banks,' he said hurriedly.

But the blooper was out. That terrier, truth, had slipped her collar. As with gas from a ruminant's gut, the remark could not be sucked back in and denied. Gordon had goofed.

In the mêlée of parliamentary debate, the mistake was perfectly understandable and was probably worth only a brief bark of cheery derision. Bark duly came there, even as Mr Brown was trying to recraft the terrible words, like a potter remoulding a wet glurp of mud on his wheel. A sentence which a second earlier had the makings of a beautiful vase had suddenly gone all wobble-droopy. 'Saved the world', eh? The hubris! It is one thing for Downing Street spinmeisters to spout such nonsense but when a Prime Minister starts to believe his own propaganda we're in trouble.

In those moments immediately after the prang it was hard to know where to look. Harriet Harman, sitting at Mr Brown's right, did formidably well not to join the general hilarity. On Mr Brown's other side sat dozy Jim Murphy, Secretary of State for Scotland (we don't need one, but that's for another day). Even the Murphy brain, not known for its acceleration, grasped that something had gone awry. Malfunction. Vehicle reversing noises.

As the sweetness of Mr Brown's word-spill became apparent and the Opposition benches threw their Order Papers in the air with delight, Mr Murphy started to sink an inch or two to his left – away from the stricken, air-gulping Brown. Those Murphy's eyeballs slowly swelled. It was as though he had been shot by a silenced revolver – single bullet, right through the forehead. The Speaker lamely tried to hose down the conflagration of laughter. Mr Brown resumed his seat, first smiling, then blushing, then scowling. His ears assumed the colour of decent claret. His hairdo somehow went from scraped-back Clooney to Frank 'oooh Betty' Spencer. Up he rose, to try to repair the damage. 'Not only did we work with other countries to save the world's banking ...' he began. But this only set everyone off again, including Cabinet ministers. Foreign Secretary David Miliband was near helpless, convulsed by chortles. Behind Mr Brown, backbench Labour MPs assumed a variety of poses. Some chuckled. A few heckled the Tories. The majority smiled wanly.

The longer the laughter continued, the crosser Broon became. There was no acknowledgement of his pratfall. Even a weak joke at his own expense could have retrieved the moment. All he needed to say was 'I may not have saved the world but there is plainly no saving the Tory Party either'. But no. All we saw was displeased perseverance, the grim determination of a waterskier refusing to let go even though his motor boat is speeding through raw sewage.

The frivolity continued when Nick Clegg began a question by saying: 'Recently, a single mother with small children came to see me in Sheffield ...' Woof! Up the House went again, this time Labour MPs joining the hilarity. Why? Because Cleggie has created himself a reputation as a lothario, claiming to have bedded thirty wenches.

'Thirty-one!' went up the hoot from various quarters. That's the circus of the Commons for you: quick and cruel.

11th December 2008

Peter Mandelson was not the only Mandy stepping out in front of the footlights.

Mandy Patinkin in Concert, Duke of York's

HERE is another Chicago bloke with a girl's name. The Royal National Theatre is, at the moment, putting on a (rather good) play by one Tracy Letts, geezer. Now we have a show-toon crooner called Mandy Patinkin, voice as high as Aled Jones before his undercarriage dropped. And yet, with a hairy chest and windy tales about his wife and sons, Mandy is most definitely a man.

The good news is that chum Patinkin has been here on a very short run and, by the time this review appears, will be down to his last three nights. He's terrible: soupy, self-referential, cliched, uninformative, platitudinous, unfunny, a bore, and not even that brilliant a singer.

Yet such is the strangeness of the musical theatre world that a reasonable crowd turned out to hear him on Tuesday, some of them even cheering the old prune.

It's a strange singing voice, swooping from what sounds like quavery castrato to something in the baritone duchess range. For the high-pitched stuff, he often keeps his large mouth agape, calling to mind a patient in a dentist's chair. God knows, the sound that emerges is worthy of any dental torture chamber.

He uses this terrible vibrato, so insistent that it gave your critic a pulsating pressure at the temples. The whole room seemed to shake, all because of that ballcock of an Adam's apple jiggling around in his throat. I became almost hypnotised by the thing.

At one point, he does stop singing (phew – sound the all-clear, men). But what follows is even worse. Mandy puts on a pair of reading spectacles, whips out a plastic A4 folder, and reads us an extract from the Gettysburg Address, doing so in a portentous, sub-Charlton Heston voice. Agony. If I'd had a pillow to hand I would gladly have suffocated myself.

When not giving us his Beta-minus renditions of various songs from musical theatre – a lot of Sondheim, be warned – he ladles us with tales of his children, beginning his yarns with 'now let me tell ya'.

There is a spiel about how his 26-year-old son has a British passport. Wow! Now how about that for something? He sees fit, furthermore, to keep breaking into Yiddish versions of Broadway classics and to give us his political views. It turns out, to no great surprise, that Mandy is pro-Obama and campaigned for him.

And still he won?

15th January 2009

The Commons mace is meant to remain untouched during debates. Michael Heseltine once swung it above his head in fury at Labour policies. Now it is intefered with again.

He jabbed a finger at Hoon and said: 'You're a disgrace!'

FISTS clenched, John McDonnell advanced down the Commons gangway towards Transport Secretary Geoff Hoon and was so darn angry, his jaw twitching with such (completely understandable) fury, that for a moment I thought, 'He's going to hit him – he's going to thwup Hoon on the hooter!'

Sadly it did not quite come to that, richly though the evasive Hoon deserved it. Instead Mr McDonnell, Labour MP for Hayes and Harlington, picked up the mace, symbol of our parliamentary monarchy, and dumped it on one of the nearby green benches. Without the mace in position, the Commons cannot properly be said to be in session. To parliamentarians the mace is sacred, like the glowing bit inside the chief Dalek's gubbins.

Well done, McDonnell, say I. Mr Hoon's announcement of a new runway at Heathrow Airport was so dishonest, so false – they did not even have the courage to mention 'runway' in the title of the thing, instead calling it a statement on 'Britain's Transport Infrastructure' – that something rare had to be done. It was the same with David Davis's eruption last year, when he walked out of Westminster in protest at Government plans for detention without charge. Our national legislature has become so warped out of shape, so paralysed by fear of the Whips, so hijacked by shysters and suffocaters and shadowy interest groups, that it is fast becoming pointless.

Mr McDonnell had just heard the Transport Secretary tell him there would not be a vote on the Heathrow runway expansion. Why the bloody hell not? 'This is an issue for the country,' murmured Mr Hoon, Hoon the robot, Hoon the policy processor who will do anything he is told, or so it sometimes seems. Hoon the minister who will not answer difficult questions, either, preferring deceit to directness.

'This *is* the country!' cried an exasperated Mr McDonnell, pointing at the floor of the Commons. Mr Hoon gave one of his bureaucratic shrugs, one of his your-view-is-of-no-consequence turns of the head. Mr McDonnell is MP for the villages that will now be flattened by New Labour's Heathrow earthwork monsters. As he had just told the House in a short, scintillating speech, his constituents will now have their homes, church, cemetery, their very souls, crushed by the greedy combine harvesters of big business. All so that foreign businessmen can more easily change flights on their way from America to the Continent.

Well, if the supposed Chamber of Democracy won't even allow a vote on something so basic to an Hon. Member's constituency – removing the bones of their dead to make way for disgusting duty-free shops and American sandwich bars – then what alternative does a man have but to seize the mace and cry to the Heavens at the insanity of it all? Mr Hoon sat stunned as Mr McDonnell stopped a few feet from him, jabbing a sharp forefinger in his direction as he said: 'You are a disgrace! A disgrace to the democracy of this country!'

And at that point Mr McDonnell lifted the mace off its moorings. Having done this he seemed at a loss to know what to do with the thing. So he plonked it on the 'awkward squad bench', where the more independent-minded Labour MPs normally sit. Yesterday, though, the bench was empty. Indeed, many of the Labour MPs in the chamber were Government Whips. There had plainly been an 'operation' to stifle dissent.

The apes have taken over our national assembly. The place is run by malevolent, state-paid, machine bullies. The Speaker was not present. Of course not. It was Thursday afternoon. Gorbals Mick often makes an early cut to his working week. He was quite possibly on his way to Heathrow Airport, in fact, to catch his wee shuttle home to Glasgow. Maybe if we had a Speaker who spent more of his time at his grace and favour mansion in London we would not need to build a new runway.

The deputy Speaker, Sir Alan Haselhurst, had no alternative but to suspend Mr McDonnell for five days. At first they thought they would need a vote on the expulsion but the Tory Chief Whip,

Patrick McLoughlin, another barrel-chested member of The System, ordered Tory MPs not to support the ejected Mr McDonnell. That's how the Establishment works. It hates elected politicians with fire in their belly. It cannot compute flair. It fears snorting impulse and regards bravery with envious suspicion because they are immune to control.

Power cannot tolerate the unpredictable. So out Mr McDonnell goes for five days, to the cheers of an admiring kingdom.

16th January 2009

Pesto's sentences came out like giant sausages

ROBERT Peston, that BBC business reporter who stretches vowels like a strand of Wrigley's spearmint gum, was up in front of MPs. They suspected he and other top City journalists were responsible for the credit crunch. The thesis was that the media, simply by reporting affairs like Northern Rock's failure, ruined investor confidence. Subtext: we politicians weren't possibly to blame.

Garrulous Peston, you will not be surprised to hear, had much to say for himself – in between the melodramatic pauses and multifarious vocal tics.

What a natural orator he is. Actually, I'm not being entirely sarcastic. You do have to crouch low for some of the sentences, like a slip fielder collecting a snick low to the left, yet somehow he manages to convey a sense of what he means. Pesto the Pellucid leaned forward, cocked his head at a slight angle, blinked double-time and the words just spilled forth. Some of them were separated by long gulfs of freefall silence, when all you could hear was the whistle of Mr Peston's parachute straps. At these points he kept his mouth wide open, like a man in a dentist's chair waiting for the cotton wool to be removed.

The fools, they let him have the first word. His reply went on and on. No BBC cameraman here, you see, to make a 'cut' gesture of drawing a pretend blade across his neck. No BBC editor to bawl 'SHADDDUP and let Huw ask a question' down his earpiece.

Beside Mr Peston sat the editor of the *Financial Times*, right eyebrow moving ever so subtly – it rose by perhaps an eighth of an inch – to indicate ennui at Pesto's windbaggery. This, I think, was while the great communicator was saying 'I mean' or 'well' (pronounced 'wellllll') or 'if you like' or 'er, er, er, er, so to speak'. He inserts these delay mechanisms the way a bricklayer uses mortar. On it went, the noise from his larynx, ceasing only for 'uh, uh, uh' and a vast hand movement, showing off a dandyish amount of jewellery.

The Commons Treasury Select Committee looked on in silent horror, appalled at the monster it had unleashed. This was like listening to a mix tape of the late Derek Nimmo appearing on Radio 4's *Just a Minute*. Mr Peston's sentences were coming out like giant sausages, as long as the Humber Bridge. Was he ever going to stop?

'I can only speak for the BBC,' he said. Nonsense, man. You could speak for much of western Europe and still have paragraphs of jerky verbiage to spare.

And then, as suddenly as the air raid had begun, it was over. He stopped talking! Stunned silence for a moment as the echo of the last stammer faded and a fleck of dust descended from the ceiling.

John McFall (Lab, W Dumbartonshire) emerged from the rubble. 'We've only got until ten to four,' he quavered. 'Could we perhaps have even briefer answers?' That 'even' was one for connoisseurs.

5th February 2009

He rose to challenge Lady Trumpington. The fool!

THAT mighty monument Lady Trumpington, sometime Tory minister and now an assiduous House of Lords backbencher, let rip yesterday. Her target: Canada geese. If you do not know Lady Trumpington you are missing a classic.

Visually, she could be an older sister of the former BBC newsreader Richard Baker. Or is there something of Ronnie Barker about her, doing one of his end-of-show drag musical turns? Bulletproof tweeds, sturdy bosom, spectacles from the same optician as Dame Edna Everage.

Jean Trumpington, 86, has a voice almost as deep as Windsor Davies, having for many years been a keen smoker. For a few years in the 1980s it was hard to say which was the greater polluter of the skies over London – Lady Trumpers or the four chimney stacks of Battersea power station. I used to have a basso profundo Great Aunt May who lived in Weybridge and whose drawing room, to my under-ten nose, carried a perpetual aroma of Gordon's gin and cheese straws. When I see Lady Trumpington I become that young boy in dust-sunlit Weybridge again, marvelling at the sheer, Raj-memsahib bombast of magnificent May.

Anyway, up stood Lady Trumpington in the Lords yesterday afternoon, during questions about the aeronautical hazards posed by Canada geese. You might expect such a fine figure of a country-woman to be pro-goose. Wrong. A Labour hereditary peer, Lord Berkeley, was incautious enough to try to rise at the same time as Lady Trumpington and challenge her for the floor. The fool! For a few seconds the two of them spoke simultaneously, trying to establish ownership of the moment. A hopeless mismatch. Berkeley may be 18th in a line of barons stretching back to 1421 but he did not stand a chance. Lady Trumpington, hearing his voice as an rhinoceros might hear the mmmneeee of an irksome mosquito, lifted her large spectacles in his general direction, fixed him with a rheumy, disdainful stare, and flicked a heavily made-up eyelid upwards by perhaps one sixteenth of an inch. She increased the volume of her tar-lined voicebox. Berkeley jabbered, stalled, sat down. Crushed.

The House had just heard Lord Adonis, Transport Minister, say that the influx of Canada geese to this kingdom was a menace to aircraft. They presented a particular problem in the Thames estuary, where the Mayor of London (one forgets his name) wanted to build a large airport. In other words: Canada geese are another reason Heathrow Airport has to have its blasted third runway. Lady Trumpington: 'Canada geese are without doubt the most disgusting birds that visit these shores!' Noble lords: 'Hear hear.' It was glorious how she hit 'disgusting', somehow working three vowel sounds into the first syllable.

She did not enter into precise details, thank goodness, but Lady Trumpington proceeded to explain that when she helped to run Kew Gardens some years ago, children and pets had their lives made a misery by Canada geese which wrecked the grass and ate anything they could lay their beaks on. 'Could they not, by any means available, be persuaded not to visit this country?' she thundered. It was pretty plain that she envisaged batteries of ack-ack guns, trained on flocks of geese and blasting them out of the skies.

Lord Adonis started to say that 'we have effective bird-scaring methods' and was going to say something else when the House lost its composure. I saw one or two lords (whom I will not identify, not wishing to expose them to danger) nudge neighbours and even point at the smouldering form of Lady Trumpington. Lord Adonis picked up on this susurration and deftly – and in a gentlemanly way – suggested that the noble baroness herself might make a damn good scarecrow. Lord knows, she had dealt with Berkeley easily enough.

Some politicians at this point would have taken the hump. Not Jean Trumpington. Her shoulders started to heave and she rewarded young Adonis with a Sergeant-Majorish chuckle.

A truly great old bird.

23rd February 2009

Gordon Brown finds himself host at the G20 meeting in London. This event is built up as a potential world-saver, with Brown himself as the hero. But how much do we journalists really see at such bun fights?

Where's the red zone? We can't say

HE could have held it somewhere such as the Royal Albert Hall or medieval Westminster Hall. Instead Gordon Brown made the world's 18 most powerful men (plus two women – Señora de Kirchner of the Argentines and Frau Merkel of Germany) hack out to some godforsaken dump on a lunar landscape near Canning Town.

The ExCel centre is a windowless monstrosity whose communist architecture matched the soulless authoritarianism of an army of yellow jackets and cheap-suited marshals.

Few of them spoke English well. Hundreds of police were also on duty, stewing in Ford Transit vans, scratching their groins and munching Mars bars.

We were greeted by a rusting ex-telephone box. 'Welcome to ExCel', said this makeshift sentry post. It had a bullet hole through one window pane and its door had long ago been nicked. Welcome to modern Britain.

We had already been decanted from one bus to another, and then another, stepping over bramble-strewn gravel and the oily puddles of wartime bomb sites. Security checks. Metal detectors. A forest of shabby pre-fabs. And then past yet more scowling Brians with squawking walkie-talkies. Finally, we reached a barn containing 2,000 pointlessly excited reporters and lobbyists, all trapped in 'the yellow zone' where they could be fed nuggets of propaganda. We were 100 yards from the G20 leaders but it might as well have been 100 miles. They, you see, were in the 'the red zone', behind be-gooned barriers, and could not be viewed or heard.

'We cannot tell you where the red zone is,' said the satirically-named Information Desk. 'We don't know.' The Info Desk was dispensing statistics about the Chinese economy and *G20 Magazine*, in which prominent 'actors and stakeholders' had upbeat articles.

A Foreign Office spin wallah dropped by to whisper, in conspiratorial tones, that the leaders had enjoyed a 'workmanlike breakfast'. I pass this on as untreated sewage. There is no way of knowing if it was true. The mood at breakfast may well have been crotchety or frivolous. There was no independent witness to say.

Everything came down through a filter of officialdom. We could not see the 'family photograph' being staged. We could not watch delegates shaking hands or communing outside meetings. We were kept well away from the 'leaders' lounge' where the politicians were able to recline on mint-green sofas.

Suddenly I saw a familiar ski-jump nose and heard a distinctive, sibilant mew. Mandelson! His lordship had been unable to resist the temptation of shimmering down to us yellow zone proles to vouchsafe a few half truths about how Mr Brown was everyone's hero and everything was going swimmingly.

Lord Mandelson, in sharp-pointed, black, suede shoes, was being interviewed by the BBC's Robert Peston. Pesto, too, was in suede shoes, the must-have item for Establishment schmoozers.

From time to time a wail of aircraft engines was heard. It was like being under attack from Stukas. Had Angela Merkel resorted to her last option? Happily not. It was merely because the ExCel centre is next to London City Airport.

Douglas Alexander, International Aid Minister, summoned us to a black-curtained briefing area. He sat behind eight bottles of mineral water and looked about 12 years old. He told us every-thing was going, yes, swimmingly. Beanpole Stephen Timms, a Treasury Minister, also appeared. An Italian journalist next to me said: 'Aiee! Ee look a-like Lurch from the Addams Family.' Mr Timms said a list of tax havens would be published. Could not say when, though. But it was all going swimmingly.

Back in the cattle hall, Lord Mandelson had reached an African news channel and was repeating his assertion that the summit was a triumph for Mr Brown. He then swept off towards the red zone but had to be told to show his badge and was nearly squashed by some lift doors. A scribe from Oregon was so dazed by boredom that, while staring into space, she walked slap bang into a notice-stand which fell to pieces.

In briefing room six, Lord Malloch-Brown was spinning some line to foreign journalists (Brits banned). I slipped instead into a top-secret pep talk by the Prime Minister's official spokesman, who firmly said I could not report anything he said. 'This is not a public event,' he said. Hang on, chum. We pay your wages. He said the summit was going swimmingly. And that Nicolas Sarkozy had eaten his starter at the Downing Street dinner.

Lucky him. Another Number 10 flunkey, Tom Hoskin, yesterday tried to secure himself a cuppa from the yellow zone cafeteria. He was told this was out of the question because he was wearing the ribbon and insignia of a red zone person. Hoskin, exasperated: 'Look, who's in charge here?' Back came the truculent reply: 'Sharon's in charge.'

3rd April 2009

By May 2009 the Commons expenses row is becoming so bad that the House starts to seek a scapegoat and alights on the man who has failed to see the disaster coming: Speaker Martin. His long, incompetent Speakership is nearing its demise.

A puce-cheeked, finger-wagging 'don't you cross me, Jimmy' tantrum – the day Speaker Martin lost the plot

WELL, people, I did warn you. The mask came off Commons Speaker Michael Martin at 3.30 p.m. and the country had a chance to see this bent, bullying berk for what he is: a purple-faced disaster for democracy.

Boy, he lost it. Gobblin', gabbling Gorbals Mick! The House had gathered to hear his wisdom on the expenses scandal. Members turned their gaze to him as sunflowers will rotate towards heaven's hot orb. They hushed. A nation stilled. The Commons Speakership, after all, is one of the prize pulpits of British life.

What followed was a puce-cheeked, finger-wagging, dooon't-you-cross-me-Jimmy tantrum, improper from any chairman of any parish meeting let alone the Speaker of a Commons in crisis. He cut off dissidents, preventing them from voicing even light criticism of his rotten regime. He hectored them and sneered at their suggestions.

This was not an objective, calm handling of the assembly by a veteran convener. It was the convulsive panic of a martinet, nerves as frayed as David Niven's dressing gown cord.

He had begun by reading, badly, a typed statement. Public articulation has never been his forte. A Speaker who can barely speak. Says it all, really. My six-year-old daughter could have made a better fist of reading that announcement. He told MPs they must bear in mind 'the spirit of what is right'. Ha! Coming from him that's as ripe as a black banana. 'The spirit of what is right', indeed. This from a quivering incompetent who has hired some of London's most expensive libel lawyers to act as his spokesmen.

'The House has to make,' he warbled, before a weird pause, as though the text was swimming before his milky eyes. Then out it glurped: 'Serious change'. As the adder will sometimes choke while chewing on a fat dormouse, so Gorbals coughed at the concept of change. He deigned to hear a few points of order. Kate Hoey (Lab, Vauxhall) suggested that it would be a waste of money to ask the police to investigate the expenses leak. Miss Hoey was going to say more but was silenced by the supposedly impartial Speaker. Fury steaming from every orifice, he told Miss Hoey: 'I listen to you often when I turn on my television at midnight.' (By the way, that'll probably be our television, but no matter.) He continued: 'I hear your utterances and pearls of wisdom on Sky News. It's easy to talk then.'

He was ranting, cross as hell, indignant that anyone should criticise his House. He sarcastically told an amazed Miss Hoey that it was okay for her to be a rent-a-quote, but 'some of us in this House have other responsibilities'. Yes you do, matey, and you have singularly failed to uphold them.

In the middle of Mr Martin's bate an orderly shimmered in and placed a cooling glass of liquid at his side. Medication? Too late. The old geyser had already blown his top. If he didn't claim to be teetotal you might have suspected he had a raging whisky hangover. But given that he doesn't take a dram, we can but conclude he has overdosed on bile, as can happen to washed-up Fred Kites when they sense an affront to their entitlements.

Like Miss Hoey, Norman Baker (Lib Dem, Lewes) and Patricia Hewitt (Lab, Leicester W) were given the bum's rush, Mr Baker for suggesting that it might now be time to publish the full gory details of MPs' expenses. Miss Hewitt wondered if 'citizens' juries' might look at politicians' allowances. Speaker Martin made clear he thought Miss Hewitt's contribution idiotic. This was as rude and impolitic a display as can ever have been seen from a modern Speaker. Utter disaster. He deserves every shovel of manure that will now no doubt be hurled at him.

12th May 2009

Gorbals Mick gulped the air like a winded welterweight

WELL, that went jolly well. Up stands the Speaker to bring clarity to proceedings and within minutes the Commons is bickering and a-boil, MPs shouting at the old purple proboscis, urging him for God's sake to go.

Another triumph. The Speaker was even attacked by Sir Patrick Parliament, the ancient Cormack, sage of Staffordshire, bard of the Establishment since the days medieval maids served foaming mead jugs in Westminster Hall.

He holed the Speaker below the trouser line with a deadly reference to Neville Chamberlain and the Norway debate. The House gasped. For Sir Patrick publicly to attack a Speaker is as momentous as news that the Tower of London's ravens are packing their spongebags and have asked for the bill. Gorbals is a goner.

And yet this idiot Speaker refused to acknowledge his fate. He's holding on in there, the last mussel in the marinière pot to open its shell. Muttley's in the cockpit and unless someone can hoik hard on his ejector seat, we're all goin' down.

Gordon Brown was there for the statement but did not stay. While Speaker Martin was droning away in a high, hesitant voice, the Prime Minister fiddled with his shirt cuffs. A moment later, as soon as the insults started to fly, Mr Brown fled. Macavity has left the building, folks. The first point of order went straight to the nasties of the matter. Gordon Prentice (Lab, Pendle), a man Lancashire can be proud of, was as clench-jawed as I have seen. He curtly told Gorbals that a motion of no confidence would be put on the Commons Order Paper today. Mr Speaker: 'This is not a point of order.' Mr Prentice, from his seat: 'Oh yes it is!' This was but the first of several examples of open defiance of the Chair. It might not sound much but believe me, the Speaker of the House of Commons has not been treated with such open contempt in living memory.

Douglas Carswell (Harwich) tried to tell the Speaker his moral authority was shot. Mr Martin's big-bellied boosters, who sat on the Labour benches with crossed arms and sour scowls, let rip with some yaah-booery. Mr Carswell is a Conservative, you see. The Martin clan warriors, when not arguing that their man is a victim of snobbery (it's like Ali G saying 'is it cos I is black?') love to put it about that the Speaker's opponents are all Tories. All this illustrates is the tribalism of Mr Martin – the root of his problems.

Things started to unravel crazily when the Speaker tried to claim that the motion against him was not 'substantive'. Richard Bacon (Con, Norfolk S), standing at the far end: 'It is! The Deputy Leader of the House just told me.' The Deputy Leader, Chris Bryant, was standing right next to Mr Bacon. A look of instant, gaseous nausea fell on Mr Bryant's face. Talk about being landed in it. The heckling increased.

Speaker Mick – who only a moment earlier had been boasting about his parliamentary expertise – was thrown by this intervention. He gulped the air like a winded welterweight. The Commons clerk, just below him, was consulted. Poor clerk. What a figure in torment. He twisted his angular body, examined his fingernails, whispered some advice. Gorbals couldnae hear it. Stretcher bearers!

Now it was the turn of David Winnick (Lab, Walsall N) to take his toffee hammer to the shattering edifice. Speaking 'with reluctance' (sure thing, David), he said it would help if Gorbals gave the House a hint of his early retirement. Speaker: 'That's not a matter for today.' Mr Winnick refused to accept this, giving him some loud lip. The session was fast deteriorating into just what this beetroot-gilled incompetent had hoped to avoid: a slagging match about his uselessness. David Heath, Lib Dem frontbencher, had a bash. Nick Clegg, his party leader, looked on approvingly. By now the clerk was doodling with a green pen. Put on the spot again by the Speaker, the poor wretch started to fiddle with his shoelaces. It could take weeks of gentle counselling to return the clerk to normality.

'Order!' bawled the Speaker, vainly arguing that rules did not permit open debate at this moment. Few people took any notice. When Sir Stuart Bell (Lab, Middlesbrough) tried to do some pro-Speaker greasing, Mr Winnick shouted: 'What world is he living in?' Laughter. Sir Stuart said that 'the majority will support this statement'. Another voice: 'How d'ya know?' Sarcastic mirth.

Natascha Engel (Lab, NE Derbys) sat at the back of the House, bolt upright, horror etched on her soft features. Richard Shepherd (Con, Aldridge) told the Speaker that 'as long as you are in the chair' there could be no salvation. A female, pro-Martin voice shrieked: 'Cheap!' Bob Spink (UKIP, Castle Point) was the only other person standing up for the Speaker. Is this formal UKIP policy? So much for them being the voice of disenchanted voters.

And outside beat the bongo drums of protest – Tamils, as it happens, but it could as easily have been English yeomen disgusted by this speakerish mule refusing to vacate his sullied stable.

19th May 2009

At last he falls.

A mafia funeral

NINE years of Speakership were soon extinguished. His little act of hara-kiri took just 70 words, 34 seconds, plus the swallowing of decades of flinty-eyed ambition. Wrap it in a black bin liner, whoosh, down the chute it goes, a lifetime's ceaseless, snarling, class-driven toil. Exit Gorbals Mick, pursued by … silence.

Michael Martin made his statement at the start of the Commons day, immediately after prayers at 2.30 p.m.. He said: 'I have decided I will relinquish the office of Speaker.' Not a soul groaned. The House heard him with stony imperturbability. No one wailed, 'Don't do it!' Members did not throw themselves at his feet in protest.

I did see a Labour woman weeping a few minutes later – Barbara Keeley of Worsley, a Government Whip, wailing like Stan Laurel after being bopped in the nose by Ollie Hardy. Ann McKechin (Lab, Glasgow N) was a bit red round the headlamps, too, but otherwise the House managed to conceal its distress manfully. It somehow managed to disguise its delight, too. Harder.

234

Westminster, so often sentimental, knew that this 'relin-quishing' – wrenching of the tiller from his sausage mitts, more like – should have been done many months ago. If deed were done, 'twere best done quickly. It's the same when matron rips a Band-Aid plaster off your bottom. Mr Martin was right to keep things short.

It was in October 2000, at the end of Betty Boothroyd's fine Speakership, that this choleric Scot, who had served as one of Speaker Betty's sidekicks, had himself inserted in the Chair. He had never been a particularly good Deputy Speaker. Those of us who had the temerity to question him early in his reign soon discovered the measure of the man. Shadowy figures arrived to threaten our livelihoods.

It was made clear to me, certainly, that unless I stilled my nib, unless I desisted from my impertinence, I could lose my parlia-mentary security pass. Thankfully the editor of the *Daily Mail* filed the protests under L for Loony.

Speaker Martin's election was a pungently tribal affair, his ticket running hard on his Glaswegian, Roman Catholic tenement childhood. No Vatican election was ever so skilfully managed. So when the likes of that bloated gargoyle Lord Foulkes accuse critics of Martin (as he did yesterday) of being 'sectarian snobs' for calling him names, let the ball be whacked straight back to them.

Mick Martin made the play on his background. It was he who made that legitimate turf. Sketchwriting is a form of verbal cartooning. The Gorbals is the best-known part of Glasgow. He was called Mick. Ergo, Gorbals Mick.

Having been elected as an old Labour bruiser, he proceeded to chair the House in the same coarse manner. It was soon noticeable that Scottish Labour MPs seemed to have more joy catching the Speaker's eye during the debates than their English and Welsh colleagues. I recall George Foulkes MP being given a lot of leeway during speeches. These two were muckers from way back.

There was a praetorian guard around the Speaker, many of them overweight Scottish men, but so be it. His burly boors were there again yesterday, scowling up at the press gallery, furious to see their sorry champ's sporran finally blasted away by the gale of public outrage. A Fleet Street colleague who sidled up to two Labour Whips to canvass their views was left in no doubt about their fury. John Prescott, invited to comment by a broadcaster, said: 'Are you a journalist?' Yes, said the man. 'Then **** off!' snapped Two Jags. They really do feel very hard done by. They will not forget this loss lightly.

Jimmy Hood (Lanark) and John Robertson (Glasgow NW) yesterday simmered beside one another with their meaty forearms crossed, two baleful beauties parked in high dudgeon. Combined weight enough to challenge your average Ford Transit van. Jim Sheridan (Paisley), who later called for sketchwriters to be banned from Parliament, was almost as pink in the face as his slain hero Gorbals. Such partisanship among MPs is destructive to a Speakership. Stupid. So counter-productive.

Yesterday, immediately after Mr Martin's announcement, Gordon Brown went up to shake the old loser's hand. Mr Cameron and George Osborne also approached the Chair, lingering in the hope that they might convey a word of gentlemanly thanks. Mr Martin chose not to turn to them to accept their approaches.

He was not all bad. Sometimes he found a soothing, grand-fatherly tone. He was particularly good on the day the Commons became overheated about the death of Baby P. But he lacked the firm smack of natural command. He forgot that the Speakership is about defending public interest as well as MPs' financial interests.

A long, inglorious line of Labour MPs had more luck than Mr Cameron yesterday, lining up to pay their respects to the departing wheezer as he slumped in the Chair which will not much longer be his. It was like a mafia funeral, pudgy *omerta* boys sidling up to squeeze his wrists and whisper a few brief words of respect. Labour's Chief Whip, Nick Brown, muttered something out of one side of his mouth, stroking the underside of Mr Martin's sleeve. Mohammad Sarwar (Lab, Glasgow C) lingered a long time.

Dark fixer Fraser Kemp (Lab, Houghton) went up and did one of those handshakes combined with a gangster's consoling wink.

Treasury Minister Yvette Cooper patted his paw like a child at an Irish coffin, not wishing to miss the chance to touch the corpse but not wanting to catch the stench of death. Commons Leader Harriet Harman brushed a hand against his shoulder, though it is hard to believe she was ever that fond of him. Behind the Chair loitered Derek Conway, the former Tory whose misuse of public money started so many of the recent problems.

The only Tories seen taking their leave of the Speaker yesterday were Nicholas Soames (who pumped his paw for 20 seconds and seemed to be inviting him to lunch), Brian Binley and Mark Pritchard. I saw no Lib Dem go anywhere near him.

In the end it all happened quickly. There was none of the 'be happy for me!' gaiety we had when Betty Boothroyd announced her retirement. This felt like something forced, something surrendered. Pity. He could have done it with more grace.

So that is it. A Speakership is all but done. Just a few gravy scrapings left, a few days to vacate his grace and favour mansion, convey the trinkets and mementoes north of the border, and tear Mrs Martin from her Marigolds. This is no time for gloating. The damage he leaves behind makes that a pointless emotion.

It's unlikely he and his mobsters would take the same view, but never kick a man when he's down, says I. Just say 'Allelluia', and hope for someone who can polish the tarnished majesty of this most mighty of public pulpits.

20th May 2009

Impossible! They voted for someone worse than Gorbals Mick

THERE John Bercow stood in the big green chair, puffed up like an amphibian that had scoffed too many vol-au-vents. 'My first thought at this time,' he said from Parliament's bully pulpit, 'is, as you will understand, of …'

He was going to mention his wife but at this point a female voice from the Tory benches shouted: 'Your wages.'

The same female voice – Nadine Dorries – heckled the Father of the House when he announced Mr Bercow's 'election as Speaker'. The voice cried: 'As a Labour Speaker!'

Rancour, partisanship, a figure whose political philosophy dodges round the place like a bouncy ball: yes, folks, the House of cheats and nodding oil derricks just got its perfect Speaker. They went and did the impossible yesterday. They voted for someone who could be even worse than Gorbals Mick. Large parts of these Tory benches refused to clap his election and they looked thoroughly sickened, sitting with arms crossed and shaking their heads. Real, gut-churning hatred. Little Squeaker Bercow has his work cut out.

The day took the format of a sandcastle-kicking competition. Each round gave MPs the chance to demolish a candidate's beautifully constructed dreams of glory.

The first round, announced at 5.10 p.m., saw Sir Michael Lord (Con, Suffolk C), Sir Patrick Cormack (Con, Staffs S), Richard Shepherd (Con, Aldridge) and Parmjit Dhanda (Lab, Gloucester) have their castles trampled on and reduced to nothing. Sir Michael mentioned that he once played rugger against the South Africans (in the days of apartheid). Not a good way to win round Labour voters. Mr Dhanda, the 37-year-old unknown who cleverly used this election as a promotional exercise (a little hard, maybe – Parmjit is a decent stick), asked: 'Do we all get it?' Get what, Parmjit? The *Beano* every week? A cuddle in the morning from our beloved?

Sir Patrick had mentioned Speaker Lenthall's celebrated speech 'that January day in 1642'. Labour MPs laughed at his tone of familiarity. Sir Patrick, gamely: 'Yes, I was there!' Sir Alan Beith (Lib Dem, Berwick) spoke but it might have been a mermaid coughing, so little impression did it make. Ditto Margaret Beckett

(Lab, Derby S). She had drawn first straw and the House was cold. It remained so.

Hampshire's Sir George Young (Con), who lost in the last round, gave the strongest speech. Ann Widdecombe (Con, Maidstone) never achieved lift-off. Widdo said it was vital a new Speaker have support on all sides. Mr Bercow, with that fake way of his, nodded firmly. Yet the only other Tory openly supporting him – apart from his oddball grunt Julian Lewis (New Forest E) – was Charles Walker, a brittle creature from Broxbourne.

In his application speech Mr Bercow spoke fluently but not quite 'without notes' as the trusting souls of the Press Association reported. He kept glancing down to his left to notes held by sidekick Lewis. Yes, a crib sheet. It's the Bercow way.

Mr Bercow had a long riff mimicking an unnamed elderly grandee who, he said, had ejaculated with scorn when asked to vote for the Bercow campaign. Ancient Sir Peter Tapsell (Con, Louth), clearly. It was interesting that Mr Bercow resorted to mockery of a Tory in his speech. The Labour benches loved this. But it perhaps gives licence to any of us who might be tempted to mock Mr Bercow right back.

Five minutes after the first ballot result I saw Sir Patrick wander forlornly out of the chamber. Not a person went up to him to say 'bad luck'. Between the votes there was milling time and we could see the vipers slithering round their eggs. Bercow-ites were active, consulting lists, number-sucking, leaning into ears. Candidate Bercow swaggered round the floor with his springy thumbs held at erect angles. His Labour-supporting wife watched from above. Albert Owen (Lab, Anglesey) slipped an arm round his side. Patricia Hewitt (Lab, Leicester W) had a long word.

The result came just after 8.30. When it was announced Mr Bercow blew out his cheeks with relief. Mr Lewis clapped him on the back. The rest of the people sitting round him looked as though they had just ingested a dodgy sardine. The response among mainstream Tory MPs? I write this having just finished speaking to one. Sickened by Labour's support for a philosophical chameleon on the grounds that he was the ultimate non-Conservative, he called Mr Bercow's election 'the worst sort of bloody political shenanigans'.

23rd June 2009

Oh well, perhaps the sketch is happier in Opposition to the Chair.

Insatiable Lembit's naughty eyebrows did a little can-can

SEVERAL people have recently taken the view that it is no longer worth being an MP. The public's vilification over expenses. The brutality of the Whips. Whingeing constituents. An impertinent press. And now Harriet Harman wants to stop them earning money elsewhere.

But there is still something about the old place, isn't there? Just look at the way Lembit Opik (Lib Dem, Montgomeryshire) behaved yesterday when a pretty girl appeared in the back gallery for Prime Minister's Questions.

She was beautiful. She was dark-haired, slender, neatly attired, attentive. While listening to the discussions she rested her head first one side, then the other, stretching her neck sinews when she suspected that men might be looking at her. She toyed with her long hair. She possessed all her gnashers and they had been polished to a peppermint gleam.

Mr Opik's radar picked her up as quickly as the golfballs at RAF Fylingdales noticing some incoming SAM missiles.

Ah, Lembit the rake! Lock up your weather forecasters and your cheeky girls. Liberal Democracy's answer to Serge Gainsbourg was on the loose. Montgomeryshire's very own Don Juan tingled like a fresh-struck bell at a Roman mass. If he had been Leslie Phillips he would have said 'well, hel-low!' Down at the despatch box, matters were taking their course, though without Gordon Brown or David Cameron. Mr Brown had departed for Italy. Destination: the Berlusconi bambini summit. Oh, Lembit, if only you could have been there, too. But Mr Opik had found consolations in the Commons. He was sitting just in front of the VIP box containing the visiting beauty. He turned round and gave her a grin which would not have disgraced Clifford the Listerine Dragon.

He may not be handsome in the classical sense but he is irrepressible. Insatiable. In the presence of this adorable creature he had come to life. His gestures acquired a Latin flair. He snaked an arm round the back of the bench and threw back his head with manly laughter. He bared his Adam's apple to her, showed her various pieces of paper, involved himself in her gaze. She loved it. Here was this parliamentarian, this important fellow, giving little her some of his surely valuable time. She cooed. He billed. They clicked.

9th July 2009

Had they all been inhaling something?

THE Commons addressed itself to an emergency question on the matter of Professor David Nutt. This Nutt was the Home Secretary's drugs adviser – that is, he advised the minister what to think about drugs, not which drugs to take of an evening after a stressful day.

But he is no more. Nutt has been crushed. The Home Secretary, Alan Johnson, 'lost confidence' in him. 'I asked Professor Nutt to resign,' Mr Johnson told MPs. Which, I think you will agree, is more of a sacking than a resignation. A sort of 'get knotted, Nutt'. Or get Nutted.

Professor Nutt. It is almost a Cluedo name. Professor Nutt, in the conservatory, with a large syringe. Poor man. It was not his fault he was called Nutt. Yet it is hard to take seriously an academic called Nutt. Perhaps this is why Mr Johnson found it so easy to dispense with him. Can we use the word 'dispense' in connection with drugs? Labour MPs were certainly in a skittish mood. Mike Gapes (Lab, Ilford South) found it hard to keep a straight face. Mr Gapes did not help himself by sitting near Stephen Pound (Lab, Ealing North), resident wit of the Labour benches. Mr Pound is one of those effervescent souls around whom it is impossible to concentrate. A name such as 'Professor Nutt' is perfect ammo for the Pounds of this world. He kept up a low burble of drollery throughout Mr Johnson's brief statement, a sort of Cornelius Lysaght racing commentary peppered with jests and repartee. Every time the name of the Professor was mentioned, the people sitting near Mr Pound started to chuckle.

Mr Johnson explained that the Prof had sealed his fate by going beyond the normal bounds of behaviour for Government advisers. He had started to fancy himself a policy-maker rather than a policy adviser. He had started to become a regular critic of ministers rather than an expert consultant. The peanut that fancied itself a Brazil.

At one point in proceedings Mr Johnson tried to refer to the 'Cabinet Office'. Alas, this came out as 'Cabinutt Office'. The slip was noticed and fed in to the general air of levity. A few of the souls in the vicinity of Mr Pound began gently to rock with laughter. Shadow Home Secretary Chris Grayling said he agreed with the eradication of Nutt but that he was dismayed by the 'unseemly row' which had ensued. Mr Grayling was trying a little hard, methinks, to find some angle of attack. By endorsing Mr Johnson's decision he was surely showing that there was no great 'row'. Chris Huhne of the Lib Dems did his best to create one. He tried to accuse Mr Johnson of all sorts of perfidy, of 'blundering into this issue', of wanting 'an army of nodding yes-men' for his advisers and of being 'ludicrously thin-skinned'.

As Mr Huhne sat down, Mr Pound murmured: 'That was weedy.' A cannabis joke. It set off Mr Gapes again. A geyser of mirth shot out of one of his nostrils.

George Howarth (Lab, Knowsley North) called the scientist 'Professor Noot'. This ignited some hog-whimpering. Hilary Armstrong (Lab, NW Durham) said that 'Professor Not does nutt hold a universal view among scientists'. Oops. That wasn't quite right. Had they all been inhaling something? The merriment had reached whinnying levels. Mr Gapes was shaking his head – a sort of 'please, stop, no more or I'll pee in my pants' expression. His near-neighbour Pound relished the absurdities, a smile playing round his natural comedian's face.

3rd November 2009

A mercifully short Queen's Speech.

Don't bother sitting ... I won't be long

ROUGHLY in the time it takes to boil a hardish egg, the Queen ran through her Government's legislative programme. She did not quite preface her remarks with a 'don't bother sitting, gang, this won't take long' but I have not seen the Duke of Edinburgh so cheerful at a State Opening for years.

Speech done and dusted in under seven minutes, and she didn't even rush her words. Normally Prince Philip sits there grinding his molars, clutching his sword with the troubling introspection of a Japanese officer shortly after Hiroshima. Yesterday he was positively frivolous. On arrival at the Palace of Westminster he prodded the Lord Chancellor's handbag (holding the speech), as if to say: 'Good and short, this time, eh, Straw?'

Her Majesty was throaty but perked up when it came to announcing her foreign trips. A tour of the Caribbean. As my children say, 'luckeee'. Commons Speaker Bercow had changed his normal minor public school beak's gown for some gold-braided robe. This was on the long side, making him look even more Squeakerish and piddling than usual. I once saw a pre-teen actor play the Lord Mayor of London. Same look. I understand from one of Mr Bercow's numerous fans in the Commons that when he entered the House before prayers, MPs on all sides burst into laughter. This Speakership is not going entirely according to plan, people.

The Supreme Court's members were showing off new robes, sans wigs. The whole point of the Supreme Court was that it separated the judges from Parliament. Why should they barge into the State Opening? Lady Hale, the only female member of the Supreme Court, was wearing a squashed little hat which owed more to 18th-century Europe than 21st-century Britain.

Lady Kennedy (Lab), everyone's favourite Celt, produced a vast pair of tinted, white plastic-framed spectacles. When she put them on she looked like the late Sunnie Mann, wife of Beirut hostage Jackie Mann. Lady Thatcher (Con) took her now customary seat near the Throne, her miraculous hairdo the colour of decent champagne. Lord Sugar (Lab) had given most of his chin a mow. How quickly he has taken to ermine. Attorney-General Lady Scotland did mwaw-mwaw kissy-kissies with Lord Carlile (Lib Dem). When the MPs turned up, Lord Janner (Lab) gave them a little wave. Lefties used to accuse the pre-1997 House of Lords of being too cosy a club but it had nothing on this lot.

Up in the galleries, Sarah Brown, wife of Gordon, was slender, pale, a fascinator jammed on her bean. It looked as though it could have picked up Radio Talk Sport on the North Circular. Nearby sat Sally Bercow, wife of the Squeaker and one of life's lineout jumpers. She was wearing fishnet stockings and a blokeish wristwatch. If Mrs Bercow fails in her bid to become a Labour politician she may have a future as a wrong 'un at a drag club.

19th November 2009

Lord Sugarpuff rotated his chops like a solo trombonist

UP he sprang just before five yesterday afternoon, Lord Sugarlump of Clapton (Lab), to make his maiden. The House of Lords slowly turned its rheumy eyes in his direction. Although outwardly polite, the old boys and old girls have their doubts about this little fella.

Before saying a word, Lord Sugar did something I have not seen from a peer. He shot his cuffs. Performed that gesture Del Boy Trotter does when he reckons he is on to a good thing. There may even have been a small tweak of the neck. He began by saying that he was the new boy on the block and that 'in your lordships' House I am certainly' – tiny pause – 'the apprentice'. At the Navy's firing ranges somewhere off Dorset, was that a shell plopping silently into the English Channel? Such a noise certainly greeted this opening wisecrack.

He delivered his speech with his left hand in a trouser pocket much of the time. Beforehand he looked nervous, rotating his chops like a solo trombonist about to play Schubert's Arpeggione. He stroked the beardlet, examined a hundred times his little cue cards and stared at the press gallery. John Prescott used to try to eyeball us in similar manner in the Commons. My counterpart on the *Independent*, staring back at sausageboy Prescott, once blew him a kiss. They don't like that.

Sugarpuff was making his debut in the Queen's Speech debate on the economy. Lord Mandelson was on the front bench, reclining so low that his body was the shape of a banana. Lord Hunt (Con) said he understood Lord Sugar was these days to be regarded as a Government spokesman on business. Across Lord Mandelson's eyes flittered a hint of nascent indigestion. Lord Hunt praised Thatcherism. Lord Sugar nodded.

Lord Razzall (Lib Dem) made a speech of slovenly dullness. Lady Turner (Lab), sitting next to Lord Sugar, spoke for us all by falling asleep. Only when Lord Razzall shut up did she come to, blinking like a hedgehog in April. A high-pitched wheeeeee made one think somebody's mobile telephone was ringing, but it was only the hearing aid of Lord Campbell (Con), perhaps telling him his eggs were ready.

Lord Sugar devoted much of his speech to his favourite subject: himself. He told us that he was the youngest of four children and that there had been a long gap before his arrival. 'Perhaps I was a mistake,' he said. Silence in the chamber. 'My mother preferred to think of me as a pleasant surprise. Some of your lordships may not agree with that.' At this there was, finally, thank God, some laughter.

He noted that his appointment as the Government's enterprise tsar in the summer was 'not met with a chorus of wild approval'. Lord Mandelson, directly in front, smiled as only he can smile. Lord Sugar growled: 'Never, ever underestimate me.' At this, Lord Mandelson's eyes rolled high to the right, as in a pantomime.

The boasting was barely begun. Sugarlump banged on about how he had once been turned down by some company and how he now owned that firm's HQ. Revenge! He gave us the old 'I started my business from the back of a secondhand Mini van' spiel and assured us that he was a diamond geezer. 'I made it by fair and honest and simple trading,' he cried. 'I'm straight, I'm blunt, I won't always be popular but I will always be honest.' My, my. It was almost as though he was sensitive on the subject.

Lord Oakeshott (Lib Dem), who has been on the end of letters from Lord Sugar's lawyers, broke convention by attacking Lord Sugar a few minutes later. He mocked him as 'the most propertied Labour peer in history', worth £730 million. 'Isn't it wonderful how well the super-rich – the bankers and the property magnates – have done out of the 12 years of Blair and Brown?' But by then Sugar had walked out.

Lord Martin, former Speaker of the Commons, also made his maiden speech yesterday. By comparison with the self-preening twazzock Sugar, Gorbals was positively statesmanlike.

26th November 2009

After leaks from the Home Office, Conservative MP Damian Green has been arrested in circumstances that are far from non-political. Police arrive at the Palace of Westminster and talk their way into Mr Green's office. Has the principle of parliamentary privilege been broken? And who is responsible for letting Plod rummage through Parliament's drawers?

Line manager? For God's sake, you're the Serjeant-at-Arms!

FOR 600 years the Serjeant-at-Arms has been a burly presence on the parliamentary estate. Serjeants tended to be ex-military men. They wore a sword, a fancy uniform and Blakeys. You felt they probably knew how to drop an elbow and charge full-speed at trouble. One did not mess with Serjeants. They were three-Shredded Wheat types. Hands like spades. Voices like Windsor Davies (or even Ruth Kelly). The Serjeant-at-Arms, after all, is responsible for security in the Commons.

That was how it continued for more than half a millennium. Then the modernisers, in 2007, appointed Jill Pay. Her predecessor, a pukka Scot and retired major general called Peter Grant Peterkin, was sacked after a rumoured falling-out with the then Speaker, Michael Martin. Mrs Pay, best known for her copperwash hairdo and brisk, clickety-click, high-heeled gait, had previously been the Commons accommodation manager. A jolly good one, too, no doubt. She would sashay round the parliamentary estate carrying a vast briefcase, of the sort generally favoured by barristers. Mrs P was clerical efficiency made flesh. Tilly the Typist.

Mrs Pay radiated competence. Her arrival as Serjeant was greeted with predictable gushing about how good it was finally to have a female Serjeant. Another blow for equal rights! Yaa boo sucks to tradition.

Yesterday Mrs Pay gave evidence to the Commons select committee looking at the arrest last year of Damian Green MP and the search of his Commons office by police. Her conduct in that controversy has attracted criticism. It was Mrs Pay who agreed that the rozzers could burst into Mr Green's office and root through his constituency files. Speaker Martin, at the time, seemed uncommonly happy to have her role in the matter magnified.

Watching her yesterday as she sat alone at a witness table, stared at by the likes of Sir Menzies Campbell (Lib Dem, NE Fife) and Michael Howard (Con, Folkestone), it was hard not to feel some pity for the woman. But it was also difficult not to wonder if the matter might have been handled more firmly by an old-fashioned military Serjeant. She was nervous. Dry-mouthed. Shaky hands. She pressed her slender, manicured fingers together, jewellery rattling at her wrists. Her lipsticked smile quivered. Her eyes, bearing perhaps a faint wash of blue liner, danced up and down.

She read a long statement. It was all about how the police kept arriving at her office in the days leading to Mr Green's arrest. They came mob-handed. They swore her to secrecy. They told her she was the person who could authorise their search of Mr Green's parliamentary office. She believed them! Punctilious Mrs Pay described her various conversations with Speaker Martin. It would be possible to read Mrs Pay's evidence and conclude that he was happy to pass the buck. 'I felt under considerable pressure,' said Mrs Pay, her voice going all weak. She tried to smile at the committee. Only to be met by granite stares.

She excused herself by saying that 'at no time did the police officers say I could insist on a warrant'. Naughty, nasty police officers. She later consulted her 'line manager'. Oh for God's sake, you're the Serjeant-at-Arms, not some grunt in Whitehall.

Under questioning from Sir Menzies, Mrs Pay said with pride: 'I am not easily intimidated!' Her evidence yesterday suggests, alas, that this is exactly what happened. The Serjeant was browbeaten and bullied. Intimidated. By a few gumshoe cops.

8th December 2009

Having long listened to Gordon Brown talk about 'boom and bust', I toddle off to see Pammy Anderson in panto.

Review of *Aladdin* at the New Wimbledon Theatre

EXPERIMENTAL theatre took a new turn last night when that well-known double act, Pamela Anderson, made her debut in the specialist genre of British pantomime. Miss Anderson, the sometime *Baywatch* star and pneumatic beachwear model, is as Californian as they come. Panto could not be more British.

So did they mesh? Did they hit it off? Did they bounce as one? Not quite. But it didn't really matter. This show is a gaudy, vulgar riot.

Big Pam is on a two-week burst – dangerous word – at the New Wimbledon Theatre in south London, playing the Genie of the Lamp in *Aladdin*. She is sharing the role with Ruby Wax, Anita Dobson and Paul O'Grady but for this fortnight it is Miss Anderson's turn – and her performance is, well, extraordinary.

It is a full hour and five minutes before she makes her first appearance, descending from on high on some celestial orb. Her first scene, which includes a Christina Aguilera hit, lasts little more than a couple of minutes but it is enough to make one dwell on the wonders of fleshly engineering. There she stands in a bright red body stocking in five-inch glittering heels, with a red, lip-shaped decoration stuck in her hair.

Last night's crowd was going bananas, whooping and cheering (and not all of them were men). Were they applauding her acting talents, or perhaps her singing voice? Not quite. They were applauding her simply because she is a one-woman Silicon Valley, a walking dumbbells, not so much a female body as a boa constrictor who has just swallowed a two-humped camel.

Wimbledon's Victorian playhouse is *en fête* for this run, for Miss Anderson is certainly packing them in. The punters, that is. Her presence, along with a slew of filthy *doubles entendres* takes panto to its most democratic extreme. Shades, here, of the 19th-century music hall and its occasional freak shows. Brian Blessed is on hand, playing Abanazar, to ensure things never dip below full frontal, vocally. Last night we had a packed house – hundreds in the stalls and circles – and yet Mr Blessed still contrived to be louder than everyone. He is an appalling old ham but he's incorrigible, and somehow, in the end, unbeatable.

The person who suffers from Miss Anderson's presence is Jonathan D. Ellis who has to play Widow Twanky. The natural laws of panto demand that the panto dame be the biggest thing on stage but Miss Anderson imbalances the dramatic scales. During the two-and-a-half-hour show she and her boobs are on stage for perhaps ten minutes, making five entrances, each to wolf whistles and jovial heckling. 'I've flown here all the way from Beverly Hills,' she says, flapping her eyelashes like a carpet beater. To which another character replies: 'I know Beverly Hills. Her father is a butcher in Streatham.' Genie of the Lamp Pamela kneels before Aladdin (Ashley Day) and says: 'Your wish is my command. Master, what is your wish?' At which some wit in the stalls last night shouted: 'Tell 'er to rub yer wick!' Big laughs.

Her legs, carrying that bizarre bulk, look as vulnerable as two Twiglets. She gabbles on stage, waves her arms around, fluffs out her custard-coloured hair, shrouds herself in some skimpy wrap and keeps giving a wannabe Hollywood star smile at the crowd. Oh, I suppose it's pretty awful rubbish, really, and yet it works. It works because she shows she's a decent sport, prepared to send herself up in a Carry On film way and it works, because, at 42 years of age, she is still perky enough to represent a challenge to that old panto cry of 'behind you!'. Because with Pamela they are most definitely 'in front of you!'.

Well done, Pam. Welcome to British vaudeville.

16th December 2009

A day of high intrigue in the House

WELL, that was mildly entertaining. Geoff Hoon and Patricia Hewitt mounted a suicide-bomb plot to assassinate the PM. They failed. So far.

Listening to Gordon Brown at the start of Prime Minister's Question Time, I wrote in my little notebook: 'Voice a bit wobbly'. Later we found out that shortly before entering the chamber he was told of the Hoon–Hewitt letter. The rest of us did not learn about the assassination attempt until 27 minutes later, when mobile telephones started to vibrate and most of the government press officers legged it from the press gallery, to make calls and find out what on earth they could tell the dingo dogs of the fourth estate.

In the service of investigative sketchwriting, your scribe waddled down to the Palace of Westminster's central lobby, that great, high-ceilinged meeting point where you normally find tourists and school parties and the occasional mouldering peer of the realm waiting to buy a few stamps at the corner Post Office.

Owing to the snow, the crowds were absent. The central lobby was almost empty. But Mr Hoon was there, giving a live interview to Sky News, burbling away, sounding maddeningly reasonable. The Sky reporter kept interrupting to try to enliven the broadcast. Five yards to his left, the chairman of the Parliamentary Labour Party, Tony Lloyd, was speaking to the BBC News Channel. Between the two men was a large statue of Stafford Henry Northcote, a Victorian politician. Will anyone ever erect a statue to Geoff Hoon or Patricia Hewitt? Hewitt! The woman whose dulcet tones could be an advertising pitch for the Dignitas clinic in Switzerland. Soon she, too, was on television, dripping moist, gulpy phrases.

Back in the central lobby, Sky News finished its interview with Mr Hoon and some of us other newshounds soon had him surrounded. He said he had spoken to 'a handful of friends' about the letter and had decided to write it over the Christmas recess, after talking to Labour activists in his Nottinghamshire constituency. He had not discussed it, he said, with former Home Secretary Charles Clarke (the Ayatollah Khomeini of New Labour). Nor had he mentioned it to Gordon Brown. 'Patricia and I just found we had both come to the same view,' said Mr Hoon, before disappearing.

This wasn't a patch (or should that be putsch?) on the upheavals which preceded Mrs Thatcher's downfall but the TV news channels were in overdrive and once that happens it is hard to stop a story going mad. Pundits were being hauled out of every corner to give their immediate thoughts. Correspondents were being made to stand out in the snow, to give an impression of urgency and of a building under siege. Some razor-cheekboned Doris was even broadcasting in a coquettish flat cap and was handed a mug of steaming tea by a policeman. Up popped the pre-Raphaelite face of Margaret Beckett, former Cabinet Minister and sworn enemy of Mr Hoon. Groans as innocent TV viewers dived for the off-switch. 'Waste of time, big mistake, should be ignored,' grunted Mrs Beckett. That's no way to talk about our Geoff – In fact she was simply referring to the Hoon–Hewitt letter.

What was Mrs Beckett's advice to Mr Brown regarding the letter writers? 'I would urge him very robustly to tell them where to go,' said Mother Beckett, lips parting to form a terrifying smile which called to mind a flatulent goat.

Almost three hours into the chaos, ministers eventually emerged to utter support for Mr Brown. They seemed to have been schooled. They all said how he had been brilliant at Prime Minister's Questions (not quite true – he was all right, but no better than that) and how they were getting on with the 'job of government'. Eventually we heard that Lord Mandelson had found a form of words which, when viewed from the right angle, could be construed as supportive. Up to a point. The immediate danger had passed.

7th January 2010

The Government has finally acceded to requests for an inquiry into the Iraq war. Unlike previous such inquiries, it is held largely in public. Will Tony Blair finally be snagged on his war-making? Or will he argue his way out of another tight spot?

Blair at the Chilcot Inquiry

TONY Blair may not have frightened Saddam Hussein much in the run-up to invasion but, by God, his performance yesterday was pretty terrifying. Messianic yet mellifluous. Baron Bellicose, the war guy in a beautiful suit. The left eye bulged like a Dalek's light bulb. All the old tics and tricks were deployed – shakes of the head, the crumpled chin, the Prince Charles grimaces – to urge us that Iraq was worth invading and that 100,000 dead was a price worth paying. Moreover, we should prepare for an encore, any day soon. He kept demanding a hardline policy against Iran.

How could a churchgoer be so set on war, yet remain so manifestly charming? He insisted that he had been keen to protect British democracy, yet he hitched us to America. Much has been made this week of the way the former Attorney General, Lord Goldsmith, magically changed his opinion about the legality of war after he went to Washington. Was there a similar moment in Mr Blair's life when he switched from CND pacifist to Neocon aggressor? His approach to Iraq after 9/11 was, he said, that 'you don't take any risks'. So what did he do? He took us to war.

Is warfare not risky? This wasn't real life, surely. It was something out of the 1960s nuclear bomb satire *Dr Strangelove*.

Having scuttled in before breakfast – to avoid the rush-hour traffic, no doubt – he had to hover in back rooms for two hours before stepping into the tiny inquiry room at 9.32. He was accompanied only by a podgy aide from his Downing Street days. A long introduction from the inquiry's chairman, that crumpled bumblebee Sir John Chilcot, meant it was seven minutes before witness Blair coughed up his first words. The long wait had done nothing for his nerves. Those inside the room said that his hands were shaking. He certainly looked a bit waxy round the gums.

The lips were parted and he wore that winded expression we used to see when he was PM and faced a groin-shrinking moment in the Commons. And then, along the nation's telegraph wires, down the cathode ray tube, came that husky, oh-so-reasonable, vicarly voice of the egomaniac ex-premier.

His hair was pretty short and the face was tanned in an ageing, cologned, Côte d'Azur charlatan sort of way. The shirt, tie and jacket presented a red, white and blue confection. Run up the Stars and Stripes. Ex-diplomat Sir Roderic Lyne was again the most persistent and obviously sceptical of the inquiry members. He stopped Mr Blair waffling. When Mr Blair started yarning away about some theory from a book, Sir Roderic said that if it was that interesting perhaps Mr Blair could let the inquiry have a copy. Now could they get on with the inquiry, please?

Sir Roderic, who surely has a future on Radio 4's *Moral Maze*, allowed himself the occasional sardonic intervention. Mr Blair's voice had acquired Americanisms. He kept doing that awful rising inflexion at the end of sentences. He emphasised the first syllable of 'Bagh-dad' and 'Af-ghanistan'. The CIA would have been proud of him.

And then, right at the end, he was given a chance by Sir John to give a peroration and his tone suddenly transformed into Shakespeare's Portia milking the 'quality of mercy' speech for every drop of emotion. He held his right hand over his left breast. He clutched his upper chest. Give her a standing ovation.

This weird creature Blair, a mixture of hard and oily, hot for yet more pre-emptive fighting, remains an incorrigible performer. He is in a class quite beyond poor old Gordon Brown. That may not be to Mr Brown's credit as a political performer or even as a leader, but it stands him in good stead as a member of the human race. Some will have watched yesterday and thought 'come back, Tony'. Personally, I thank Heaven the maniac has gone.

30th January 2010

Gordon Brown could wait little longer and has finally called a general election. The Commons gathers for its last Prime Minister's Questions of a tired parliament.

Last PMQs before the election

THERE sat the Cabinet on the Government bench, possibly for the final time. Sailors in a leaky submarine. As in *Das Boot*, Wolfgang Petersen's 1981 film about a U-boat, they retained their professionalism but demonstrated scant enthusiasm for the cause to which they found themselves lassooed.

Last PMQs of the parliament. One or two glanced at their skipper, Gordon Brown. Dougie Alexander, the Overseas Aid man, recruited to his boyish face an expression almost of fascination. Edward and Yvette Balls, most committed of the Brown hairshirts, nodded and tried to smile. They were in a minority. Yvette was washed out. Hair lank. Clothes crumpled. That young woman could do with a holiday and a large bowl of trifle.

Chief Whip Nick Brown, at the end of the bench, was impassive, his butcher's chops in stubborn repose. Occasionally he nodded, acknowledging some universal truth, but otherwise he vouchsafed no more emotion than a boulder. Jack Straw seemed sad. Harriet Harman rubbed her hands. Beady, greedy, needy Harriet. We haven't heard the last of her. Jim Murphy (he's the Scotland Secretary with the doleful voice) clenched his jaw. Alistair Darling turned a flank away from Mr Brown and chatted to Alan Johnson. Once perky Mr Johnson has taken a beating as Home Secretary. His cheeks are bruised by tiredness. He has been in the post but months but it has added years to him. Finally, David Miliband sat with arms crossed, giving away nothing save an air of faint disgust. What lies ahead for all these people? And what of the ones who have already said they are leaving?

Andrew Mackinlay (Thurrock), one of the really good guys, sat sparky eyed, interested still, down on the Labour awkward squad bench. It's a crying shame that he is going. But few will miss the likes of Anthony Steen (Con, Totnes), who yesterday hovered behind the Speaker's Chair. A silly, self-absorbed man. Nor will many notice the departure of the Father of the House, Alan Williams (Lab, Swansea W), a non-event of a patriarch.

During the main exchanges, David Cameron ran circles round a slow-witted Gordon Brown. Mr Cameron mentioned some top businessman who had just criticised Labour. Dim but cheery Ronnie Campbell (Lab, Blyth Valley), referring to the businessman, shouted: 'He's probably a Tory!' Mr Cameron: 'No, he's an adviser to the Government. But he's probably a Tory now. So are half the country!' Mr Brown tried to nick this approach, when later referring to people he met in Kent on Tuesday ('they are now staunch Labour supporters') but it didn't really work.

Mr Brown also stole an old Cameron jibe at Tony Blair – 'he was the future once'. This won little, if any, reaction. The PM jabbed the name of Lord Ashcroft at the Tories a few more times. This was more successful in cheering up his backbenchers. Nick Clegg tried to borrow the old Cameron tactic of using the second person singular, attacking Labour with, 'you've failed, it's over, it's time to go'. Not bad. Mr Clegg also referred to Brown and Cameron as 'he and he'. This made the House laugh, which was perhaps not the desired outcome.

At the back of the Labour benches sat James Purnell, once thought a future leader of his party, now quitting the Commons. All the puffery of power was gone. In a similar position on the Tory benches: Sir John Butterfill, that old booby from Bournemouth who boasted to ITV's hidden cameras that he was likely to go to the Lords. Won't be now. Sir Patrick Cormack

(Con, S Staffs) and Bob Marshall-Andrews (Lab, Medway) tried to catch the Speaker's eye one last time. Squeaker Bercow, who can usually be relied on not to do the decent thing, declined to allow these two honourable, unpartisan parliamentarians one last hurrah.

And then it was over. 'Bye bye!' yelled the Tories as Mr Brown left the chamber. They said that to Tony Blair before every election, too. But this time it might be true.

8th April 2010

The election campaign has seen remarkable progress in the opinion polls by the Lib Dems. Cleggmania has hit Britain! Up to a point.

Now it became clear why no one had touched the Lib Dem sarnies

ARMANDO Iannucci, who writes political satires, was announced yesterday as a celebrity fan of the Lib Dems. I accuse the admirable Mr Iannucci of naked self-interest. A Lib Dem rally yesterday in Streatham, south London, provided enough raw material to keep satirists like him in beans for weeks.

First there was the gospel singing which preceded the arrival of (atheist) Nick Clegg. Six female crooners of varying vintage yelled Christian hosannas, not all in tune. 'You can do everything with God, Amen,' ululated one. 'All things are possible in Jesus' name. It's time to shine again.' The microphones popped. The electric organ warbled. Then she and her chorus started clicking their fingers and waggling their bottoms as they went into a number called, 'Jesus is a winner man, a winner man, ooh yeah.' Refrain: 'We're on a winna, winna, winna, winning side.'

All this was enjoyed by a crowd of 150 oatmealy Lib Dems, mostly white. The mood was middle-class, self-denying. Free food was laid out at the back of the room but it was only 11.30 a.m. and Lib Dems do not eat between meals, thank you. Soapy men held toddlers high on their necks and boogied to the Afro beat. A bearded fellow held his hand high and swayed, lost in evangelical bliss.

Brian Paddick, a former senior policeman, watched from the back of the hall. Mr Paddick once tried to become Mayor of London and, though unsuccessful, did fine. It would have been good to hear from him yesterday. Instead we were subjected to a warm-up routine by Floella Benjamin, one-time presenter of *Play School*. She was dressed in the sort of white trouser suit worn by the man from Del Monte. 'I can see a lot of my *Play School* babies here today,' gushed Miss Benjamin, who sounds even more posh than Mr Clegg. 'We can make a huge difference. Nick has spoken and we say "yes! yes! yes!".'

In fact, at this stage Mr Clegg had not spoken. He had not even arrived. When he did walk through the door there was wild cheering. A couple of Labour supporters had infiltrated the event and tried waving 'Vote Labour' placards. These were swiftly hidden by a forest of 'Vote Lib Dem' symbols.

Mr Clegg was accompanied by his señora (she's the one we were told would not be taking part in the campaign because she was modern) and by the local Lib Dem candidate, Chris Nicholson. He is a partner in a City firm, KPMG, and has been accused, in Parliament, of pocketing £800,000 in bonuses. He has also given some £283,000 to the Lib Dems. A teenage girl sang, 'I'm just a poor wayfaring stranger, a travelling man in this land of woe.' Oh, puh-lease! Then Floella Benjamin yanked back the microphone and begged us to give a big hand to, 'a great man, a man who has vision and empathy, with all people'.

Could she really mean the Cleggster? She could. 'He thinks for you. He sees for you. He has the vision for you.' Britain would be better, she said confidently, 'with our leader leading the country'. Fast spiralling out of control, she added: 'He's a wonderful man! A family man! Beautiful wife! The love they have together is a love they will give to the country!' Now it became clear why no one had touched the sandwiches. They would have barfed them all up.

Mr Clegg, when he was finally given the floor, proved less exciting, but he did accuse David Cameron of being cocky. Given that we had just had God's name welded to the Lib Dem cause, this seemed a minor misdemeanour. Mr Clegg, drawing himself to his full magnificence, also promised: 'No more Lord Ashdowns!' I think he meant Ashcroft. But Mr Iannucci would have enjoyed that moment.

4th May 2010

The Lib Dems lose seats in the general election – Streatham votes Labour – but Mr Clegg's party does well enough to join the Conservatives in a coalition Government. Floella Benjamin, surprise surprise, becomes a Lib Dem peer.

Mock pouting, misty gazing

TO the Downing Street garden, to admire the ceanothus and wistaria and two other fresh blooms, Messrs Cameron and Clegg. The new Prime Minister and his deputy – I almost said vice-president – held an outdoor news conference. They stood beside one another at equal-sized lecterns, lovey-dovey as two cooing ptarmigan.

The nation's drinking classes may have taken a glance at the TV screens and feared they were seeing double. Like that old joke about Mike and Bernie Winters, it was a case of: 'Oh no, there are two of them!' Comedy heaven. British showbiz has a new double act. No doubt there will be comparisons to Ant and Dec, Torvill and Dean, Brighton and Hove, maybe even Peter Cook and Dudley Moore in the 1969 film *Monte Carlo or Bust*. Or, given the level of political mwah-mwah, was this more Mills and Boon?

Behaving like this, these two would have trouble being admitted to the American army. It's a 'bromance', as movie moguls say. We had 'Nick and I' this and 'David and I' that, plus some mock pouting and misty gazing. As Mr Cameron spoke, Cleggy nodded and tried to clench his jaw. The Prime Minister said he had thought about forming a minority government. But once he and Nick had talked about it they had realised how much more inspiring it could all be if they went the whole way. So here we were now in sunshine, on grass, spring leaves on the lime trees, the acacia sprigging. All we needed was a glass of Pimm's – thank you, Giovanni – and it could have been the Henley Royal Regatta. Blossom drifted from on high. Right on cue, birds tweeted. Or was it Percy Edwards standing in the wings?

As we entered, I noticed a wormery – a metaphor for the world of coalition politics, some might say. An etiolated fig tree stood forlorn sentry by the wall. Horticulturally, the Downing Street garden is tidy but a touch municipal. Trimmed box. Shrubs in planters. One dank pond and a surfeit of shade.

Mr Cameron spoke of 'a new progressive partnership'. 'Progressive' is a spongy word previously owned by Labour. Now it is being hijacked by Tories. What we are seeing is the occupation of the centre ground. The Thatcherites will like it no more than the Miliband brothers. 'This is a Government that will last,' said Mr Clegg, pushing a midge out of his air space. The clock on Horseguards struck. Someone reminded Mr Cameron that he had once called Mr Clegg a joke. 'Did you?' asked Mr Clegg like a betrayed Juliet – but not meaning it. 'I'm afraid I did, once,' said Romeo Cameron. Juliet playfully pretended to storm off. 'Come back!' cried Mr Cameron. Laughter. A rare sound in Downing Street of late. What a relief those Labour thugs, the Campbells and Co., have gone.

The power posing was a whole subplot in itself. Mr Clegg stood away from his lectern, perhaps to look independent. He snaked an arm round Mr Cameron as they concluded the event. This is an old trick, a way of projecting yourself as the senior partner. But Mr Cameron did most of the talking and, being a little chunkier, probably won the gravitas contest. He is the PM, after all, and three months older. Mr Clegg's yellow tie needs to go. It makes him look washed-out. Mr Cameron tans more easily and his voice is smokier. All of which, of course, is pop nonsense, mere imagery. We learned little about the Government's policies – nothing, certainly, about its tax-raising intentions – but that was not the object of the exercise. This was about establishing an upbeat tone for the early days of the project.

There had been precious little optimism in the air on Tuesday night, when Gordon Brown left under a cold, blackening sky and Mr Cameron had given a workmanlike but unexciting speech before entering Number 10. Now we had something brighter and the voters were being shown two party leaders who, not without risk, were cooperating in the national interest. I suspect that may play well.

13th May 2010

Index of names